A Knock at the Door

Wayne Bisek

Author proceeds from
A Knock at the Door
will go to Buckets for Hunger, Inc.
to continue the battle against hunger.

"A Knock at the Door," by Wayne Bisek. ISBN 978-1-60264-815-9 (softcover), ISBN 978-1-60264-816-6 (hardcover), and ISBN 978-1-60264-817-3 (Ebook).

Published 2011 by Virtualbookworm.com Publishing Inc., P.O. Box 9949, College Station, TX 77842, US. ©2011, Wayne Bisek. All rights reserved. No part of this publication may be reproduced, stored in a retrieval system, or transmitted in any form or by any means, electronic, mechanical, recording or otherwise, without the prior written permission of Wayne Bisek.

Manufactured in the United States of America.

I dedicate this book to all of those people who have touched my life. They helped me understand the meaning of love, happiness, forgiveness, generosity and kindness. It is dedicated, especially, to my wife for teaching me how to love, to my children for constantly reminding me how great it is to laugh at life, to my siblings for giving me the strength to survive, to my parents for helping me to discover that there is good in everyone, to my friends for accepting me for who I am. This book is dedicated to the strangers and the acquaintances who reached out a hand to help me at a crucial time and never asked for anything in return. I am a better person because of all of you.

Lastly, I dedicate this book to God, who never gave up on me and never left neither my side, nor my heart.

Table of Contents

Foreword

A Knock at the Door is a great example of the remarkable impact that positive attitude can have in one's life. The person who knocked on the Bisek family door with a badly needed Christmas basket had an incredible impact on one of the Bisek children. Wayne Bisek, a fourth grade student at the time, realized how much that gift basket meant to his struggling family. But, why did it have such an impact on Wayne? We may never know. What we do know is that Wayne remembered and was inspired to help others. Once he got started, he never quit.

I have worked with Wayne for over twenty years in the fight against hunger. During that time, I have shared many conversations with him about his life and my life. We have discussed everything from health, sports, charity, religion and family. The stories that Wayne has included in this book are great examples of the depth of feeling that he has for all of those aspects of life.

Somehow through all of the trials and tribulations of his early life, his physical issues and his psychological battles, he has forged a successful life with the love of family and friends. Wayne has found happiness, love and peace through genuine acts of forgiveness and introspection. This book provides a lesson for all to stop and smell the roses and appreciate the miracles of our own lives.

During the 1960s, I had the privilege of playing professional football with a great team, the Green Bay Packers. Every member of that team sacrificed and worked hard in order to succeed and to reach our goal of winning the NFL championship. For the last nearly twenty years, I have been a part of another great team, Buckets for Hunger, Incorporated.

Over two decades, Buckets has paid out over $2,200,000 in grants to food pantries. Buckets passed the mark of ten million pounds of food raised for the hungry and is now looking at twenty million pounds. Wayne and his team of volunteers have provided food and hope to thousands upon thousands of grateful people who otherwise may have gone to bed hungry. They (we) have made a difference!

(Jerry Kramer, 2005)

Jerry Kramer

Five time NFL Champion

Introduction

I am proud to have Wayne Bisek as a friend and I am in awe of his survival. *A Knock at the Door* is a courageous and at times, gut wrenching account of Wayne's dreadful childhood and triumphant life.

For many years I have known this man with the biggest heart in Wisconsin; this man whose existence placed him in a position to either quit or challenge the fates and become a winner in the game of life.

Neither Wayne nor I are a product of a life of privilege. While we came from different parts of the country and different cultures, as kids Wayne and I both experienced one of life's cruelest realities; hunger.

Because of the type of person he is, Wayne founded Buckets for Hunger and serves as the organization's president today. Tons of food has been distributed to thousands of people through the group's efforts. We have yet to find a way to measure the amount of caring that has been provided.

I have had the privilege of helping Wayne deliver healing and caring through the gift of food by working with "Buckets" and the effort is personal for me.

My mother, dad, seven brothers and sisters and I lived in New Jersey. I must have been about nine-years-old when my dad told me the real Santa Claus was going to stop at our house. I was scared beyond words when I saw the big white Santa standing at our door holding sacks of goodies. Instead of toys and games, the huge bags contained food and our family had a Christmas dinner for the ages. My dad, Leslie, ever the teacher, made sure I understood the real spirit of Christmas and the spirit of Santa that was embodied in the man and the food that arrived at our door through an act of compassion.

I was floored to learn that Wayne Bisek, at age nine, heard a knock at the door on Christmas Eve and a man on the other side was holding sacks of groceries. Wayne and I both understand that food fills emptiness in the stomach, the act of giving fills emptiness in the heart.

If we are to trust the words of Luke 12:48, "From everyone who has been given much, much will be demanded," nothing would have been demanded of Wayne Bisek because he had virtually nothing as he was growing up. Instead, he has given much to many.

My great friend and great teammate Jim Taylor, one of the toughest men I have ever known, has been moved to call Wayne a hero as a tribute to his life and his work. I believe Jim's description is exactly right.

Wayne Bisek represents the best in all of us and when you read *A Knock at the Door* you will know why.

May God continue to bless him and his labor.

Dave Robinson #89
HOF 2013

Dave Robinson
Pro Football Hall of Fame 2013

(Standing, Left to Right: Nick Collins [Packers], Melanie Bisek, Tramon Williams [Packers], Cole Bisek, Vivkie Carroll, Antonio Freeman [Packers], A.J. Bisek, Wayne Bisek. Front, Left to Right: Jerry Kramer [Packers] Dave Robinson [Packers] Frank Winters [Packers], 2011)

Wayne Bisek

Author's Note: David Robinson was just inducted into the NFL Hall of Fame in August of 2013. He was a member of the All-Decades of the Sixties and is also in the Green Bay Packers Hall of Fame. Dave was a key player for four NFL Championship teams with the Packers in the Sixties.

Preface

MY NAME IS WAYNE Bisek. I am a fifty-seven-year-old man with a wonderful wife, three great adult children, and I am currently experiencing a mid-life revival.

First, I must tell you that I am a man of many flaws. Underneath my usually controlled public persona, I still have substantially more feelings of anger than I would like to admit. Competitive sports still mean more to me than they should. After fifty years of life, I still have not learned that some of my opinions and thoughts should be kept quiet. As a father, I have made too many mistakes in the lives of my children. As a husband, I need to improve substantially in my ability to communicate effectively with my wife.

In attempting to do this review of my own life and all of its wonders and joys, I have also relived the errors that I have made. As my father and mother before me and as their parents before them, I have done things that have hurt my children. I shall regret those mistakes forever. Even now, I can vividly recall all of those instances when I spoke before I considered the damage that I could do.

More than anything in this world, I wanted to be a kind and loving father. I wanted to be a father who never hurt his children's feelings. I never wanted to be a "green screaming monster" for any of my offspring. Unfortunately, there are times when I have not been faithful to those promises. However, I will tell you in all honesty that the pain of regret for all of those moments cut me to my very core.

After writing this book, I realize that while I have made mistakes with my own family, they have always fully understood how deeply I love them. In return, they have delivered unto me an unconditional love that I did not believe in for many years. They have loved me in spite of my many personality flaws, personal quirks, and character faults.

The revival comes into play in a simple way. Together, my children and my wife have inspired me to acknowledge and accept all of the love that has existed in my world. For a large part of my life, I did not just look at the glass as half-empty; I felt as if no one had even given me a glass. My own family has changed that attitude. They have helped me to realize just how full my glass has always been and continues to be. Every day, they help me fill that glass a little more.

It is through them that I have now begun to realize that I have had many wonderful gifts from God that I have not fully appreciated. There is a whole list of those gifts in this tome. There is a collection of miracles that God has brought into my life and a list of times that God's Divine Intervention has affected the people I love, as well as myself. There is even a tale of one instance of God's actual presence in my life. Finally, there is the tremendously powerful realization that God has been with me every step of the way and that is why I am here today.

Same Glass, New Eyes

I HAVE ALWAYS BEEN a raging pessimist. For the entirety of my first seventeen years on this earth, nearly every day was filled with anger, violence, and utter disappointment. The two most consistent activities in our "home" were arguing and yelling. Norman Rockwell could have spent an entire year with our family looking for one shining moment of inspiration, but he would have gone away as a frustrated artist with a whole new perspective on the American family.

Unlike the Walton family of TV fame, we were never taught to enjoy the simple things of life. We were never made aware of the profound happiness that can exist in a home filled with love and respect. Instead, we learned a very different, but valuable, life skill. We learned to survive.

All five of us children learned how to get from one day to the next. We learned how to meet our friends at their homes so as to never have them come to our stark, angry world. We learned how to prepare for our leather-strap spankings after evening prayers. We learned that by eating faster we could leave the supper table more quickly. Thus, we could escape from the constant arguing between Mom and Dad. We learned how to avoid discussions with our friends about Christmas gifts and birthday celebrations. Somehow, we learned to find strength in each other. We learned to believe that someday we would leave all of this behind and find a new life.

I personally learned to block out specific memories of my youth that were especially painful. I learned, very early, that Dad did not care for me to be around him. I learned that no one, neither my parents nor the vast majority of my teachers, "expected" me to ever become anything worthwhile or to attain any professional-type position in life. In hindsight, I learned what it meant to be born on "the wrong side of the tracks."

But, eventually, I also learned to move on with my life. I learned that I could set my own goals and have my own dreams. I learned that with hard work I could give myself the chance to move up in life. Eventually, I learned of the profound impact that the love of a good woman could have on my life. Later still, I learned how to understand that my mother and father were not entirely responsible for their behavior and parenting skills. I learned that they were only the products of even worse home-life environments. I learned that I would have to accept and assume complete responsibility for my future. Finally, somewhere around my thirtieth birthday, I learned about genuine forgiveness.

The whole process of evolvement has been rather gradual. In fact, I know that I am still not as optimistic about life as I could be. There are still a great many times when I focus too much on what did not happen or what I did not obtain. There is still a part of my personality that is too quick to spot the downside of the situation. It is as if there is an anger deep inside of me that is ever-present, just waiting to come to light. Yet, I am now so much more aware of that persona and so much more capable of controlling it than I ever was before these life-changing events took place.

As a result of this gradual change in outlook and approach, I have come to realize a few things. One of the main revelations I experienced was that there are a great many amazing episodes and inspirational incidents that have occurred in my life, and I have let so many of them escape without appreciation. Scientific reasoning may be used to explain away some of the events, perhaps. Certain people may attribute other incidents to "dumb luck." I am sure that there are individuals who would even cite "wishful thinking" as the best explanation for some of the events.

But I believe in a Supreme Being. I believe in God. I believe in a "higher power" that watches over us, yet allows us to decide our own fate through free will. I believe in a God that is loving and forgiving. I believe in a God that occasionally saves us from our own mistakes and poor decisions for various reasons. And, I believe that the role and influence of God in my life has been both constant and profound.

I believe that each and every one of us spends too much of our energy in search of happiness, success, and enjoyment. Unfortunately, the search never seems to lead anywhere important. All of those self-help books are correct in stating that our life is not and should not be about a destination, but more about the journey.

A Knock at the Door

My journey has been nothing short of remarkable. In fact, I have come to appreciate that I have had an entire list of gifts, divine interventions, miracles, and even an extremely powerful occurrence with the actual presence of God in my own personal space. Now, I want to share these experiences with everyone.

My writing skills are probably not sufficient enough to convey the power, depth, and impact of these very special occurrences in my own short lifetime. But, I do believe that each of them is a substantial reason for me to reconsider my viewpoint on life. Each of them can evoke in me emotional responses starting with fear and progressing to sorrow, surprise, joy, appreciation, awe, and wonder.

I find it somewhat sad that it has taken me fifty years to recognize these tremendously positive happenings in my own life. Yet, I am pleased that I am finally so aware of them. In the past, I would have become somber and depressed by the simple act of reminiscing about some of these "close calls." My entire focus would have been on the near-tragic aspects of some of the episodes. So much of my energy would have been spent on worrying about the possibilities of dire consequences. With my former prevalent perspective, I would have missed out on the enormity and abundance of these many blessed events of my life. Even with the glass overflowing, I would have complained about the size of the glass.

Hopefully, the dominance of that negative perspective is gone. My new goal will be to experience happiness in what I have and in what I have been given. That change has already begun to take place with the simple undertaking of the making of this list. I have taken a step away from the fracas that has been my life so as to understand and appreciate the various gifts that I have already been given by God.

My list includes a number of instances involving my loved ones or myself in which I believe God reached down his powerful hands to save me or to save someone in my family. The list includes at least a few circumstances in which some other kind and caring human being reached out to touch my life in a positive way. In addition, there are several times in my life that I made a decision to extend my hand to someone else and, in return, my own life was made more complete and more joyous. Yet, without any doubt, the single most profound item on my list is quite obvious. It is the torturous night during which I experienced the actual presence of God next to me. There was no radiant light and no deep baritone voice ala James Earl Jones. There was not even a quiet, calm

10

voice in my head; there was just the amazingly moving aura of God there with me in the very early hours of that transcendental morning.

In a recent movie, I heard an interesting comment about the gifts and miracles that take place in our lives. The statement was made that "most miracles occur in hindsight." That is how I feel about my situation. Maybe it is different for others. Maybe other people immediately comprehend and acknowledge the occurrence of a miracle or a gift. Maybe all of those "glass-half-full" people need no time at all to spot these events. If that is the case, then I am happy for them. I am guessing that if you immediately understand the awe-inspiring nature of the event, then its impact would be even greater.

It has taken some years of distance and some substantial evolvement on my part to stop and take inventory of the complete list of gifts, miracles, and divine interventions that have happened to me and to the people that I love. As a result of these revelations, I am now beginning to see the glass as more than half-full. Maybe I have found a new pair of eyes that allow me to finally see what has actually been there all along. For the first time in my life, I do not want to just survive; I want to thrive.

Immaculate Conception II?

ONE OF THE MOST basic concepts of our human existence, I believe, is the need to understand our own history. There seems to be a desire in all of us to understand and appreciate our parents, the two people who are directly responsible for bringing us into this world. I suppose we are hoping that by learning about them, we will more deeply understand ourselves and why we are the specific compilation of physical traits and personality characteristics that we are.

Dad approximately 1951

My father's name is Adrian Adam Bisek. In his prime, he stood about six feet tall. He packed two hundred pounds very tightly into his muscular body. Dad was a handsome, rugged man with a deep baritone voice that demanded attention when he spoke. I remember quite clearly that he was a tough guy who took no guff from anyone. I never saw him back down from any physical challenge, whether it included a human, animal, or inanimate threat.

He grew up on a small farm with seven siblings (two others died in infancy), his mother, and his tyrant of a father. In fact, my paternal grandfather was the only man that ever put fear in my father's eyes. Dad was the first-born son (1929) and the second child born into the family.

Dad was a very strong student until he was forced to quit school in the eighth grade to work as a woodsman to help the family. It was a trade that he extended into his adult life for many years. Unfortunately, it was a very dangerous way to make a living. One of his partners was killed when a tree

12

fell on him, and Dad once had several hundred stitches put in his left arm as the result of another serious accident. For many years, he used a team of horses to skid the logs after he had felled them.

Dad served in the military in the Korean War as a truck driver. He received two service medals for battles that he survived.

I am told that my father was quite the ladies' man. He enjoyed dancing and was very much in demand as a partner for the women at any and all wedding dances. For a gruff, physical, uneducated man, he was quite smooth on the floor.

Unfortunately, my only remembrances of my father from my youth are simple. I yearned for him to show me any sign of affection or love. I wanted nothing more than to sit next to him or on his lap. I wanted deeply to hug him and to have him return the sensation of tenderness. I was so unbelievably proud that he was my father. Ironically, he never took me into his heart throughout my entire youth and adolescence.

My mother's maiden name is Gertude Valeria Sonsalla. She was one of the hardest working people that I ever knew until she developed Alzheimer's disease later in life. Physically, she was a pleasant looking woman with attractive features.

Like Dad, she also grew up on a small farm, but with six siblings. When mom was only twelve years old, her father had her mother placed into a mental institution. It is now thought that he placed her there so that she would not interfere with his habit of abusing his own daughters. At that point in time, a husband could place his spouse in a mental institution without great difficulty.

Mom approximately 1951

My mother was a simple, uneducated woman who developed one of the best credit ratings in the entire community. She never could afford to pay a lot per week toward the items that she had purchased on lay-away programs at the local clothing

13

and shoe stores, but she never missed a payment and people always said she was as honest as the day was long.

I was in high school when she worked outside of the home for the first time. Her job was that of a scrub lady at the local chicken hatchery. It was dirty, difficult work, but no one did it better than she did. No matter what kind of labor she performed, from ironing clothes for the neighbors to cleaning the bathrooms at the Hatchery, it would be a job well done. No one ever built up a better credit rating with no discretionary income than my Mom did. And, I seriously doubt that anyone ever was able to "stretch" a dollar as far as my Mom could. Somehow, she managed to buy some groceries most weeks, a piece of clothing every once in awhile and she even sent us to a movie on a rare occasion.

No matter how intimidating my father was to other people, including me, he never seemed to frighten Mom. She argued with him toe-to-toe at every meal that I can remember. Mom had an unbelievable sense of strength in spite of her difficult life. She did everything that she could to provide for me and for my siblings; she was one tough lady.

However, in addition to looking to our parents to learn about ourselves, we also turn to our siblings. Our brothers and sisters can be reflections of ourselves in many ways.

Marilyn, Maggie, Karl, Me, Richard approximately 1965

That effort to utilize an in-depth study of our parents and each other was somewhat difficult for me and my siblings because of the complexity of our family makeup. I have one sister, Maggie, who is ten years older than I am. She was the product of an unwed pregnancy that my mother had when she was approximately twenty-three-years-old, many years before

14

she ever met my father. My mom's doctor had to explain to her how this had happened, since she did not learn about it in school, and her own mother was not there to explain, either.

Next in line is my brother, Karl, who is my elder by two years. He was also conceived before my mother was ever married. While my father and mother were married in August of 1951, he was born only five months later. Apparently, Mom had gotten pregnant while Dad was in basic training in a different state. The Army granted him a furlough to come back for the wedding. When Dad realized the details of the situation, he got an annulment of their marriage. That meant that Karl's father is not the same man who is my father. A third man was my older sister's father.

The court records are rather extensive involving the on-again, off-again marriage of my parents. They were originally married on August 18,1951 (as I mentioned above). Dad then filed for an annulment in September 1952, and it became official on September 26, 1953. I was born on January 23, 1954, approximately five months later. However, the most devastating official record that I have discovered is my own birth record. I don't know how or why it would have been recorded on an official document in this manner, but I swear to you that it exists. Whenever I see it or think about it, my heart tears apart. My official birth certificate actually reads: "Mother-Gertrude V. Sonsalla"; " Father—___none." *

That's right! My birth certificate actually states that I do not have a father.

Eventually, my parents had two more children after me. My brother, Richard, is three years younger than me, and I have a little sister, Marilyn, who is two years younger than Richard. So, our family tree includes five children by three separate fathers and a husband and wife who were married (1951), got an annulment (1953), remarried (1956), separated (1971), and finally officially divorced (1974).

By most classic definitions of the phrase, we would have been considered a confused and dysfunctional family. Yet, through it all, we kids developed a unique bond. For instance, I am fifty-seven-years-old, and I have never heard any one of my siblings use the terminology of "half-brother" or "step-sister." I have only known Maggie, Karl, Richard, and Marilyn as my two brothers and two sisters. Together, we managed to help each other survive seventeen years of arguments, beatings, psychological torment, emotional pain, poverty, and humiliation. We survived the misguided efforts, or lack thereof, of Mom and Dad to parent us.

By height: Maggie, Karl, Me, Richard, Marilyn.
Approximately 1959 or 1960

For many years, I have stated to my own wife and children that I have almost no happy memories of my childhood. It is difficult to look past so much hurt and pain to try and find one incident or moment when I might actually have felt loved. When a child knows only disappointment, sorrow, anger, and stress, it is asking quite a bit of him or her to spot a single ray of sunshine.

Night after night, year after year, we learned that there would always be certain constants in our family life. We knew that every time we planned to go to a friend's house, something would happen to anger Mom or Dad at the last minute so we would be banished to our rooms. We knew that at every meal, there was a great chance that Dad would get into a screaming match with Mom. We knew that birthdays were not really celebrated as much as they were painfully endured without fanfare or gifts or even simple acknowledgement. We knew that hugs and kisses were things other parents did. We knew better than to ever expect to hear the words "I love you" spoken in our home.

Now, as a middle-aged man looking back at a difficult and painful life, I realize that something good did happen during those years that I spent with my four siblings. While I can now accept the fact that love was an emotion that never visited our family circle, a tremendous bond did occur with all of us. At various times in my life, each one of my siblings has played a major role in my happiness and success.

Being the eldest by eight years, Maggie played a major role in our unique version of a family. My sister had the grave misfortune to have spent her youth in an extremely dreadful environment. As the child of an unwed mother in a small, rural community in the late 1940's, many people ostracized her. At the Catholic grade school that she attended, the local priest had an especially humiliating practice. He would bring her to the front of the classroom and tell everyone that "this is what a bastard child is." Then, he would explain that she was the product of a sinful mother. Almost fifty years later, her good friends from those childhood years still anguish with her when they talk about those classroom sessions with the "good" priest.

In addition, Mom and Maggie's living quarters at that time was nothing more than a wooden-plank-floor home with clapboard siding located only a hundred yards away from the local livestock yards. It was an absolute run-down shack with mice and bugs and no decent heating system. The place was right out of *The Grapes of Wrath*. But, the dire and stark physical nature of that living space was nothing compared to the emotional environment.

Once my brother and I came along, Maggie's workload increased to include watching over us. It was just the beginning of a long list of things that my sister would do for me over the years. When I was approximately seven or eight-years-old, she started to take me to movies at the local theater on many Sunday afternoons. I never had to even ask her to do it. It was just a generous gift that she gave me from her own hard-earned money, to take me away from the house for a couple of hours at a time.

Another favor that she did for me involved my fascination with President John F. Kennedy. During the aftermath of his tragic and shocking assassination, I sought out any and all literature about him. Maggie did everything that she could to satisfy my yearnings for information and documentation about him. I still remember that she brought me magazines with stories about him or his murder. In fact, I still have all of those tattered magazines. They still remain as some of the most treasured gifts anyone has ever given me.

I never had any idea who Maggie's biological father was and still do not know with absolute certainty. Even Maggie never knew with complete confidence who her biological father was up to the moment of her death at age 63. However, I do remember that my Dad did not treat her with anything but contempt. She was not his daughter, and he showed his resentment bluntly and frequently. There was one incident that I can recall vividly that clearly showcased this resentment. After what seemed like hours of screaming and threats between Dad, Mom, and Maggie, my sister smashed her arm through the glass window on the front porch. Blood was splattered all over the walls and the floor. If my memory serves me correctly, I believe Mom got the bleeding stopped, and Maggie ended up in the emergency room later that night.

In the late sixties, Maggie fell in love and married a local farm boy named Dick Andre. It was the best thing that ever happened to her. He survived Viet Nam, came back home, and took over his father's dairy farm. To my knowledge, he filled Maggie's life with love, joy, and respect. They had a great partnership in every sense of the word.

During the summers of my seventh and eighth-grade years, Maggie bestowed another great gift on me. She and Dick took me in to live with them on their farm. It was a truly wonderful time in my life because Dick and I became fast friends. We both loved sports, and he was a genuinely caring man. He and Maggie showed me that it was possible to be happy. He made me laugh so much in those two summers. No matter how long the day had been, Dick always found the time to play catch with me, to talk sports, or to just joke around with me. He treated me as a young man, no matter how childish I acted. I found it hard to believe that no matter how inept I was at farm work, he did not berate me or chastise me. Instead, he found a way to make me laugh at myself and move on to the next chore. Dick became a father figure to me in no time at all. Nearly every night for those two summers, he and I closed out our day's work by sitting down and watching Johnny Carson.

More importantly, however, he demonstrated the importance of moral values, strong integrity, and ethical behavior. For a young man enduring puberty at the time, my brother-in-law was an excellent source of information and influence. Dick and Maggie showed me more love and joy in those two summers than I had experienced in my entire lifetime before then.

My older brother, Karl, provided an even more difficult situation for my father to deal with. It seems that while Dad was in the Army, my mother became pregnant by a man who was the real love of her life. Unfortunately, he had no desire to give up his unmarried status. Instead, she convinced Dad to marry her under the guise that she was pregnant with his child. When Karl was born five short months after the wedding, Dad told his fellow soldiers the great news. He could not understand why they were either laughing at him or giving him these strange, quizzical stares. To his dismay, he came to understand their reactions when the platoon's chaplain explained the problem.

Karl was born January 18, 1952. That was 294 days after Dad had left Arcadia to join the Army. Since a normal pregnancy lasts thirty-eight to forty weeks (266 to 280 days only), he could not possibly be Karl's father. He had gone for basic training March 30 of 1951. He came back to town to marry Mom on August 18, 1951. After the wedding, he returned to military life and was sent to Korea for the war in May of 1952. Dad was uncomfortable discussing the situation with anyone, so he finally asked the chaplain for help. That is when the chaplain explained to Dad that the baby could not possibly be his. This situation made for a horrible relationship between Dad and his wife's second child.

In fact, Karl has informed me that Dad broke his nose more than once. Apparently, I had such a strong desire to escape from the situation that I completely blocked out any and all memories of those incidents, except for one.

I do recall one chaotic night when Karl was about sixteen and he wanted to leave the house. Dad forbade him to go and Karl was threatening to do it anyway. As he attempted to leave the kitchen, Dad grabbed him by his arms and twisted them behind his back. As I stood there and watched this mismatch, I remember thinking that Karl's shoulders were going to be completely dislocated. I was only fourteen-years-old and no physical match for Dad, but I remember yelling at him to leave Karl alone and to "stop hurting him." Even now, thirty-some years later, I can still see the look of pain in my brother's eyes as he was being manhandled by Dad.

In many ways, Karl was my inspiration and my idol. He was the epitome of the late-sixties cool man on campus. Almost everyone liked him; the girls thought he was good-looking, the guys liked the car he drove, and the athletes respected his speed on the track and football field. Karl was a great guy to have as an older brother. In fact, he was cool enough to teach me how to drive in his own car. For an eighteen-year-old guy to do that for a younger brother takes a lot of guts and love.

However, my memories of growing up with Karl involve a lot of pain. He was hurt badly playing football as a starting quarterback in his junior year of high school. During a varsity game, a tackler grabbed onto his facemask and severely twisted his head and neck. It resulted in very painful muscle tears that haunted Karl for months afterward. Karl also suffered from painful boils on his back. There were many nights that I would be lying in bed next to him, and he would be absolutely writhing in pain. He would just be consumed by the throbbing and piercing sensations. And, this was all on top of the problems with Dad.

Yet, Karl was always there for me as a big brother. He never once made me feel slighted or humiliated. In fact, he did everything possible to protect me from anyone and everyone who thought about harming me. One particular incident occurred when I was in sixth grade and had accidentally hit a softball into a group of seventh grade guys during recess. They immediately took off after me, threatening to tear me apart when they caught me. I circled the playground at least twice when Karl noticed what was going on. At once, he let those three guys know that they would not be touching me unless they went through him and his two friends. That memory of Karl unhesitatingly defending me is still quite clear in my mind.

As for my younger brother, Richard, he has always inspired me because of his single-minded focus on becoming the best mechanic that he could possibly be. His passion for cars and motors began when he was only seven or eight-years-old. While Mom and Dad were still married, Richard absolutely idolized Dad. They were together constantly and Dad inspired him to take apart motors and put them back together in even better working order than before the planned demolition. Everywhere that my father went, Richard was in tow. As a result, Richard became an excellent mechanic and now runs his own successful business.

Richard is the mechanical wizard of the family. He had absolutely no interest in schoolwork or sports, but he always had an avid interest in motors and how they function. He has taken the skills and interest that he first learned from our father, and he has honed and sharpened them. In fact, he has taken them to a whole new level. Every time I talk to him about cars, I am amazed at his knowledge and at his ability to decipher a mechanical issue. In addition, his persistence is astonishing. He never lets a problem beat him, no matter how complicated or challenging it is. Whenever I consider where I am in life, I think of Richard and how far he has taken his talent by building himself a profitable business out of his favorite pastime. I have learned great appreciation for craftsmen as a result of observing him.

Lastly, my younger sister Marilyn was the only other family member left with me and Mom once Richard married his wife, Renee. Karl was in the Air Force and stationed in the Phillipines and Maggie was on the farm with her husband. Together, Marilyn and I made the best we could of the situation while I was in high school and she was in grade school when Dad left the family. She had always been Daddy's little girl and was devastated when he left.

Yet, she fought hard to keep her identity and self-esteem. She participated in the few sports programs offered for girls at the time, and she was a cheerleader in addition to being an excellent student. Her competitive nature and perfectionist attitude were great assets in her own internal battle to deal with the loss of our father. At a time in her life when she could have hung her head and looked for pity and sympathy, she chose instead to redouble her efforts to succeed academically and socially in her high school years.

We became very close during that part of our lives, and she inspired me to be a better big brother than I thought I could be. She inspired me to seek out opportunities to improve my own lot in life. When I opened up my own clothing store in town, she was my main employee. Even at sixteen, she could handle the duties of managing the store and serving as a sales clerk while I was away on business in the Twin Cities. I learned a great deal about parenting skills from our relationship, and I know that I am a better father to my daughter because of the lessons that Marilyn taught me. She put a smile onto my face every day for a great number of years, and for that, I will be forever grateful.

Early on in my life, I came to understand that my family was uniquely structured. There was always a "soap-opera" feeling about our family because of the combination of various fathers. Almost every day was filled with nasty reminders from Mom and/or Dad about our different bloodlines and different heritages. Profanity and violence were both ever-present in our homes. A negative atmosphere permeated our lives, as neither one of our parents ever accepted any responsibility for any aspect of our plight. Everything that happened in our lives was blamed on someone else.

But through it all, we five siblings developed a strong bond. It is difficult to describe it as genuine love, since we all knew so little about brotherly and sisterly love. Our bond, I believe, can be more aptly described as similar to one in which a group of people survive a tragic nightmare or overcome devastating circumstances in order to move on to different, separate experiences. In some ways, it was a bond similar to a group of hostages held in captivity for years who slowly, individually, escape to find happiness.

It boggles my mind to consider that through all of our years of despair, disappointment, pain, and suffering, my siblings and I never abandoned each other. We may have been a wildly dysfunctional family, but we were a family, nonetheless. No matter how many various fathers were involved in the makeup of our family, we always remained brothers and sisters. Those gifts of commitment, respect, and consolation to each other were priceless. We shall, each and every one of us, take them to our graves.

I am very proud to say that a large part of my identity centers on my brothers and sisters. Together, they helped to forge who I am and what I have become in my life. I am made up of bits and pieces, good and bad, of each one of them, and I am proud of it.

Back row: Karl, Maggie, Me.
Front row: Richard, Mom, Marilyn.
December 2002

* The County Clerk in Trempealeau explained to me in 2011 that it was common practice in the 1950s in that county to state "none" in the line for the father's name if there was any dispute or question.

Un-American Gothic

SEVENTEEN YEARS OF MY life were spent enduring the tumultuous relationship of my mother and father. I have almost no recollection of the two of them showing each other any form of affection or respect. They were two people who were almost completely unhappy with each other.

Mom and Dad 1st wedding Aug 1951

For their first marriage to each other, Dad was a man who felt trapped in a relationship where he was supporting the children of other men. He had almost no interest in making the marriage work because he felt he could not trust his wife to be faithful to him. For their second marriage to each other, Mom was a woman pushed into a legal union by welfare agency workers who were no longer interested in providing aid to a woman who continued to have children out-of-wedlock.

In fact, I have now come to understand that there was a very simple reason for their disdain for each other. My older sister, Maggie, shared the reason with me many years ago. She informed me that Mom was always in love with another man. However, marriage was not something that he was particularly interested in. Therefore, Mom married my Dad simply because he was willing to get married. Unfortunately for all of the parties involved, it was probably the worst decision of their lives.

My only memories of their relationship were simply unhappy. Mom and Dad seemed to be constantly arguing; it was as if they were always in a state of absolute anger with each other. There are only a few occasions in my memory of the two of them getting dressed up and going out to socialize, but usually, Dad was either working his logging business or in one of the local bars carousing with his buddies, avoiding coming home. Literally, every moment of our lives was filled with tension. We never knew if our parents were about to explode at each other or if they were going to abruptly turn their venomous tirades at one of us kids. It was always only a matter of time before the animosity came out into the open.

Supper was the only meal we consistently ate together as a family, and I only remember it as being tortuous. Dad would yell at Mom about the meal being tasteless. Mom would scream back about a lack of money to buy food or about the fact that the food had been reheating for hours while he was at the local bar after work. Because of those circumstances, I developed a nasty habit of "speed eating" through those meals. To this day, my wife talks about how I don't eat a meal; I simply inhale the food. That habit, I am sure, is a result of my desire to escape from the supper table that was more of a "war" table.

I believe that it is only natural for a child to have to blame someone for a lifetime of unhappiness and disappointment. As a result of their eventual divorce and of a lifetime of living in this environment, it took many years for me to stop choosing sides. Eventually, I came to two important conclusions. First, I decided that their marital problems were not of my making. Second, it finally hit me that there was nothing to be gained by my attempts to ascertain which of them was the bigger culprit in our dysfunctional family's many problems. Instead, I chose to expend my energy in appreciating the positive impact that they each had on my life. While it was obvious that they never should have married each other and that they never should have tried to raise a family together, they did each have some worthwhile personality traits that have become a part of me.

In the classic painting, *American Gothic,* the husband and wife team of farmers portray a strong sense of pride and of accomplishment. Yet, there is an obvious humility in their faces and attitudes. In completely separate photographs, taken years apart by different photographers under different circumstances, my Mom and Dad project those exact same qualities, attitudes, and values.

In the mid- seventies, the local County Board of Supervisors hired a professional photographer to create a pictorial history of the people of the area. He toured all of the small towns in the county asking people from all walks of life to pose for these pictures. There were wedding photos with dancing grandparents and giggling toddlers. There were funerals with processions of tearful family members and friends. There were pictures of men and women at work performing the tasks of their everyday lives.

Mom 1975

That photographer captured the essence of my Mom's character with one click of his camera's shutter. She is posed at work at the Hatchery where she toiled as a "scrub-lady" for many years. In the picture, she is leaning over a sparkling clean stainless-steel tub. She is wearing a hairnet, and she is proudly displaying one of the tools of her trade, the scrub brush. Her somewhat stern, yet proud presence depicts the same set of values and beliefs as the farm couple in *American Gothic*. She knows exactly what her position in life is, and she is very proud of the fact that she performs her duties as well as anyone possibly could. There is a genuine sense of dedication and effort. In one clear, clean photograph, it is obvious that this hard-working woman would never give you less than her best effort for the day's pay.

Another belief that my Mom passed on to me was her commitment to the payment of her debts. In spite of the dire circumstances of our family's financial situation, Mom had a line of credit in every store in town. It did not matter that our family always lived "on the wrong side of the tracks." We did not always have food on the table, and for a large part of his early adult years, my father had a horrible history of not paying his debts. Yet, my Mom could charge items or do "lay-away" purchases in any retail store in town. She never missed a weekly payment to any merchant, and she never bought more than she knew that she could pay off in a few months. On any number of occasions, I witnessed my Mom being treated as if she was the most valued costumer in town. Mom almost never had the cash to buy an item on the day she picked it out, but in a few months, it would be in our house.

My mother instilled in me a set of values based on two philosophies. The first was that no matter what the situation, you should never steal anything from anyone. I can still recall that people in my hometown always talked about Mom as being "as honest as the day is long." The second philosophy is that no matter what work you do, you should do it to the very best of your ability. My mother taught me by her example that there is no shame in pure and simple hard work. Even at eighty-four years of age, she would never stop working hard as a volunteer at church events or other programs.

In addition to those attributes, my mom has done everything that she could possibly do to be a good grandmother to all of her grandchildren. In spite of the fact that she lives on a fixed and very limited budget, she never fails to send a card and a couple of dollars to every grandchild on their birthdays. In addition, she has delivered to every grandchild a "hope chest" filled with dish towels and hand towels. The wash towels are all hand-embroidered by Mom and take hours and hours to produce. Even when she was in her late seventies and early eighties, she painstakingly embroidered these dish towels for every one of her thirteen grandchildren.

Mom also took the time to teach my kids how to play several card games. To this day, a game she taught them, "Whist," is one of my children's favorite to play. During those card game sessions, Mom let loose, laughed, and seemed to thoroughly enjoy herself. She has a wonderful sense of humor, which had been hidden for so many years.

As with my father, I believe that Mom could have been a good parent had she married the right person.

In another picture that is eerily reminiscent of the photo of Mom at work, Dad is captured on film posing with his power saw and a just-felled tree. His appearance is long and lean in the body, and he is somewhat narrow at the hip and broad at the shoulders. A slight smile conveys a high level of confidence and a great degree of pride in his work. In the photo, it is obvious that he is a man who is very comfortable with who and what he is.

Dad approximately 1956

It is most likely that a significant amount of my physical characteristics are derived from my father. His barrel chest, his thin sturdy legs, and his naturally taut biceps have been passed on to me. I believe that he could have been a gifted athlete; however, he was never given the opportunity.

I grew up basking in the shadow of a man who feared no one and who was comfortable with anyone. Other than his own father, I never witnessed my Dad cowering from anyone. No man ever made him back down under any circumstance.

Yet, I also saw grown men from all walks of life socialize with him. Business owners, professionals, farmers, laborers, and local politicians all laughed and drank with him. They all greeted him openly and happily. I believe that my Dad was, and is, a guy's guy. Men admire his strength, candor, and absolute lack of fear. Women, on the other hand, love his sense of humor, his cocky demeanor, and his flirtatious attitude. Dad always has walked with the swagger of a rock star and he has pulled it off successfully.

In spite of the absence of parental skills, he had a major influence on my personality and character. It is because of him, I believe, that I am never uncomfortable around people outside of my socio-economic strata. It is because of him that I learned never to back away from my beliefs and never to back down from an enemy. While my weapon of choice has usually been my acerbic tongue rather than my fists, I mimic his "fear no one" attitude.

Furthermore, without any education beyond seventh grade, my father has managed to be self-employed for nearly his entire adult lifetime. He was an independent logger for many years, and then became a salvage yard operator for another twenty plus years.

Like my father, I have also been self-employed almost my entire adult life. He managed to inspire in me an entrepreneurial spirit. For better or for worse, I have never felt intimidated by any opponent on a field of athletic competition, in a classroom, or in a political arena. And, somehow the message that no one was "above" him was instilled in me. His total comfort with people from every socio-economic status in town taught me that we all put on our pants the same way, one leg at a time.

Whether he planned it or not, his demeanor and behavior has had a profoundly positive impact on my life, personally and professionally.

In a *Twilight Zone*-like twist of photographic irony, that same photographer who captured Mom's *American Gothic* pose at her job also caught me on camera for the same project. He visited me at my clothing store on the very same day, in fact. My snapshot shows me standing in front of a rack of clothing in my newly established business. Perhaps it is an attitude and an atmosphere that only I can detect in the three photos, but in all of them, the subjects seem to project the same message: we are all very proud of the work that we have done and of our accomplishments. Even if only to me, it is obvious that we are mother, father, and son.

Me 1975

My parents were definitely not "Ozzie and Harriet Nelson" as far as their parenting skills. However, my parents did provide me with a great many character attributes and physical features that have served me well during my lifetime so far. For that, I am forever grateful to the two of them.

Slow-motion Football and Deer Pen Baseball

I'M NOT EXACTLY SURE of the month, or even, for that matter, the year in which my family left the farmhouse that we were renting to move in to the small city that became my home for the next twenty-plus years. If memory serves me correctly, it was just about the time that I was going to start second grade at St. Aloysius. I remember that the home we moved into was located just across the street from a small park. It was a rather large, two-story home with four bedrooms and a dirt basement. No one would have mistaken it for a mansion, but it was not a dilapidated shack, either. The major attribute to this house and location, though, was the fact that it was two doors away from the home of one Andy Pellowski.

Andy was a freckled-face, slightly pudgy, always happy kid who was about five years older than me. He was the youngest of eight children in his family. Each and every one of them seemed to love life. Even his adult married siblings visited Andy and his parents quite often. Their family was always warm, kind, and loving. Every time I was at his home, I was made to feel welcome and treated like just another member of the family. It was a stark contrast to the home life in which my family existed.

Andy's most obvious character trait was his obsession with sports. He went from baseball to football to basketball and track. Andy was never a star athlete by any stretch of the imagination. The elite positions of quarterback, running back, and wide receiver in football were never his to play. Center on the offensive line was his spot. On the baseball team, he was a back-up outfielder, not the pitcher or shortstop. Yet, he never seemed to lose interest or to stop smiling. Andy introduced me to whole new concepts of sports activity and attitude. Even with the age gap between us, we became instant friends. I guess when you are the last of eight children in a family you probably tire of being the "little brother."

Therefore, he sort of adopted me as the younger brother that he never had.

Since Andy was in seventh grade and I was in second grade when I first moved in to town, our friendship started out with the typical trucks and guns games. But, it did not take long for Andy to become my mentor in an area that would thrill and haunt me, alternately, for my entire lifetime: sports.

It started out with Andy getting me to play one-on-one, slow motion, backyard football games. The "field" was only fifteen feet wide and thirty feet long. It was bordered on one side by the backend of a small, wood frame handyman's shop. One end was a brick building that housed a mechanic's shop for a local cheese plant. One sideline consisted of three small pine trees, and the other sideline was the back end of still another small repairman's shop. I would snap the ball to myself and then step s-l-o-w-l-y toward the designated goal line some thirty feet away. I would get my four downs to move the ball over the goal line, and then Andy would have his turn to do the same. I am not sure how we did all of the running and tackling in slow motion, but we were quite satisfied with our game.

Another football game we played by ourselves required the detailed knowledge of all of the names of the quarterbacks and top receivers of each of the NFL teams then in existence. Andy would always play the quarterback, and I would be the wide receiver. He would explain the pass routes that I was to run and then we would determine, by our completion ratio, just which team had the best quarterback and receiver combination on that particular day. This game was always enjoyable until one unfortunate pass pattern execution by me. I miscalculated the depth of my cut for that "stop and go" route. Andy then added to the problem by overthrowing the pass. Andy's spiral and my pass route intersected at an inopportune location—the telephone pole located at the lot line of his parent's property. I jumped and stretched out my arms to caress the ball just as my face smacked into the side of the pole. Needless to say, I took the brunt of the impact and ended up with a bruised cheek, a cut lip, and a black eye.

Summertime and late spring always brought out Andy's joy in cheering for his beloved New York Yankees. When I moved into town, I had never known of the Yankees, Mickey Mantle, Roger Maris, Whitey Ford or any other sports personality. I did not know what a baseball bat or glove even was, much less did I own one. Over the course of those next four or five years with Andy as my best friend and mentor, I learned every minute detail of the Bronx Bombers, The Mick, Yogi, and "the house that Ruth built." Once the snow disappeared from the Wisconsin ground, Andy would bring out his bat, glove, and a couple of worn out, fuzz-flattened tennis balls. One of his brothers even gave me his own weather-beaten leather baseball glove that he no longer used. It was great.

Andy taught me a game of baseball challenge that his older siblings had developed over the years, right there in his own driveway. Andy's house was about fifteen feet from one side of his crushed-rock driveway, and on the other side of it was a Quonset-hut type of building that stood about twenty feet from the crushed rock. The building was covered with a shiny, silver metal material that went from the ground on one side to the ground on the other side of the tall half-circle-shaped building. The one-car garage faced the street, and the driveway was probably sixty feet in length followed by a three-foot wide sidewalk and the two-way-paved street. On the other side of the street, approximately one hundred feet from the garage door, was the eight-foot high fence surrounding the deer and the pheasant pen of the park. (The bird pen always contained about two hundred young pheasants, and it had mesh fencing across the top so as to keep the birds from flying out to freedom. The deer pen usually housed three or four deer that looked as underfed and uncomfortable as a wild animal can when kept in captivity.) Down the center of the street was a solid white painted line. The batter would stand about six feet in front of the closed garage door, and the pitcher would stand about forty feet away, and the game would begin.

The pitcher always called balls and strikes. The batter received credit for a single on any ball hit hard into the house or the silver building. Any ball caught in the air or on the ground by the pitcher was an out. A ball hit against the fence was a double. Any time a hit landed on the top of the pheasant pen or inside the deer pen, the batter was awarded a home run.

Every time a "new" hitter stepped into the batter's box, the player's name would have to be announced along with all of his vital statistics as of last Sunday's paper. The pitcher would call out his "name" and his "statistics" prior to taking the mound. And every ball hit went to "somebody" playing a particular position. We would play this game for hours, just the two of us. Yet, even in writing this now, I truly do not remember if Andy dominated me or if I got the best of him in these little battles of sports skills. I do remember that I absolutely loved to do this, and I do not recall ever arguing with Andy about a strike call or what the final score was for a single game.

As we outgrew that game, we moved over to the large confines of the deer park. There Andy and I would take turns playing offense and defense. One player would take the bat and ball, toss the ball into the air, and try to hit it over the fielder's head. We had to try to avoid hitting one of the five large oak trees or the telephone wires that stretched through the park. As usual, we kept score each and every time that we played. As with the other games, I don't recall who won more games or played better. I just remember playing the game and laughing for about as much of the time as we spent actually hitting and catching the ball.

Gradually, our circle of playmates increased as Andy brought over his friends and relatives, and I brought over one of my brothers and some of our other neighbors. Our games involved a mixture of age levels, gender, and player skills. As a result of Andy's personality, as well as his kindness and his obsession with sports, I grew to love sports of all kinds, too. During a very difficult time in my life, Andy and his family taught me about a whole new way of living and a whole new concept of family.

I have always told people that Andy Pellowski taught me everything that I know about sports. Andy is directly responsible for showing me how much pure enjoyment can take place when the focus is not so much on the game and the score as it is on the friendship and the camaraderie. Andy Pellowski, his parents, and siblings showed me how good it can be to have a family. Every moment that I spent with Andy was truly a gift.

Author's note: Andy and I remained close friends until the day he left for the war in Viet Nam. His tour of service took a heavy toll on Andy and he was never the fun-loving and always-smiling "older brother" that I knew in my youth.

Birdman, Old Man Doc, Stuff and the Family

THE LA LIBERTE HOME was only about one-hundred-fifty yards away from my front door, in terms of actual earth. It seemed like it was a universe away, though, in terms of family dynamics. For about six years of my adolescent and young adult life, the James and Ruth La Liberte family was my salvation. Their group of sons and daughters managed to fill my life with laughter, excitement, and a sense of belonging. At a time in my life when I desperately needed a different role model and male-influence other than my own father, Doctor James La Liberte became a part of my world.

Back row: Paul, Mark (baby), Ruth, Jim.
2nd row: Steve, Chris, Mary.
Front row: Lisa, John, Jim.

The La Libertes lived just in the next block of our neighborhood. Their home was a two-story, shuttered-windows-with-awnings framed house. They had a detached two-car garage with a basketball hoop hanging on the edge of the roof. As you walked into the back doorway of their home, there was a set of steps that led directly upstairs to three bedrooms and a bathroom. The two oldest boys, Paul (young Doc), and Steve (Stuff) shared one bedroom, while the eldest daughter, Mary, had the "open" second-story landing as her "bedroom without walls." Her younger sisters, Lisa and Christine, were the occupants of the other upstairs bedroom.

On the first floor, there was a den located just inside the backdoor entryway. It had a door that led to the finished basement, complete with a ping-pong table and an old sofa. There was a set of steps in the den that led up to the kitchen and dining areas. The dining room/sun room had windows that opened to the den on one side and to the outside of the house on the other. On the other side of the kitchen was a living room that led to Jim and Ruth's bedroom. Next to their bedroom was another bedroom that was shared by the three youngest boys, John (Birdman), Jimmy (little Jim), and Mark, the baby. A second bathroom was also located on that floor.

I knew every inch of that home like it was my own because that is how the La Libertes always made me feel. Old Man Doc, especially, always treated me like I wanted my own father to treat me. Doc La Liberte was a successful dentist who was about twenty years older than me. He was a rather thin, bespectacled man who never seemed to be without a smile and a humorous comment. It was not at all unusual for Doc to join in a basketball game in the driveway with Young Doc, Stuff, and me. If there was a basketball or football game on the television, then it was more than likely that Old Man Doc would be sitting with us in the den commenting on the game. If my memory serves me correctly, then I believe that Old Man Doc went out of his way to say hello and to have a conversation with me literally every time I was in or near their home.

Old Man Doc had the type of personality whereby he seemed to never be upset or irritated. No matter what kind of trouble that Young Doc, Stuff, I, and the other guys caused, he always seemed to deal with it calmly and effectively. He never acted as if he was yelling at us so much as he was asking us to "knock it off." It was difficult to continue to misbehave when he was so "cool" about the manner in which he was reprimanding you. James La Liberte, in my eyes, was the quintessential father figure. He was a professional man who loved kids, sports, life, and his wife, Ruth.

Old Man Doc La Liberte always made me feel good about myself, about my accomplishments, and my future. He never missed a chance to pat me on the back after a football, basketball, or baseball game. Usually, he would start off with a joke about some play I had made. Then, he would get around to congratulating me on my efforts. If the truth were to be known, I would have to admit that I always looked forward to seeing him after a game because he made me feel good about who I was and what I had done.

Ruth was always the harried mom looking to somehow manage this brood of children. She always seemed to be just one more juvenile act away from losing her cool completely. Yet, it was obvious that she loved each and every one of her kids deeply and profoundly. Just about the time that you thought she was mired in a state of frustration and anger, she would break out into a laugh or make some funny comment.

I must tell you that one of the main reasons for her concern was my presence. She was well aware that I was interested in her eldest daughter, Mary, and she was not about to let me get near her. Since Mary was in seventh grade and I was a sophomore when we first started to notice each other, I could understand her angst. Ruth was absolutely vigilant in her approach to protecting her daughter from the likes of me. With the reputation that I had with girls at that time, I don't blame her at all for that attitude.

Mary and I were close friends all the way through my high school life. Ironically, we never went on a date in spite of the fact that I spent more time with her than I did with any of the girls that I did date. I always found it so easy to talk with Mary about anything and everything. She was always more mature than her age implied and it did not hurt that I found her to be a very attractive girl. Our relationship was always filled with "boyfriend-girlfriend" tension because I would see her nearly every night when I was over visiting and carousing with her brother, Paul. She and I would laugh, converse, and hold hands, yet I was always dating some other girl closer to my own grade level.

At first, I could not ask her out because her mom would never let it happen. Then, later on, I could not ask her out officially on a date because I was going steady with a girl in my class. The real irony is that I had this great relationship with Mary for longer than any other girl in my youth, and I always wanted her to be my girlfriend. The fact is that I showed her more respect than any other girl that I went with in high school. Yet, we never did become a couple.

Paul, Young Doc, was a tall, lanky guy who was a good student and a very good friend to me for many years. He and I spent a great deal of time together from the moment that his family moved to town. We both enjoyed sports a great deal, and we challenged each other in school academically. Doc was more into the sciences than I was, but we still ended up in the same classes for much of high school. In spite of the fact that he did not play football, he enjoyed watching it and discussing the game. Basketball was the game that he really reveled in throughout high school. While he was never a star, he worked hard at it, and he always made it fun for me to practice with him in the driveway. Doc was the kind of friend that you respected because you knew he would be straight with you and treat you fairly at all times. Plus, he had a good sense of humor.

His younger brother, Stuff, was a real card. He had a nickname for everyone that he ever met (long before Chris Berman and ESPN). Plus, every one of them made you smile. Stuff was a top student in his class and a pretty good track and field athlete. Like his brother, he enjoyed basketball the most and he was pretty decent at it. I think in a lot of ways Stuff was a reincarnation of his father. He had his ever-present smart-ass smirk, and he was willing to talk to you about any subject for as long as you wanted to do so, and much more.

Mary's younger sisters always made me feel like the "cool" big brother whenever I was over to visit after school, where we all ended up shooting hoops or watching television. I had to go home for supper, but afterwards I headed right back over. I spent the entire evening at their house most of the weeknights.

It was not unusual for me to be seated on one of the car seats that they used as a sofa in the den with Chris on one side of me and Lisa on the other side while I tried to talk to Mary, Young Doc, or Stuff as the television set blared. With all eight of the kids and me there, the television needed to be on full-blast to be heard over the din of all of those mouths yapping and yelling at the same time. I loved every minute that I spent there.

They were a family in the truest sense. The kids yelled, screamed, and fought, and the parents coped as best they could. I remember thinking that the noise level at my own house was at about the same decibel range, but there was a much different feeling in the air at my home. At the La Libertes' home, I always sensed that underneath all of the racket and the jostling, this was a family that genuinely cared about each other. At my home, the air was always thick with tension and nervous apprehension.

I spent countless hours with that family in their home and I came to feel as welcome as if I was another one of their children. Without any doubt at all, I am sure that my attitude and outlook on life and on family were salvaged because of the La Libertes. For that great gift, I will be forever grateful.

Author's note: "Old Man Doc" La Liberte and his wife now live in Eau Claire, Wisconsin, and I recently introduced my entire family to them on a trip through that area. I had arranged to get together with them so that I could read the chapter to them about their role in my life. My family, Old Man Doc, Ruth, Paul, and his wife, Mary, and Mary, the daughter, met us. We all had an absolutely great time reminiscing, laughing and teasing each other. Old Man Doc is still a great guy, and Ruth is very happy and substantially less harried now that their children are all adults. Paul is still the person that I remember as my good friend and his sister, Mary, is still the very classy lady that I recall from so many years ago.

The Grace of God

THERE, BUT BY THE grace of God, go I. Most people utter that phrase as they observe someone who is less fortunate than they are. With me it was different. During my youth, I would observe the happiness and love that my friends had in their families and I would think, "There, but by the hand of God, could I be."

Growing up I became closely acquainted with my own intense feelings of hatred and anger. Yet, I spent eight of my formative years attending St. Aloysius Catholic School and being taught daily about God's kindness and about the loving nature of God.

Every school day of those eight years, the School Sisters of Notre Dame and the lay teachers of St. Aloysius drilled into me that God would always be there for me. God would always forgive me for my many, many sins and God would show me the way to eternal happiness. God was the Supreme Being that I could always look to for comfort and solace. God was my Savior.

But I could not get myself to understand how this loving and kind God would place a child so hungry for love into a family where the parents had no basic understanding of the simple concept of love. I spent a substantial amount of time peering into the mirror and wondering why God had put me into this particular dysfunctional family. It seemed to me that all of my friends had homes where hugs were shared, hands were held and smiles creased the faces of kids and parents alike.

Life at St. Aloysius Catholic grade school instilled in me a deep sense of values and a great many of life's lessons. Principal Sister Mary Alvin and her cohorts demonstrated every day by their own commitment to God and to all of us unruly children that there was a greater calling in life. Each one of them had relinquished their own personal opportunities for financial success, marital bliss and for professional goals in the business world. They had dedicated their lives to teaching young

Catholic boys and girls the fine points of English, Mathematics, Geography, Art, Music, Reading, Writing and all of the other subjects necessary for a complete education. But they also shared with us their deep belief in God and the church.

Whether it was Sister Mary Johnna, Sister Mary Rochelle or Sister Mary Bertrandis teaching Religion, the primary message was always the same. I was a sinner and so were all of my young friends. Every one of us deserved to be completely consumed with guilt. We all needed to constantly beg for God's forgiveness. Secondarily, those nuns also shared with me that God was also this wonderful Omniscient and Omnipotent Spirit that watched over us and kept us safe. They somehow found the time to tell me about the other side of God. They infused in me a deep belief that wherever I was, God also was.

Throughout all of this teaching there seemed to be several main concepts and precepts that existed in our Catholic faith. For example, every one of us children who experienced that education came to understand that we all have a soul, a conscience and a free will. We came to realize that God did not necessarily cause things to happen in our lives. God simply allowed us to make our own choices about the opportunities for good or bad behavior. Each of us had our own conscience to look to when it came time to determine the path that we would choose to take with our lives. Every one of us came to know that once we left this world our souls would be transported to a venue in the next world.

The options were Heaven, Hell or Purgatory. Purgatory was for those who were not quite ready for an afterlife in God's glorious presence. It was a temporary "waiting station" for our souls. We would move onto Heaven when enough people on earth prayed for us to do so. Hell was that most severe and permanent of prisons where we would experience an eternity without the opportunity to be with God. Heaven, on the other hand, was going to be an existence wherein all of our wants, needs and desires would be gone forever because of the eternal peace and joy that the abundant aura of God's presence would provide.

But I would be completely remiss in sharing my Catholic grade school experience if I did not share some of the "lighter" side happenings of those eight years. For example, on those rare occasions that I actually ate lunch at school, I had to learn how to get past Sister Mary Alvin's plate inspection in order to be able to head out to recess. No plate was to ever be returned unless ALL of the food was eaten and the milk carton was completely empty.

Sometimes that meant that I would have to load up the noodles and processed cheese into my pants' pockets in order to make it out to play football.

In sixth grade I began to notice one of God's best works. The young girls who were my classmates suddenly became very interesting to me. Their parochial school uniforms started to take different shapes and when I would "accidentally" bump into them they felt nice and soft. Sister Mary Bertrandis, though, was hell-bent on squelching my newfound attraction to the opposite sex. Every time she caught me talking to a girl I would have to do push-ups. I think by the end of the school year I had sixteen-inch biceps and a raging set of hormones to boot.

Throughout these eight years of Catholic influence, I spent a great deal of time and effort as a mass server. I would be assigned, first with my older brother, and then with one of my good friends to serve either 6:15 a.m. mass or 8:00 a.m. mass every morning for a week at a time. The early edition never had more than five attendees while the latter mass was for the entire school of 250 kids who wanted to be anywhere else but there. (I did learn a valuable second language though as a result of my duties. I can't begin to tell you how many times Latin has come in handy for me in airports and fast-food restaurants.) On those very many occasions that I got into trouble for laughing during mass or for intentionally pouring too much wine into Father's chalice, we had to suffer the wrath of Sister Mary Alvin.

Sister Mary Alvin was a stern rigid nun who had apparently been trained by a master in the art of spreading fear into the hearts of young Catholic boys. With one cold hard stare from her steely brown eyes you could almost feel your trousers beginning to get very damp. Very early on in my grade school life, I learned to deal with Sister Mary Johnna's hard knuckles running down my spine after she had caught me talking in class. I grew to accept Sister Mary Gertrude's loving use of the wood ruler slapping across my hands when I wasn't paying close enough attention. I even found a way to enjoy all of those recesses spent writing words and definitions from the spelling dictionary because of some misbehavior. What I never learned to overcome, though, was Sister Mary Alvin's 1960s version of the "Hannibal Lecter" eyes. When she did it to me, I just knew I was about to be mentally tortured to the point of breaking. Every time she finished with me, I vowed to avoid any future bad behavior. Then a week or two later I would be right back in that same awful position.

In spite of all of the quirks and idiosyncrasies of that Catholic School, I did receive a great education in all subjects, including Religion. The juxtaposition of that constant creed about a loving God next to the constant hellhole of my family life somehow struck a chord with me.

My belief in God did allow me to escape from the torturous mental and emotional anguish that was my home-life. No matter what disappointment or frustration had occurred with my parents, I turned to God. Mostly, I asked for Him to help me understand why these things happened. Other times, I asked why He let them continue to happen. For some reason, though, I always felt safe in church talking to God. I always knew that God was listening and that He was giving me the strength to deal with my circumstances. I always knew that I needed God to be with me and I knew that I wanted God to be on my side.

When I left grade school and moved into high school I discovered the unbelievable pleasure of sexual exploration with so many young girls. But since I never wanted God to be far from me, I ended up going to Confession every Saturday. My guilt never let me go long without asking God for forgiveness. I always knew that I would be back the next week confessing the same sins, but I knew that I always felt tremendously better after having purged my soul of those misdeeds. While all of those nuns had been effective in teaching me about guilt, I had also remembered the details they shared about God's ability to forgive me "seventy times seven" times for my transgressions.

I'm in front of the third girl from the left in the top row.

From the time that I first went to St. Aloysius grade school, throughout all of high school and my adult life, God has always played a major role in my moral decisions. God's presence always provided me with a "comfort blanket" in my times of difficulty and in my times of challenge. While God has not always answered my prayers with a resounding "yes," God has always given me the opportunity to feel "heard."

There is a long list of examples of those times when I have asked God to help me or to aid someone that I care about deeply. There have been many instances when I just asked for God to be with me, to be at my side or to give me the strength to face a challenge. It was a long time ago that I stopped asking God to give me something materialistic or even something intangible. I have learned that usually all that I want from God is a little boost. I usually just need God to help me find the courage, stamina or fortitude to perform up to the best of my ability at whatever I am doing or whatever experience is happening.

Occasionally I will ask God to help me find peace and comfort in difficult times. Even the simple act of praying to God can become a mantra for me when I need to relax or to overcome a fearful situation. For example, prior to my double by-pass heart surgery, I memorized the twenty-third Psalm. It became my mantra of comfort and solace.

For nearly all of my fifty-seven years on this earth, I have sought out God to be my Comforter, to be my Consolation, to be my Stabilizer and to be my Spiritual Guide. And I can honestly state that God has been all of that and more for me. Without God's presence and influence in my life I cannot even imagine where I would be now.

So in spite of this cathartic review of the life-changing gifts, the wonderfully generous miracles, the inspirational occurrences of Divine interventions and the absolutely soothing single experience of God's actual presence in my life, there is something else even more profound about my relationship with God.

For as long as I can remember, God has been my constant companion. It did not matter if I were questioning His actions or if I were sinning against His commandments. It did not matter if I was near death or near complete mental breakdown. It did not matter if I were begging for His Guiding Hand or if I was seeking out His Wisdom. It did not matter if I simply wanted nothing at all from Him. All that I remember and all that I know is that God has been my constant companion and for that I am forever grateful.

There, because of the Grace of God, I have been. There, because of the Grace of God, I have survived. Here, because of the Grace of God, I now am.

Author's note: In early Spring of 2012, I ventured to Elm Grove, Wisconsin to visit with Sister Mary Alvin at the School Sisters of Notre Dame Retirement Center. Her order now has the nuns use their birth names so Sister Mary Alvin is now known as Sister Arline Jaeger. I thoroughly enjoyed my three hours of conversation and a complete tour of the facilities. I grew to appreciate Sister Arline as a devoted and devout woman. I now understand, in retrospect and through the eyes of a parent, that she was only doing the job assigned to her as principal of St. Aloysious Catholic School in Arcadia so many years ago. I see now that she was and is a woman dedicated to serving Jesus and serving her order of nuns in whatever role is necessary. Even at age 82, she is still working hard to serve God and her fellow nuns.

Hometown Hero

AT ONE POINT IN MY LIFE, I attempted to overcome my fear of water by visiting a psychologist. He informed me that the most effective method that he had utilized for dealing with such a phobia involved "desensitizing" therapy. Without going into all of the details, suffice to say that as part of the process he asked me to share with him a "moment" or experience in my life during which I was totally relaxed and comfortable. My response surprised me a little.

Senior Year Fall 1971

The first such experience that hit me was not necessarily a "relaxed and comfortable" circumstance. It had occurred on a high school football field during my senior year of high school. It was in a game against Bangor, a member of our school's athletic conference at the time. They were going through a bit of a tough time in their football program and we were expected to do reasonably well that year. Even though we had a new coach and we had only had a 4-5 record the previous year, our team had gotten off to a good non-conference start to the season. Our record was 2-0 going into the night.

For that year of football I never came off of the field until we were substantially ahead in the score. I was a running back on offense at the time and I played outside linebacker on defense. Kicking duties were also assigned to me. Coach had informed me before the first game of the season that he expected me to be a leader on this team and that he would do everything possible to help me reach my ultimate performance abilities.

A Knock at the Door

The evening got off to a bad start for me when I left my helmet back in the locker room in the high school. I must have looked like some kind of an idiot as I led calisthenics and stretching in pre-game warm-ups and I was the only player without a helmet. Luckily, Coach Fredrickson forgave me for my absent-mindedness and we found a substitute who had the same helmet size as I wore so that I could play.

For this game, Coach had informed us that if we did not have a fifty point lead at the half, then all of the starters would have to run two miles the next Monday in practice. That is correct; I did write "a fifty point lead!" Coach had high expectations for us and wanted to give us incentives to achieve our full potential. Of course, none of the starters would ever see any second-half game action if we did get that much of a dominant lead.

On this night our offensive line was opening up huge holes in their defense. The play calling was nearly perfect by our quarterback, my closest friend, Mark "Arnie" Arnold. Before the first fifteen minutes of the game were done, I had already had a 57 yard touchdown run and a 54 yard touchdown run. In fact, I had only carried the ball five times and my offensive line had helped me to gain over 130 yards.

At one point I remember the referee handing me the football for another kick-off and when he did he said, "It's too bad you won't be playing much longer tonight. I'm having fun watching you." That comment made me feel pretty cool. To have a ref tell you something like that doesn't happen very often.

Then in the second quarter their punter had gotten off a beautiful spiral from the fifty-yard-line that sailed over our returner's head and out-of-bounds at the four-yard line. For the first time all night, we were backed up against the wall. When we got into the huddle, my quarterback friend Arnie told everybody, "Listen up, we're doing a new play."

He then proceeded to draw out the directions on the palm of his left hand. He had diagrammed a play wherein the two wide receivers ran post-patterns to the center of the field taking their defenders away from the sidelines. Then he had our fullback step up into the pocket to protect him in the end zone so he could try to hit me with a little flare pass. My job was to step up about four yards from my starting position in the backfield (about seven yards behind him to start with) and simply cut directly to the left sideline and look for the ball.

I still remember it like it was yesterday. I made my four steps straight into the backs of our offensive linemen and planted my right foot hard. Then I cut sharply out to the left sideline. After I made a pivot and took two quick steps, I turned my head toward Arnie. This beautiful, tight spiral pass was already floating toward me. It felt soft as a marshmallow when it landed in my outstretched hands and I cradled it in my left arm, immediately. When I turned to check out my circumstances, I realized that I was only about a yard out of the end zone and about twelve yards from the sideline. A linebacker was trying to close in on me to tackle me. I just gave him a slight stiff-arm in the chest and turned the jets on to get to the outside. Once I turned the corner on him I could see nothing but 100 yards of grass ahead of me.

That is when my "moment" started. I hit full-stride at about our ten-yard line and headed toward the other end zone as fast as I could. I knew that there would be tacklers trying to use the "angle" to catch up with me. But, I was sort of carried down that long expanse of turf by the cheers of the crowd immediately ahead and to my left and by my teammates standing and screaming along the sideline (only a few yards away from my pounding feet) as I raced by them. For the entire run, it seemed like I was being swept along by a tide of excitement and joy.

Now I know that the adulation that I felt for those instances and those Friday night games for that year was not really love. But it sure felt like it to me. That moment only lasted about fifteen seconds, but they were the fifteen happiest and longest seconds of my life to that point. Who knows maybe I will never lose the sensation of an entire crowd standing and cheering for me as I sprinted down that sideline.

I can honestly tell you that I think about that touchdown, that night, and that year less and less. It is now to the point where I have to be nudged into even discussing it. The starters did all end up running the two miles that next Monday since the half-time score was ONLY 47-0. Yet, whenever I travel back to my original hometown, it is inevitable that someone will ask me to talk about those "glory days." A lot of them though remind me of the night that I got kicked out of the biggest game of my career because of an unsportsmanlike conduct penalty. With the good there is always some bad, I guess.

No matter what, I know that that "moment" in my life will always bring a smile to my face.

Brief Encounter

I BELIEVE THAT IT was during the late summer of 1974 that I had the pleasure of meeting Judith Ann Rackley. For nine wonderful days, I spent every lunch hour and every evening in her company discussing life, love, God, and the world.

Interestingly enough, I remember very few details of her physical being. What I do recall is that in many ways, she was somewhat nondescript. She was neither overweight nor supermodel-thin. Her face was pretty, but not stunningly so. Her hair was thick and curly, but you would not have confused her with Farrah Fawcett of the 1970s.

What did absolutely fascinate me about her was her mind.

It all started rather innocently on a warm and bright Saturday morning in June. My good friend, Jim Haines, and I planned to hit the softball fields to get in some extra batting practice. We did this quite often at that point in our lives. We would rotate pitching and hitting. Then we would chase down the softballs and start all over again.

On this particular day, two young ladies wandered over to the fields and offered to help us gather the balls so as to save us more time for hitting practice. They seemed friendly and attractive enough for us to acquiesce to their request immediately. As I remember it, we enjoyed several laughs and some general teasing during the hitting and fielding session.

Once Jim and I decided to call it a day, we sat down and introduced ourselves more formally. Judith and her friend informed us that they were in the middle of a "coming of age" experience. They were trekking across the United States by hitchhiking. Their trip was only a part of their plan to "become one with God." The level of their sincerity and commitment was extremely obvious, even to a couple of eighteen-year-old, hormone-driven, constantly-consumed-by-thoughts-of-sex guys.

Since Jim already had a steady girlfriend at the time, he was not overly interested in a longer, more in-depth discussion with the two young ladies. However, that night I showered and returned to the park as quickly as possible. At first, I just spent some time helping them set up camp right there in a corner of the park. It didn't take much effort because they had nothing more than a pup tent. All of the time that we worked and talked, I was completely intrigued by Judith and her endeavor.

Over the next week or so, Judith, her friend, and I spent every moment possible involved in deep philosophical dialogues. At some point, though, I told them that I was truly concerned about their safety as they planned their next move across the countryside. Conversely, the two of them were convinced that God would watch over them and guide them to safety so long as they were intelligent about their decisions. They admitted that they had had several instances wherein a degree of discomfort and apprehension had been present. Yet, their genuine trust in God's divine hand and in their ability to discern the appropriate people that they should befriend provided them with ample strength to continue on their journey.

I remember that I spent that whole week consumed by the thought of Judith and how she filled my life with challenging ideas and thought-provoking concepts. I could hardly stay focused at my bookkeeping job because the time moved too slowly without her next to me.

It was not until the third day of their stay that I spent any time alone with Judith. However, I do remember that we did nothing more than continue our conversations about every subject imaginable. We sat on the high school football field bleachers and stared into the dark night. As much as I wanted to take her into my arms and to press my lips against hers, I knew it was unnecessary. The depth of my feelings for her was so strong that I was content just to be sitting next to her.

As each day passed, Judith and I spent more and more time one-on-one while her friend read books or walked throughout the city. I was enjoying a connection with Judith that I had never experienced prior to this. Here I was with this young, interesting, and not un-attractive woman, yet I had not made even a slight pass at her. I was so intrigued by her and respected her so much that a physical/sexual relationship had not been necessary.

A Knock at the Door

Somewhere around the fifth day of her visit, we mutually realized that our emotions were beginning to come into play. We knew that, eventually, our hearts and our hormones were going to reach a point of no return. So we sat across a picnic table under a moonlit sky as millions of stars shone above us, and we did something that I had never done before and neither had she.

At first we just reached out to each other and held hands. I remember wanting desperately to take her in my arms and to hold and kiss her. But I did not do that. Instead I looked deeply into her eyes and soul and my heart nearly burst.

"Have you ever kissed someone with your eyes?" I asked her.

"I believe that I just did now," was all she said.

We stayed there basking in the loving warmth of our emotions for what seemed to be an hour. We never so much as caressed. We simply held hands and gazed into each other's eyes.

The next two days passed much more quickly than I wanted. We walked, talked, and listened to Olivia Newton-John sing *I Honestly Love You*. We both admitted that it was very possible that we were falling deeply in love. Yet, she never flinched in her plans to continue her journey to become one with God. As strongly as she thought she felt about me, and as much as I wanted her to stay, she felt even more deeply that she had to leave in order to follow-through on her commitment to God.

On one of the last nights that I ever saw her, Judith told me that she did not believe in anything materialistic. Therefore, she had made the practice of never taking anything with her or leaving anything behind with the people that she had met on her journey. But she wanted me to have a hand-written note. In that two sentence letter, she told me to "please don't lose your love because love is the mainstay of existence." She signed it, "God be with you always."

In looking back now on that beautiful week of my young life, I don't remember any long and tearful good-byes with Judith. There was just that one time when I pulled around the corner in my car to head back to their little campsite only to see that they were not there anymore. I remember my heart sinking and my brain thinking that I should hit the road and find her. But, I did not do that. For some inexplicable reason, I let go of her forever.

Eventually, I found another woman later in my life who gave me these same thrills and who challenged and intrigued me in the same ways and even more. This time I did not let her go, and I eventually convinced her to be my wife.

Author's note 1: For whatever reason, Judith Ann Rackley was a part of my life for that one week, and I never saw her again nor did I ever seek her out. Maybe I subconsciously thought that the reality of attempting to rekindle those tremendous feelings could never live up to my memories of that one single week.

Author's note 2: In a somewhat odd circumstance, my wife nudged me into trying to find the actual note that she had given me. It took several attempts to scour my closet to find it buried in with a hodge-podge of old letters and cards, some of which belonged to my wife. The irony is that without having seen this note for at least a dozen years or more, the salutation of "God be with you always" was very familiar to me. For the last several years or so, I have signed all of my letters, emails and other correspondence with nearly the exact same words.

While I am sure there is no deep meaning to that coincidence, I find it somewhat interesting.

A Special Birthday

CAN YOU FATHOM THE number of situations in which you have been involved wherein a matter of inches was the difference between life and death for you? To go even one step further, can you begin to grasp how many lives would be altered had that gap of several inches not existed in your life? Do you understand that there are incidents that occur completely outside of your own life that eventually play a major role in your life?

My wife is here today and is the mother of our children and has touched the personal world of so many people because of a simple matter of several inches in one direction at one exact moment of her life.

It was May of 1977 when she was a student in the nursing program at the University of Wisconsin in Madison. At the time, she was twenty-one years old and putting herself through school by working several jobs. She was an attractive, brown-haired young woman who stood about five feet two inches tall and weighed no more than one hundred ten pounds soaking wet. During her high school career, she had toiled long and hard to maintain excellent grades, and she ended up in the top five in her graduating class of two hundred-plus students. Her goal was to be a registered nurse, and she was well on the way to achieving that position.

Vickie's high school graduation photo

While in the nursing program, she was required to attend several clinical classes at the UW hospital. They were also difficult and challenging sessions, but she truly enjoyed them. She found her forte was not class work so much as it was the "hands-on" experience of the clinicals.

One late afternoon, she had just completed her assignments, so she headed out from the hospital to walk to her apartment. She remembers that it was a very bright sunny day, and that there was nothing of particular importance on her mind. The last thing that she remembers is that she approached an intersection in front of the hospital. She is not clear as to whether or not she was somewhat blinded by the sunlight or if she simply looked and did not see the approaching truck. Either way, she stepped off of the curb to cross the street. Apparently, she was then struck in the head by the mirror of a truck as it went by her. She collapsed into the road and from that point forward, her memory of the incident is completely absent.

The driver did stop and come back to help her. He called an ambulance, and she was rushed right back to the very hospital from whence she came. She lost consciousness and lapsed into a coma immediately upon being injured. The doctors were quite concerned that the impact of the blow to her head had caused a lot of pressure on her brain. So, they carved a piece of her skull out in order to first relieve the pressure and to implant a monitoring device.

For the next four days, Vickie's parents and family members spent every waking hour praying for a miracle. Throughout the entire ordeal, the medical staff poked and prodded her with medical tests and procedures. They did everything possible to bring her back to consciousness. But, with each passing hour, the fear of significant brain damage grew. At some point in time, the major concern became whether or not she would be a "vegetable" with no cognitive abilities if and when she did return from her deep sleep.

Then, on May 23, as her father prepared to spend the day at her side praying, a miracle happened. After all the procedures and medical opportunities were exhausted and all that was left was to wait and pray, Vickie suddenly awakened and recognized her father. He held her hand and rejoiced at her dramatic recovery. His daughter had been brought back to consciousness on his birthday.

It took several months for Vickie to return to normalcy, but she did come back with all of her brain functions and abilities. The only loss of memory that she suffered was of the accident itself and of its weeklong aftermath.

Thirteen Miles of Treacherous Turns and Too Many Tequilas

IT WAS ONE OF those all-too-many times when I let my little brain (read: penis) do the thinking. I let my hormones take over for my brain too many times in my early twenties. On any given night, when I allowed my sex drive to overcome my conscience and values, it was quite possible for me to risk serious bodily harm to myself and to others. One particular Saturday night in 1978 was just such an occasion.

Earlier in the week, this special young lady had stopped into my clothing store to purchase several items for her brother. She was a slender, young woman with a curvaceous body and very pretty brown hair. Her demeanor and personality were both of an extremely attractive nature. However, the characteristics that really intrigued me were her intelligence and confidence. She was quite sure about her future and how she was going to achieve all of her goals. In addition, she was poised enough to have won a statewide beauty pageant. While she had planned to make those few clothing purchases quickly, she ended up staying for over an hour.

Our conversation was lively, challenging, and, of course, occasionally flirtatious. At that time in my life, I fancied myself as a bit of a poet. Several of my own poems were displayed in a calligraphic form on a couple of large posters in the store. She commented that she found them to be quite good. She was pleasantly surprised by the quality of my writings. In spite of the fact that I had never spoken to her prior to that day, we talked as if we had been friends forever.

Eventually, she decided that she needed to get back to her homestead so that she could wrap up these newly purchased items for her brother's birthday party that night. But, before she departed, I invited her to visit again prior to going back to college in Madison on Sunday. She informed me that it was a good possibility that she would do just that.

Sure enough, it was only two days later that she was back. This time there were no purchases to be made. We just enjoyed several hours of philosophical discussion filled with serious thoughts and tinged with substantial laughter. It was as if we were long-lost lovers in the process of uncovering a passionate affair, but it was currently still beneath the surface.

After two or three hours of interesting and entertaining discourse, she asked me if I would come out to her farm that Saturday evening. Apparently, her parents were gone for the weekend, and she was planning a huge party for all of her friends in the valley. It did not take me long to agree to make an effort to get there.

However, that Saturday evening, several of my close high school friends were home for the weekend, and I ended up bar hopping with them. We started immediately after attending the 5:15 p.m. mass and sharing a pizza. The drinking began with some tequila swilling. I will tell you that I was not a drinker in high school at all. In fact, other than a year or so in my early twenties, I have never been much of a drinker. But this was right in the middle of my "drinking era."

By ten o'clock that evening, I had partaken of at least seven or eight shots of tequila, and I was feeling pretty giddy. I remember sitting on the doorsteps of a local business while I shared a couple more laughs with Doc and his girlfriend, Mary. They were both much more sober than I was at the time.

Suddenly, I recalled that there was a party in Waumandee that I wanted to attend before it got too late. If my memory serves me correctly, I believe that they made some effort to dissuade me from driving out there. But, they failed because my hormones were again in control of my intellectual capacities.

In hindsight, I am amazed that I would have even considered getting into my car, much less driving sixteen miles to the party. The last thirteen miles were some of the most treacherous hairpin-curved roads in the area. There was one sharp curve after another and several double back turns. To make the drive even worse, they all occurred while climbing, first up a steep hill and then traveling down into the valley on the other side. This trip was always a challenge when I was sober, and on this particular night, I was definitely not that.

A Knock at the Door

On at least two separate occasions on the trek that night, I actually stopped the car completely because I was on the wrong side of the road. Luckily, I was not a fast driver whenever I was in this condition or I would not be telling this story now. I am sure that the trip took me at least twice as long as it would have had I been sober. Somehow, though, I steered that vehicle around all of those twists and turns and avoided the trees and the ditches and the oncoming traffic (which was probably no more than a few cars anyway), and I arrived at her home for the party in one piece.

Thankfully she was a smarter person than I was because she convinced me that the evening would be much more pleasurable if I were to cease drinking alcohol for a while. I took her advice and switched to consuming gallons of water.

The rest of the night's events shall remain private memories for me and for the young lady. The important issue is that, once again, God guided me through the entire trip of impending danger in spite of my own horrible judgment. For whatever reason, God had a bigger plan for me, I believe. I am certain that without his Divine Hand reaching down that night on that road trip, I would not and should not be here today.

Author's Note:
Luckily, the world has changed for the better when it comes to young people watching out for each other more fervently than our generation ever did. My own sons have had such evenings of partying and reveling, but there is always a designated driver that ensures the safety of all in the group. I look back and I know that I deserved to get a handful of traffic tickets, and that I should thank God every day for having survived that idiotic decision that I made to drive so drunk.

But, I believe, that the reality of it all is that God saved me that night.

A Thrilling Response

THE SINGLE MOST TOUCHING and memorable moment in my life revolves around the day that Vickie became my wife. It is especially memorable to me because she was a somewhat reluctant bride. She likes to remind me, even to this day, that she did not say, "Yes" to my proposal for a while. It took a substantial amount of persuasion on my part to convince her that it was a good idea for her to marry me.

For approximately six years before she ever met me, she had dated someone else. He was her high school sweetheart. They had planned their future together and everyone in their family assumed they would marry some day. However, their relationship changed when she moved into town after college. She had received a scholarship from the local hospital while she was attending the University of Wisconsin in Madison. Part of the arrangement for the scholarship was that she had to work at the hospital for one year after she graduated.

That is when I came into the picture and complicated things. Through some friends of mine who were also nurses at St. Joseph's hospital, I arranged an introduction. Miraculously, Vickie and I hit it off from the very start. Our phone conversations would last for hours and we discussed every subject under the sun.

During the next eleven months after our initial meeting, our relationship had many tumultuous ebbs and flows. Vickie broke up with me at least four times. She kept telling me that she enjoyed my company, but that she did not really love me. Of course, I refused to give up because I knew that I had found my soul mate. With that stubborn persistence that has always been one of my trademarks, I increased my efforts to win her heart. Eventually, finally, she realized that in spite of all of my faults and flaws, I was the right one for her. The struggle to win her over was a long, arduous, and at times painful, experience. But I was thrilled with the final outcome.

Therefore, our wedding day meant so much to me because it was the culmination of that experience. But even more importantly I knew that for the first time in my life someone genuinely loved me for who I was. I believed that I had a legitimate shot at happiness. Vickie had become my best friend and my confidante. She was the person that I wanted to cry with when I needed to. She was the person with whom I loved to celebrate every victory. She was the person who knew just exactly what to do to spur me on in the right direction no matter what the situation. A thousand times before this, my friends had heard me tell them that I had found "the ONE." This time there was no doubt at all. She was "the ONE."

I was in a state of near-euphoria when Father Klink turned to her in front of my family and friends and asked her those unforgettable words, "Vickie Carroll, do you take this man to be your lawfully wedded husband?"

I could barely wait to hear her respond. When she said, "I do," I could hardly contain my joy. That moment is indelibly etched into my memory. If there is such a thing as a "moment" that forever changes your life for the better, then that was my moment.

Move Over Indiana Jones and James Bond

I WOULD NOT CHOOSE Marlon Brando's character in the great 1954 movie, *On the Waterfront*. I would not choose Harrison Ford's classic character, Indiana Jones. I would not select even the ultimately cool alter-ego role of Sean Connery's James Bond. No, the movie character that I would love to be in real life is much more subtly successful. He is much more psychologically interesting and appealing. The single, unequivocal choice of my favorite movie character of all time is George Bailey in the Frank Capra Christmas classic, *It's a Wonderful Life*.

George's story takes place in a much simpler time and in a community right out of a Norman Rockwell picture. Bedford Falls is a city filled with gorgeous old Victorian homes and picket fences lining the front yards. George is trained well in the fine art of both generosity and compassion. His wise, caring father and his gentle, kindly mother are perfect role models. He spends his young life surrounded by a loving family and good friends. The tremendous influence of his parents is the foundation for his own compassionate attitude but he takes that love of mankind to a whole new level. He spends his entire lifetime placing the needs of everyone else ahead of his own goals, dreams, and ambitions. Somehow he manages to find a position of some esteem in the community and a certain level of business success.

At every wrong twist and turn in the lives of his family, friends, and clients, George concocts a plan to save them. At his first job as a pharmacist's delivery boy, he realizes that his boss, Mr. Gower, is extremely distracted and distraught one day. So, he pays special attention when Mr. Gower asks him on that day to deliver a prescription. As a result, George saves the life of the recipient, and he helps Mr. Gower avoid prison because the druggist had accidentally substituted poison for the proper drug.

A Knock at the Door

As a boy enjoying a beautiful winter day with his brother and some friends, he is suddenly put in a position of danger. His younger brother, Harry, drops through the ice and is drowning. George jumps in to save him, but in the process loses hearing in one ear. As a result of the accident, George is unable to enlist in the Army for the war, but his brother goes on to be a war hero when he saves an entire shipload of soldiers from eminent death.

In another instance, he saves the citizens of Bedford Falls from some of the ravages of the great depression by using his honeymoon money to fend off a "run" on the Building and Loan. While almost everyone in town is in a state of financial panic, George persuades the Building and Loan patrons to believe in each other through the tough times.

Through his beloved Building and Loan business, George helps many local people fight their way out of the slums by providing money to build their own homes. He manages to find a way to grant loans to individuals who are hard working but a little down on their luck financially. George single-handedly allows the working-class people of Bedford Falls to improve the quality of their lives.

Our beloved George even turns down the prospect of total financial security for himself and his family when he is offered a new job at the arch-rival bank . He knows this would not be good for the people of Bedford Falls. Another time, he is offered the possibility of cashing in on some "insider" information on his friend's company, but all he can think about is the chance to bring his friend's factory to town so more jobs will be available for the good citizens of Bedford Falls.

Whenever his family or friends need George for any reason at all, he puts their needs ahead of his own desires. Time after time, he sacrifices his own dreams, goals, and wishes in order to help a friend or family member who needs him. George seldom gives the impression that he is thrilled to do these things. In fact, on many occasions, he is downright reluctant to change his course of action. Yet, he does each and every one of these acts for one simple reason and with one simple motivation: love of his fellow human beings.

In one last show of the depth of his love for his wife and family, George ponders taking his own life because he, mistakenly, believes that he is worth more dead than alive. It is the only way he can see to save his family from social scandal and financial ruin. Just when all seems lost, George suddenly and dramatically is given a tremendous gift.

All of those folks whose lives he has touched over the years reach out to help him. They bestow on him all of the money he needs to remove him from his predicament with a heart-wrenching, tear-inducing demonstration of their own love and admiration for him.

It took me a great many years to understand why, exactly, I empathized so intimately with George Bailey. In fact, it took me almost thirty-five years of psychological torment and almost a year of professional therapy to understand my own situation and what George Bailey had to do with it. George Bailey was loved by everyone in Bedford Falls, except for the miserly grinch, Mr. Potter. Every time I see the last scene of the movie where the entire town shows up to save him, I cry because I want that same love so desperately.

After my near mental breakdown, my therapist explained that I was a classic case of "love deprivation." My own siblings have told me about examples of how my parents would take turns using me to anger the other party. For example, late in life, I found out that for the first five years of my life, my Mom told my Dad that I was not his child. My Dad would then ignore me or mistreat me in favor of the last two children in the family because he knew that they were his own offspring.

In my adolescent and young adult years, I took a different view of being "loved." I sought out "love" in the form of physical conquests of girls at first, then young women. I came to believe if a young girl let you "make love" to her, then it meant that she "loved" you. So as soon as the latest girlfriend allowed me to experience that act with her, I would move on to the next one because I wanted and needed as much "love" as I could gather in order to replace what I had not gotten at home from my Mother and Father.

My life changed with one tremendous gift that God gave to me. Vickie Ann Carroll came into my life, and she actually loved me for who I was. In spite of all of my faults, all of my flaws and my many neuroses, she genuinely loved me. She committed to staying by my side through whatever I did or did not do. She urged me to become a better person, a better father, and a better friend. She showed me that all families have problems of some kind, and that you don't run from them. Rather, you acknowledge them, you manage them, and you work to eliminate them.

A Knock at the Door

This wonderful woman showed me what real love actually was. She gave me the greatest gift that anyone can ever bestow upon someone. This great lady taught me **how to love**. She showed me that in many instances, we love someone, not in spite of their flaws, but **because** of their faults and failings. Those idiosyncrasies and misgivings are what make us unique, interesting, and challenging.

Vickie helped me to realize and understand that love allows you to disagree at times; it allows you to be imperfect; it involves written and spoken acts of consideration and appreciation; it requires acts of forgiveness; and it should always be unconditional between family members. For the first time in my life, I genuinely appreciated what love actually is.

Now, my own children have taught me that unconditional love is possible because no matter how gruff I get, they always come back and hug me and hold me. In turn, that love has mellowed me, refined me, and redefined me. Between my God, my wife, my children, my long-ago therapist, and my own effort, I have received the gift of having been taught how to love.

I spent nearly thirty years of my life constantly searching for someone to love me, but I never knew how to accept love. I never learned how to actually love someone in return until I met Vickie. Ever since my wife taught me how to love, I have found that the dividends returned are phenomenal. Happiness is something I now understand and experience. I have actually found love, and I have actually given love. Thanks to this priceless gift from my lovely wife, I now know what George Bailey felt like at the heart-warming end of that movie.

It is rather interesting that as our family has grown up together, we have developed a Christmas tradition of viewing *It's a Wonderful Life* every Christmas eve. Every year, we laugh at the change in George Bailey's demeanor as he turns from a loving father into an angry, violent, and suicidal maniac. It takes a visit from an angel named Clarence to help him understand and to see the riches that he already has in his life. It takes the countless prayers of his friends and family to convince God that George needed His help that night. Every time we watch this classic, my kids and wife turn to me to watch and listen for the tears to stream down my face as George's hundreds of friends come out to save his life and to let him know that they genuinely love him. And every year, the tears do come down my cheeks.

62

Wayne Bisek

Yes, George Bailey helps me to realize what a wonderful gift it is to know and understand the concept of love. However, my lovely wife, Vickie, is the one who gave me the great gift of teaching me how to love.

Attagirl, Vickie.

The Day That I Became a Father and a Son

IT WAS VERY LATE in the evening when my very pregnant wife informed me of the much-awaited news. Her first contraction had just occurred. As a registered nurse, she was well aware of the oncoming situation and of the imminent pain-filled, yet glorious, event that was about to take place.

All of those months of attending LaMaze classes had served at least one purpose. For a first-time father, I was not overly concerned about rushing to the hospital. I calmly suggested that we start to time the gaps between the contractions to determine whether they required medical attention or not.

My actual concern was that my then-favorite singer, Kim Carnes, was scheduled to perform her big hit, "Bette Davis Eyes" on the *Tonight Show*. Since that was only ninety minutes or so off into the future, I thought it would be no problem. I asked Vickie if she could possibly delay the move to the hospital until after I had heard and seen the rendition. She told me that she would be glad to attempt to delay the birth of our first child so that I could enjoy that musical and visual delight to my heart's content. Yeah, right!

Luckily, for me, the contractions were not as strong or as frequent as to require immediate action. Instead, we matter-of-factly prepared for the trip and the several-days-hospital-stay. We spent about an hour or more packing clothes and making the necessary telephone calls to relatives concerning the situation. Then, finally, after Ms. Carnes' much-anticipated performance, we decided it was time to journey to St. Joseph's Hospital.

As I recall, all phases of the check-in went off without a hitch. Of course, the fact that Vickie had been working at this very hospital for the last several years helped substantially. The medical staff members were all friends of hers and were all very aware of the minute details of her pregnancy. In addition, as a life-long resident of this rural community, I was well acquainted with all of the doctors and nurses who were about to assist my wife in delivering our little baby into this world.

Once Vickie was resting in the hospital bed and hooked up to all of the monitors, it was much easier to time the contractions as we viewed them electronically. Naturally, she was relatively calm and in total control for the first several hours. Even though the contractions were somewhat erratic at first, they were definitely persistent and building in pressure. My job at that point was rather simple: I was supposed to "coach" her breathing pattern and to attempt to make her as physically comfortable as possible. I remember now that my supposedly simple duties became increasingly more difficult as her birthing experience became more intense and more focused. My role developed into the "stopper." I was to "stop" her from following through on the impulse to "push" our baby out before it was time to do so.

I am here to tell you that that is not as simple of a task as it sounds. Imagine the woman you love enduring the sensation of having her nerve endings pulled and snapped and slapped every sixty seconds. Imagine the woman that you vowed to spend your entire life with crushing your hands with her tiny moisturizer-softened fingers while you are attempting to "comfort and console" her. As I stood there next to the woman of my dreams, the love of my life, I could not help but wonder how in hell I could last any longer as a "loving and supportive coach" to this maniac of a human being. All she seemed to be interested in doing was screaming at me to "let me push! let me push!" Somehow, we endured those several hours as we waited for her body to adjust itself to accommodate the expulsion of the seven and one-half pound object of tissues, muscles, bones, and a skull.

Eventually, the time came when the doctor made the decision to move us to the delivery room. Once we were there, the intensity of the circumstances increased exponentially as all five people in that room anticipated the beginning of a new life. All five parties wondered quietly and internally whether or not all would be fine with the child and the mother. Would he/she have all of the requisite fingers and toes? Would the child be properly placed for the entrance into this different world? Would the umbilical cord not transform from a life-giving link between mother and child into a life-threatening noose of tissue and flowing blood? Would my petite young wife be able to tolerate the entire physical trauma associated with childbirth?

The answers were all almost immediately forthcoming as the delivery team went to work. All of the vitals were captured throughout the procedure and the cool efficiency of the situation and the environment helped maintain a genuine sense of calm and of effectiveness. We were constantly aware of every facet of the medical condition of my wife and child. I was finally granted permission to have Vickie push our baby out into the world to begin life on his own.

As I stood there holding the hand of my now heavily-perspiring, nearly completely disheveled (but still lovely) wife, I could not help but recall a conversation that I had had weeks before with a good friend of mine. He was attempting to help me comprehend the exact level of profoundness that this moment would involve. He knew that I loved sports and that I very nearly lived for sports. So, he explained that the absolute wonder that overtakes you when you score a touchdown or hit a home run is only 1/1000th of the awe that you feel when you see your child come into this world. I remember, quite vividly, that as I held her hand so tightly and worked with her so closely to breathe and push and breathe again that I had never prayed so intently for anything in my life.

And then, the doctor announced that the head was out and that the shoulders were coming through fine. I peered over the hospital sheet to see my child. At that moment, I felt more love flowing through our tightly enjoined hands than I ever thought existed. My heart swelled with pride and humility simultaneously, and I absolutely knew in that moment what it meant to be genuinely overcome with happiness. I hunched over Vickie and I used every bit of energy to hold back a flow of tears of joy. And then, somewhat abruptly, Doc calmly removed the tiny feet of my son from Vickie's womb and stated, "It's a boy!"

At last, we could all now see for our very own eyes that our newborn son appeared to be a very healthy physical specimen. All ten toes, all ten fingers, and all of his extremities appeared to be present and normal. His body was covered with amniotic fluid and splotches of blood. He wriggled and rolled around as Doc handed him to me to hold for the first time ever. He was breathing comfortably, and his little heart was beating so rapidly that I could nearly see it pounding away feverishly as his mind wondered what had just happened. The sound of his very first cry pierced the air.

Wayne Bisek

AJ May 1982

I cannot even begin to describe the sheer adulation that I felt at that time. I had just witnessed the very birth of my own beautiful, healthy son. I was a father. I was a Daddy. I was more deeply moved by this experience than by anything else that had ever happened to me up to that point of my life. I made so many promises to myself, to God, my wife, and to my newborn son that I cannot even fathom what all I had committed myself to do.

I promised to be a kind, loving, and supportive father. I promised to teach him everything that I knew about everything possible. I promised to keep him safe, and I promised that I would do everything possible to make him happy. I promised to be the best husband that I could be for my wife. I promised to help my wife to be financially comfortable and to always be her best friend. I promised to never give my son a reason to feel anything less than my absolute, unconditional love. In short, I promised never to be like my own father had been to me.

Yet, I knew, right then and there, that I could not and would not teach my son to hate someone he had never known. I could not continue the long line of animosity and of estrangement that had plagued my father and me. I decided that I would invite my father and his second wife to be a part of my son's life. Vickie and I determined that we would offer them the opportunity to be genuine grandparents to our son.

After calling dozens of friends and relatives, I finally dialed up my Dad's number. His second wife, Dottie, answered, and I informed her who I was. I told her that my son, Ashley Jordan, had been born, and that they were invited to our home to see him. Within one week of his birth, my Dad and Dottie were in our kitchen for this breakthrough event.

I remember as if it happened yesterday, the look on my Dad's face when I gave A.J. over to him to hold. I could almost literally see the weight of a decade of hatred and hurt washing away from him. He held onto him with the sincere love of a proud grandpa. He rocked him softly and smiled at him proudly.

A Knock at the Door

This big bear of a man, with hands chiseled and thick and scarred from years of hard labor, held my son so sweetly and gently as if he had comforted infants his entire lifetime. This man, who never had backed down from anyone at any time for any reason, was now putty in the hands of my week-old boy. It was then that I realized that the gift that I had given to my Dad of inviting him back into my life was coming back to me already. At that very moment, I understood that A.J.'s birth had provided me with *two* wonderful gifts. At his birth, I had become a father and I had become a son.

Author's note: For the births of my second son, Cole, and my only daughter, Melanie, I accompanied my wife during childbirth. In each of those two cases, my heart was just as filled with love and excitement. Each experience was unique unto itself and both were absolutely unforgettable moments in my life.

First Walk

A MOMENT THAT I will never forget involves A.J. He was just over a year old when we lived in my hometown in a large two-story Victorian house located on the corner of Main and River Streets. It is a very rural community with an ever-constant population of about 2,000 people and it is lined with small "ma and pa" shops, restaurants that make homemade pies and neighbors that know and care about everything that you do. It had always been my home and I thought it was going to stay that way forever.

Vickie and I were in our second year of wedded bliss and she was well aware that I was absolutely thrilled to be a daddy. A.J. had progressed from that developmental stage wherein he was no longer a baby just responding to various actions from Dad. He was now able to "play catch" and toddle around the house. But the major move upward that I was waiting for was the first trip down the main street sidewalk with my son in tow.

When it finally happened, I was thrilled beyond explanation. Vickie has always thought that I wanted to marry her because I just did not want to wait any longer to become a father. She may be right.

That moment that A.J. and I stepped out the front porch door and onto the sidewalk together was a memory that fills me with pride. There he was this little version of me. He was so happy to just reach up and grab my finger with his tiny hand. And then we took off, attached by this union of hand and finger and unconditional love. I am sure that not a single car passed by us without noticing my immense smile and my obvious fatherly pride. In all honesty, I know that I thoroughly enjoyed every second of that four-block trip to my brother's furniture store. It was one of the rare times in my life that I was in no hurry to move on to the next moment. Until the day that I die, I know that I will always be able to vividly recall the complete feelings of that day and that event.

69

Perfectly Planned Parenthood

OUR SECOND SON, COLE, is that very rare human being who can honestly state that his birth was absolutely perfectly planned.

It was 1983, and I was working with Mutual of Omaha, an insurance company. One of the products that they offered at the time was a maternity policy. It was designed to help couples cover all of the incidental costs of having a baby, even beyond the normal deductibles and co-insurances in place with health insurance at the time. It was very reasonably priced, and it only had one exclusion. The pregnancy had to result in a delivery at least ten months subsequent to the purchase date of the policy.

So, on January 14, 1983, Vickie and I purchased a maternity policy that would pay us $500 if our child was born no sooner than November 14, 1983. This meant, of course, that we had to avoid any possibility of conception until- that's right, February 14th, Valentine's Day.

Just think about that for a minute. A young, relatively newly married couple is looking to have another baby. They have gone thirty days without risking conception, and they make a $500 "bonus" when they do get pregnant. The first day that is acceptable for them to try to conceive is Valentine's Day. Sure enough, our romantic evening was spent attempting to conceive a child, and that is exactly what happened.

Once we knew that our second child was on the way, we began to plan for another set of LaMaze classes so that I could be helpful in the delivery room. Since the first shot of utilizing the breathing program was so successful, it only made sense to do it again. But, one day, while I was watching *The Today Show*, I saw a demonstration and discussion on the "LeBoyer" method of birth delivery. It fascinated me immediately.

In this method, the delivery room lights are dimmed as low as possible, there is classical music playing in the background, the mother is submerged in a tank of water from the chest down, and the baby is bathed in the tank immediately upon birth. The idea is to make the child's introduction to the world substantially less abrupt and more familiar.

I remember that the report mentioned that it was an extremely popular system in Russia at the time. In fact, they even showed a film of an actual delivery in Russia in which the woman was, literally, in a tank of warm water as she gave birth. The father assisted with the delivery by washing the baby off in the water and then severing the umbilical cord after the doctor had tied it off. It all seemed to make so much sense to me.

Sadly, Vickie's doctor was not overly enamored of the concept. He felt that it was still "too experimental" for his level of comfort. I assured him that the Russians had been using this method for over thirty years and that both Vickie and I were interested in having our child brought into the world in this manner.

It took almost the entire nine months to convince him, but we finally got him to concede to a long list of accommodations. He did allow the lights to be dimmed to an acceptable medical level. We had Vivaldi's Four Seasons playing in the background. The staff all spoke in quieter tones, and I was allowed to cut the umbilical cord once Doctor Yray had tied it off. I then bathed our little blue-eyed boy immediately. All in all, the experience was pretty cool.

I remember quite vividly that the moment Cole came into this world an immense rush of love and joy swept over me just as it had when A.J. was born. As soon as Dr. Yray confirmed that Cole was healthy, he announced, "Oh, very broad shoulders just like his brother!" I am not sure that any father could have been more filled with pride than I was at that very moment.

It did not take too long, though, for all of us in the delivery room to notice that apparently it had been a rough and long birthing experience for our son. His head was not nearly as round as most newborn babies. Instead, it was much more of a cone shape. The doctor had to spend some time reassuring both Vickie and me that it would return to customary shape in a day or two. It was quite normal, he explained, for the skull to be oddly defined as the result of a prolonged delivery.

As I recall, Vickie and Cole joined A.J. and me at home in just about two days. A.J. seemed to be thrilled about the idea of this new "toy" that we had brought home for him. I was completely excited about the thought that I now had two sons to teach about life.

Cole

Much to our dismay, Cole quickly demonstrated to the entire family that he was going to be a slightly different baby than A.J. had been. He would awaken us once or twice every night at some God-awful wee morning hour to be fed or changed or just to be held and rocked. On its own, that would have been livable. But, he took it several steps higher in frustration.

It would always start with just a couple of whimpers from his crib in the middle of the night. Then, either Vickie or I would proceed to handle either the diaper or the not-so-subtle request for nourishment. But, when it came time to return him to bed, he never went back smoothly. Instead, it seems, he had this unbelievable sixth sense about him. Whenever we thought he was back into a deep sleep, or any sleep at all, he would shock us back to reality with a mind-boggling, window-rattling series of screams. He would tease us at least three or four times per nightly visit by allowing us to think that he could be returned to bed. Then, as we would try one more time to place him in the crib with the gentleness and concern of a man handling a bottle of nitroglycerin, he would scream out again. Honest to God, I don't believe that we were ever able to return him to his crib without at least an hour of this torture. This nightly ritual lasted for at least the first year of his life.

Eventually, though, he did acclimate himself to our household and to the family, and we all came to appreciate the wonderful, healthy gift that we had been given.

The Highest Treetop

ON NOVEMBER 22, 1963, President John Fitzgerald Kennedy was shot to death riding down Dealey Plaza in Dallas, Texas by Lee Harvey Oswald. I was in my fourth grade class at St. Aloysius Catholic School when I heard the news. At nine-and-a-half years old, I was absolutely struck by the outpouring of love that resulted from that tragedy. Every television network had pictures of men and women all over the world in tears. Even news reporters like Walter Cronkite could hardly contain their emotions.

The more that I saw and the more that I read about this much beloved man, the more I yearned for all of that love. It was obvious to my subconscious, at least, that the best way for me to earn that much love was simple: I just had to become the President of the United States, and then I needed to be a victim of assassination. I now find it remarkable that I immediately decided that would be my top goal in life. I was so desperate to feel love that I was willing, at less than ten-years-old, to die to attain that kind of love from total strangers. It was a moment in time that changed my life forever in so many ways.

As I recall, there were a great many times during the next four years of Catholic schooling that I was asked to complete a questionnaire about my life choices. Every one of them eventually asked the question, "What is your goal in life?" It was followed by a list of possible careers such as attorney, doctor, teacher, farmer, nurse, and so on. I am sure that the diocese was scouring those documents for as many potential future priests as possible, as that was always one of the options. Whenever I filled one out, I wrote in an option that was not listed. Next to "other" in the categories of future careers, I always stated my goal as follows: to become the President of the United States.

Once word got out to my friends and, the teachers and nuns of the school, I received a lot of attention. The nuns would talk about the fact that "If you shoot for the moon, then you will probably at least hit the highest

73

tree top." My friends started to tease me about my dream by calling me "Mr. President." For a number of years, everyone in my class and several other classes talked about my wanting to become the President of the United States. Unfortunately, no one ever grew to understand that my motivation was not the office, the money, or the power. No one ever realized that I simply wanted to enjoy the outpouring of love that I thought the office would bring with it. Even I did not realize the real reason for my desire to reach that goal until I was thirty years old.

It was because of my twisted understanding of politics that I, indeed, became involved in running for office. During my junior year in high school, I was elected as class vice-president. My senior year, I was voted onto the student council. I enjoyed the positions, but it took me ten years before I decided to run for office again in 1982.

This time, I sought the position of council representative for my ward in Arcadia. I was twenty-eight years old and quite vocal about the business and political workings of my hometown. I spoke with my wife, Vickie, about the possibility of putting my name on the ballot against a twenty-four-year incumbent. He was a businessman in town and was actually a decent man. I just thought it was time for someone to challenge the status quo of our city's operations.

The campaign was relatively clean and straightforward. I simply ran on the theme of "change." I went door-to-door throughout the ward that covered approximately one-hundred-fifty homes. It was interesting and rewarding. When the results came in on election night, I had beaten the incumbent. Little did I know that the next two years of my life would be filled with tension, stress, constant battles at council meetings, and even a public betrayal by a good friend.

During those two years as a councilman, I learned about the real inner workings of the political world. Even in a town of barely over 2,000 inhabitants, there was a substantial amount of intrigue.

At one point, I uncovered a situation involving a city employee's ineffective work habits. The person had caused the city to be fined a large number of times. In fact, the records showed that the fines were in excess of $26,000. The council voted to accept all of my findings as true and accurate. Yet, my fellow council members voted 5-0 to retain her while acknowledging that all of my findings were true. I was advised by our

74

city attorney to abstain because I had submitted a motion to fire the employee.

Every time that I left my home to attend a council meeting, my wife would half-jokingly ask if I had placed the bull's eye target on my back as I headed out the door. For two years, I was treated as an absolute outsider. I was the guy rocking the boat. I was the guy asking the questions. I was the guy that no one wanted to be seen talking with on the street.

During those two years, I became even more committed to finding the truth and serving the people of the city. That attitude drove me to make a major decision. After much discussion with Vickie, I decided that I would run for mayor.

The race was between me and the incumbent, who had already served fourteen years in the position. He was someone that I neither trusted nor respected. Once I made the decision, I went for it all out.

Again, I went door-to-door. This time I covered the entire city of about five hundred homes. I talked to anyone and everyone that answered the door. I learned so much about the people that I had not known before this adventure. I campaigned cleanly and honestly. My ads simply espoused my ideas, credentials, and plans.

I soon discovered that this job that paid approximately $2400 per year in salary was, for some reason, heavily coveted by a small group of the mayor's supporters. During my campaign, some very interesting and startling activities occurred. One lady who had vocally supported my candidacy received a death threat. Several business owners were told to take my signs down or suffer the consequences. ALL of my campaign posters and signs were vandalized. At one point, a flyer was distributed to every home in town. It listed every council member, council candidate, department head, and utility commission member as being opposed to my candidacy. At least two people on the list informed me directly that they had not given permission to use their names. I toyed with the idea of asking for an injunction against my opponent's action, but an advisor of mine convinced me not to do so.

I lost the election by a vote of 600 something to 400 something. The loss stung deeply, but I took pride in the fact that I had garnered more votes in this losing effort than any other winning candidate had ever received in the city's history.

Almost immediately after the results were published, I ended up in the hospital. I was not sure if it was simply a case of being both physically and emotionally exhausted or if I had caught "swine flu." With all of the hand-shaking and face-to-face campaigning that I had done, I could easily have contracted it. Unfortunately, my doctor had prescribed a medication that was killing my white blood cells, which were already low due to my illness. Luckily, my wife (who was a registered nurse at the same hospital at the time), questioned the treatment. Her dedication to her career and to me helped put me on the road to recovery.

The loss of that mayoral race took a heavy toll on me, both physically and emotionally. Yet, there was much good that came out of that defeat.

Once I had been elected to my council position, I decided that I needed to pursue further education if I was to properly serve the citizens of Arcadia, I sought and received my masters degree in public administration in 1984. Ironically, one month after I lost the election, I was offered a position with the city of Elm Grove, Wisconsin. I took the job and moved away from my hometown at the age of 30 with my wife and two sons.

Now, in retrospect, I see the path of my life. Had I not become interested in politics because of JFK's assassination, then I never would have sought my master's degree. Had I not sought that degree, then I would not have received the job offer in Elm Grove. Had I not moved to Elm Grove, then I would not have gotten the offer for the job at the town of Madison. Had I not taken the job at the town of Madison, then I would not have ended up in my current career. Had I not found this career, then I would not have founded Buckets for Hunger, Incorporated. None of what I now have would be here. My path to love, happiness, and God is a result of believing that I had to die as the President of the United States in order to earn everyone's love.

Perhaps I have reached the highest tree top by virtue of my position as President and Founder of Buckets for Hunger, Incorporated. Ironically and happily, my drive to find love through political success did, eventually, help me find love, happiness, and God. And I did not have to die to discover it.

Long Distance Labor

ON JANUARY 2, 1986, I began my short-lived and tumultuous career as a Town Administrator for the Town of Madison, Wisconsin. It was a mixed blessing because it gave me the opportunity to further myself professionally, but it forced our family to relocate for the fourth time in less than two years. There was one more fact that made it even more traumatic and challenging. Vickie was due to deliver our third child on January 24. That meant that we would be nearly three hours away from her doctor and the hospital that we were planning on using for the birth.

We moved into our bi-level ranch home on January 23rd. It was a modest three bedroom home with a two-car, walkout garage located under the bedrooms, a finished basement, and a nice yard. It was located in a subdivision on the outskirts of the local village.

Because we didn't know any neighbors and we had no friends or family located anywhere near the area, we asked Grandma Dottie to stay with us until the birth. That way, she could watch our two young sons when I ended up having to take Vickie to Menominee Falls. Since the boys loved Grandma Dottie's visits, we thought it would work out great to have her there.

On January 14, Vickie and I went in for another doctor's appointment to check on how the baby was doing. As the doctor examined her, the tone of his voice switched from uplifting to concern. He pointed out to the two of us that our baby was in a breach position. He informed us that the position of our child in Vickie's womb was not conducive to a normal delivery. As I recall it, he was very careful about how he chose his words when describing the situation. He definitely attempted to comfort us as much as possible. Yet, he still wanted us to understand and appreciate the potential hazards without alarming us.

He then scheduled a "turning of the baby" session for the 17th. Upon arrival for the procedure, it was discovered that the baby had flipped around and righted itself so the "turning" was unnecessary.

Vickie and I left that doctor's appointment with a whole new sense of the value of a normal childbirth experience such as we had had with the two boys. We knew that we could only hope and pray that our baby would find a way to stay positioned properly so as to avoid the breached birth circumstances.

It was a typical stark, cold and windy Wisconsin January 29th night when the contractions started. We had just finished celebrating Vickie's birthday when the action began. She informed Dottie and me at about 9:30 p.m. that we should begin packing our clothes to head up to the hospital. I got on the phone and let her doctor know that we were on the way. The boys were still up and told us they wanted us to bring Melanie home from the hospital, not Rachel, and not a boy. (Since we were hoping for a girl, we had had the boys pick out a name for the hoped-for baby sister. We had settled on "Melanie" as the name until I decided that I thought the name should be Rachel.) Everyone was very calm about the whole ordeal.

However, when we climbed into our Toyota van to take this exciting trip, it suddenly hit me that I was going to be driving for over two hours with my possibly-minutes-away-from-delivering-a-baby wife sitting in the seat next to me. Then I also considered that the roads were snow-covered in spots and that Vickie's history of deliveries was for relatively short labor times. I began to ponder the wisdom of attempting to drive across the state of Wisconsin at 10:00 o'clock at night on January 29 in order to have my wife give birth to our third child.

Before long, Vickie noticed that I was beginning to exceed the speed limits by a good ten miles an hour or more out on the interstate highway. So, I decided to put on my flashers to let the other drivers know that I was in an emergency situation. Luckily, there were not a whole lot of other motorists out at that time of night. We covered a lot of miles in a relatively short time, and the whole while, Vickie did a great job of keeping me aware of the timing of the contractions.

Eventually, we got off of the main highway and headed through the last two small towns on the way to the hospital. Since the contractions were now close enough apart to warrant genuine concern about the imminent birth, I continued to cruise through the towns at a somewhat high speed. I had just told Vickie that it was looking like we would make it without any problems when I saw the flashing red lights trailing me through the intersection.

In spite of my desire to proceed onward with the cops in chase, Vickie calmly persuaded me to pull over and inform them of our dilemma. I will never forget the stern look on the officer's face when he approached me on the driver's side window and flashed the light at me.

"What's the big hurry, sir?" he queried.

"Actually, officer, it's my wife over here," I said as I nodded toward Vickie as she attempted to control her breathing during another contraction.

"She's about to give birth and we have to get to the hospital in Menonimee Falls right now," I added.

The policeman just leaned over to validate my comments and then looked back at me and said, "Oh, I see. Let's get going. I'll lead you. I know just where it is."

He proceeded to run back to his vehicle and jumped into the driver's seat. He then pulled into the lane next to me, passed me, turned on his lights and flashers, and off we went.

Within minutes, we were at the hospital and being ushered into the delivery room. Everything was all set to go when we arrived, and that was a good thing because it only took about two hours and our little daughter was officially out into the world on her own as of 2:00 a.m. We were thrilled to have a girl. When the nurses asked if we had chosen a name, we looked at each, smiled, and simultaneously said, "Melanie." We knew her brothers would be excited about this and feel like they had named their sister, thus making it more of a family affair.

Melanie

A Knock at the Door

Even though she was a third child, I can still recall the wonderful sensation of happiness that took over me when the doctor announced that we had a girl. After having had the two boys, I am pretty sure that Vickie was hoping for a daughter. Before too long, the doctor added that she appeared to be very healthy and quite normal. I guess that since we had been somewhat concerned about the possibility of a breach birth problem, we were ecstatic when everything went so smoothly.

As soon as morning hit, I started calling all of the relatives on the other side of the state to let them know about the new female family member. I then headed back to our new home to pick up Grandma Dottie and the boys. In my excitement to bring them together with Vickie and Melanie, I somehow managed to lock us all out of our new house, though. I ended up having to break into our home by taking a window completely off of the house and having A.J. go inside to unlock the doors for us.

In spite of all of the difficulties and challenges, the whole experience was well worth it when I saw the look on the boys' faces as they met their baby sister. At four and two years old, they were both enthralled with this new little person that was their own sister. It added a whole new perspective to the exciting and joyous occasion.

Mel's Skull

IT WAS A SIGHT that no father should ever have to view. My precious little daughter was lying there writhing in pain. Her voice was shrieking out this horrendous scream that shocked every one of us and made the hair on the back of my neck stand rigid. Her blood-curdling wail had brought me charging across the basement floor. And there I saw her with this cold, agonizing stare of fear in her young eyes. Next to her was a pool of thick, dark liquid that immediately took me to a level of concern that I had not previously known. My only thoughts were that my baby was going to die.

We had arrived only minutes before the accident. I was going to attend a training session in Minneapolis for my new career as a financial advisor. My wife and I had decided to take the whole family to visit her sister and their family while I went to school for the five required days. It was a long, difficult trip over two hundred miles with our three very young children. There had been miles and miles of questions and diaper changes and potty breaks. The two boys filled the entire trip with "are we there yet?" comments starting at the stop sign at the end of our own neighborhood street, and it did not end until we pulled into the in-laws' driveway.

My wife's sister and her husband were providing us with the quick tour of living quarters for the next five days. They had just explained how they would be putting down carpeting on the basement floor several days after our visit. Until that renovation, it was an uncovered cement floor.

We were all at the end of the hall finalizing the sleeping arrangements when something happened that rocked our whole world for the next several weeks. Apparently, our daughter had managed to work herself free from the infant seat that she had been sleeping in for the trip. Our beautiful, little eighteen-month-old girl had tried to crawl down the steps in that backward fashion that infants have, but she had slid off to one side. It was the side that had no railing and no wall.

A Knock at the Door

I still do not know how close to the top she was when she went off of the edge and dropped onto that cement floor. Her head must have smashed into the floor with full force seconds before her screams shocked our world.

As I picked her trembling body off of the floor, I was horrified by the sight of a dark, reddish-purple puddle of ooze next to her head. Instinctively, I ran my hands over her head and found no blood. A small measure of relief filled me when I realized that the pool of liquid had not come from her body. It was, in fact, a puddle of plum pudding baby food that had burst out of its container as a result of the fall. One major concern was eliminated, but we were not out of the woods yet.

My wife and I took turns comforting her and before too long it seemed as if she was back to normal and that she was none the worse for her experience. She was soon smiling and laughing and the entire group of family members relaxed somewhat. My wife then called the local hospital's emergency room, and the medical personnel advised us to watch for any more signs of discomfort and a fever. They also told us to bring her in for x-rays and a CAT scan if she began to throw up.

Only a few hours later, our night was abruptly disrupted by Melanie's startling squeals. She was tossing and turning, almost violently, as we held her and attempted to comfort her. However, it was to no avail, and Vickie and I decided to take her in to see a doctor immediately.

Upon our arrival at the emergency room, the medical staff quickly determined that it would be necessary to take an x-ray of her head. The personnel were not very family friendly. The x-ray technician informed Vickie and me that we would not be able to be in the room with Melanie while they took the photos. We would have to wait outside while she and a nurse worked on the procedure. Then, they placed a halo of steel on her head. I know it was necessary in order to stabilize her cranium and to protect her from further injury, but now my little girl was obviously in a state of fear as she was having this metal device screwed onto her head while her Mom and Dad were nowhere to be found in this darkened cavern of a room. To this day, I do not know how they restrained me to that outer room so many miles away from holding my darling daughter as she screamed in pain and terror and confusion.

Eventually, they allowed us to come into the room to retrieve her and to hold her. They took the x-rays without speaking to us at all. As per the custom, we were then ushered back into the examination room to await the doctor's review of the film. When he entered the room, he was completely stoic. He simply placed the film on the viewing area on the wall, turned on the backlight and quickly informed us "everything's okay." With no sense of emotion, at all, he explained that there was probably nothing wrong with Melanie and that we should just continue to observe her behavior over the next several days. If the symptoms of high fever, discomfort, and vomiting presented themselves, then we were to bring her back in to see a doctor again.

As a rule, my wife was always the strong one during any medical emergencies. As a registered nurse, she had dealt with physical trauma hundreds of times with hundreds of people. She was always calm, unnerved, and completely in control of her emotions. I, on the other hand, carry my emotions on my sleeve. I tear up watching sentimental movies even when it is my tenth time viewing them.

On this occasion, Vickie was different. There was a genuine sense of fear and of concern in her demeanor. She was no longer the coolly-reserved medical professional dealing with a simple health situation. She was a mother with a baby daughter in physical distress. I noticed it and understood that on that day I would have to be the strong one. I prayed for God to give me the strength to comfort Vickie and to watch over Melanie and to keep her safe. I prayed every second of every day that week for my daughter and for my wife.

Those next four days seemed interminable as I spent them commuting from the home of my wife's sister to my business classes. It was nearly impossible to maintain any focus during the training sessions as I could only wonder how Melanie was surviving the ordeal. Her behavior was somewhat normal during the daytime hours, but the nights were unending bouts of tears and screams of agony. She started running a high fever the second night after the accident. Luckily, the fever subsided relatively quickly and she never had experienced any incidents of regurgitation. We made it through the week and eventually drove back home. Gradually, it seemed life was on the road to normalcy again.

The interesting twist, though, was we found out that while we were in Minneapolis we had received a letter at home from the hospital where we had taken Melanie for treatment and diagnosis. It was an apology from the doctor that we had seen there. Apparently, he had spoken out of turn with his reading of the x-rays. The radiologist had informed him that Melanie had a severely fractured skull. She was to seek medical assistance and hospitalization, immediately.

Melanie

Once again, God had answered my prayers by aiding Melanie through her injury and back to health. Another little miracle had been bestowed upon our family as our tiny daughter managed to survive the terrible fall and the severely fractured skull without any long-term ramifications.

My Night with God

AN ABSOLUTE DARKNESS SURROUNDED me, as I lay there, motionless, only inches away from the love of my life. My arms seemed as if they were about to fly away, completely of their own accord; yet, those same arms felt as if they weighed two thousand pounds each.

My very worst nightmare kept flashing into my brain. The visions of my one true love, Vickie, on our bedroom floor motionless—not breathing, gone from me forever—were terrifying. Furthermore, the horrifying, recurring thoughts of my three beautiful children lying in a crumpled, lifeless heap made me want to die right then and there. I knew that I could not possibly live with the destruction and death that I had caused to the very people who filled my life with love, hope, and understanding. I was going to have to take my own life, too.

My mind tossed and turned as violently as the late summer storms that ride roughshod over Wisconsin towns each and every year, tearing down multi-generation-old homes and farms and altering the lives of families and friends. I lay there surrounded by fear and doubt, and I wondered what I had to do to stop these horrid visions of suicide and homicide. No single night of your life should ever last this long; no fiendish nightmare should ever fill your sleep to this degree.

I lay there on that cool cotton sheet, fighting my own dizzying whirlpool of thoughts, visions, torment, and anguish. I thought that I had absolutely no ability to screen my own thought process or to determine my own actions. Never had I ever experienced this kind of fear.

Oh sure, I had had many of those other "failure" dreams before, when I would awaken startlingly in the middle of the night. I would sit rigidly upright in bed and stare out into the hallway "knowing" that someone was out there lurking. Someone was going to come into my peaceful bedroom to hurt me, and then they would harm my family. The dream was always the same for years; some faceless intruder whose intentions were not clear would confront me. I would try to scream for help or to wake up my family, but I could not speak. I could only mumble incoherently and helplessly. The sense of doom would consume me, until I would be awakened from my dream by someone or something.

And yet, this specific maelstrom of murderous nightmares and self-loathing thoughts was so many times more real, more vivid, and more frightening than before. I could only lie there and pray as fervently and devoutly as I knew how to do. I could only beg God to give me the strength to understand what was happening and why, and to somehow fight my way back to some level of sanity. My only sane thoughts were very simple: I needed to ask God to come to me and to save me and my family from this evil presence, from this fiendish excuse of a human being—from myself.

It took every last ounce of courage and fortitude for me to sit up in that bed and to painstakingly take one step at a time out of my den of dreams and into the hallway of horror. I moved ever so meaningfully toward the phone in the kitchen. I honestly believe that I have never been more focused or single-minded in any endeavor as I was in striding down that path from my bedroom to the phone. I know I must have run to that phone in near desperation, yet I don't know that I was able to even walk without constant self-encouragement. My legs had now joined with my arms in this state of confusion. They were simultaneously separate from my mind, heart, and soul, but closely tied to my thoughts, nightmares, visions, and hallucinations.

Somehow, I made it to that phone and dialed Father Tony's number. As a priest, I am sure he has had many early morning calls depicting a sudden death or some drunken confession or even tear-filled self-revelations. I am just not sure how many times he has experienced the suicidal and homicidal ramblings of a man on the verge of a nervous breakdown. He listened intently and caringly as I bluntly informed him that I needed him to be in my home with me immediately. He simply hung up the phone and appeared at my doorway minutes later.

I know that he attempted every angle to reach me, to comfort me, and to console me. He spoke in the gentle, soothing voice of a man whose lifetime had been spent in the presence of grieving families who were angry at God for various and sundry reasons. Father Tony questioned me, listened, and responded with sincerity and genuine concern and love. And yet, it was not enough.

86

The visions still persisted and my heart raced with the knowledge that I had no control over my own mind.

It had become obvious to me that the loving presence of my gentle wife and the good intentions of our family priest were not enough to help me face these demons of my mind. I wanted so desperately for this night of anguish and torment to end, but it just simply would not.

Then something very strange and unique happened. It was neither sudden, nor startling, nor shocking. It was more quiet and sedate. It was more enigmatic than dramatic. I simply became aware of this tremendous presence in the living room with me, Vickie, and Father Tony. It was a presence of astounding love and comfort and which filled my every thought, hope, and desire; it was a sensation of complete safety and divine proportions. It simultaneously covered me like a comforting, warm blanket and swept over me like a gentle, cool breeze on a hot summer day. The presence held my hand and calmed me down, reaching around my entire body to hold me while I cried out tears of relief. I felt the actual presence of God in that room.

I sobbed with happiness knowing that I would survive and so would my wife and children.

Yet, I never actually shed a single tear; I just felt them because of that presence. There was never a radiant booming voice or a shocking white light. There was never a sudden bolt of sunshine through the night sky, and I did not see a burning bush or a crying Madonna. There was just an overwhelming aura of love and comfort and peace and safety. It was the presence of God in my life, in my home, in my living room, at my side. That night in that room, with those people under those dire circumstances, I deeply needed the presence of my God, and it happened.

Throughout my life, I have been involved in many conversations concerning Heaven and God. I have always shared with those people that it is my opinion that when we reach heaven, God's presence would be so powerful as to make all problems, worries, and concerns disappear. The simple aura of this Supreme Being would rid us of all wants, desires, and needs.

That is what happened to me that night in my home with God's presence in my living room. I became overwhelmed with a sense of love, comfort, and strength, and my fears, visions, and demons were all gone. A genuine peace came over me— total tranquility replaced near insanity.

Only a few hours later, I found myself in the emergency room of a local hospital. God had given me the strength to seek professional help for my problems. In hindsight, it is almost humorous to think back about that emergency visit on a Sunday morning. I remember barely getting inside that office to sit down when I poured out my tale of midnight terror and horrific hallucinations. I cried like a baby for almost an hour with the doctor. Then he proceeded to tell me that he already knew that there was no possible way that I would hurt my wife, children, or myself. He explained that the fact that I had left my job as a town administrator had rekindled issues of success/failure in my life.

For various reasons, I had psychologically learned to associate being loved with being successful. Therefore, my "failure" to keep my job caused me to believe that I would lose the love of my wife and children. The visions of their demise were my way of viewing the loss of their love. It was as if they had all died, and I had driven them away because of my professional failure. The thoughts of my own physical demise were simply my way of paying for my failure.

My complete psychological recovery took some time. However, I have never again suffered through another night of terror, nor have I ever endured the hallucinations and visions that tormented me until God actually came to my side that night so long ago.

Forgiveness

"GIVE US THIS DAY our daily bread and forgive us our trespasses, as we forgive those who trespass against us."

"Forgive us our trespasses, AS WE FORGIVE THOSE WHO TRESPASS AGAINST US." It took me too long into my own life to understand that I could not seek forgiveness unless I gave forgiveness.

Sometimes, the pain and suffering that we experience is so profound that it is difficult to let it go and move on to another period of our lives. Yet, eventually, I discovered that without extending the olive branch of forgiveness, I would never find my own happiness. So much of my thought process was grounded in revenge and hatred that I did not have the time to appreciate the joy and love that was in my life. For me, a great deal of those negative feelings involved my childhood.

I believe we are all products of our environments, and that we are especially all influenced by our families. Whether in positive or negative ways, our families affect our views on life. There are times that the absence of family, through death or abandonment or other means, can genuinely influence our personality and psyche. There are other times that, perhaps, the presence of our family members can do more harm than good. I am not sure which would have been better for me, personally. However, I do know that I no longer blame Mom and Dad for all of my character flaws and psychological nightmares.

It took nearly thirty years and countless life experiences before I came to this realization. And, this realization still did not occur until I fully understood that my parents, too, were products of their own environments.

Neither my father nor my mother understood what it meant to feel love or to give love.

A Knock at the Door

My father was raised in the 1930s and 1940s by a man who could have come straight out of a Charles Dickens novel. My paternal grandfather was a tall man for his time. He stood about six feet tall, as I recall, with long, thick arms that were taut with muscle. His waist was neither slender nor rotund, and I remember him being substantially thick and broad in the chest. His most prominent feature, however, was his demeanor. He was an angry, vicious tyrant who treated his own children as if they were slave labor. They had to put in long, hard days toiling on the farm in constant fear of his next violent tirade. If they malfunctioned in any way, then they would suffer the very dire consequences. I personally remember Grandpa Adam lashing one of his sons with a bullwhip because of a problem that had occurred in the barnyard.

Even as a more-favored grandchild, I remember nothing good about my grandpa Bisek. What I do recall is that he never smiled and that I absolutely hated to visit him. He was a vile, gruff, and intimidating man who put you in a constant state of fear. Even as a small boy, I was mindful of the constant potential for danger and violence whenever we were at his farm.

Since Grandpa Adam was well aware that Maggie and Karl were each the products of separate indiscretions (out-of-wedlock pregnancies) by my mother, he always said that they did not "belong" to my Dad. Therefore, Grandpa Adam would refer to them as "bastards" whenever we came over for a Sunday visit. I even remember that on several occasions he pointed a loaded shotgun at Karl and roared out, "I should just shoot you, you son of a bitch!"

Grandpa Adam suffered from severe gout near the end of his life, so he had his bed moved into the living room. That allowed him to be able to watch television more comfortably. I remember that he would lie in that bed in obvious torturous pain, and yet he could still strike fear into anyone who ventured into his lair. His grown sons would cower in his presence. As strong and fearless as my own father was in any other circumstance, I never saw him question or challenge his father in any way, shape, or form. No matter how belligerent Grandpa Adam was towards my mother, to me, or to my siblings, Dad simply and begrudgingly accepted his behavior as a fact of life.

As was the case for most farm boys back in that era, Dad had to quit school at a very early age (thirteen, in fact) so he could assist with the farming. Dad was also sent out to labor for another man who was in the logging business. Whatever he earned was to be handed over to Grandpa Adam. Now, I understand that it was a different time and that men did not display emotions openly, child labor was a staple of farm life, and the father of the family was the absolute dictator of the household. However, I am also aware that, in many cases, family life meant a genuine existence of moral and spiritual values. It involved the sharing of workloads in a teamwork environment. With a great many families, difficult times served only to heighten the amount of love shared by siblings and parents.

Sadly, my father, his siblings, and his hard-working mother never experienced that arrangement.

My mother, Gertrude, was the fourth of seven children in her family that lived on a small farm in Trempealeau County. Her home was also one wherein the father was a completely self-centered despot who treated his wife and children with contempt. In what few photographs that we have of him in his early life, he appears to have been a rather wiry man who stood just a little short of six feet tall.

Grandpa George kept Grandma Clara pregnant for the first decade of their marriage, and then he apparently tired of her. So, in order to get rid of her, he had her placed into an insane asylum where he kept her for over forty years. Almost immediately, George moved another woman, Linda, in to live with him for the rest of his life. Poor Grandma Clara died a frail, mindless woman alone in a nursing home.

It took Mom over sixty years to share some of her youthful memories, but she now tells me that her father actually had a nickname for her. It is a Polish phrase that means "second cow." His pet name for her mother was the Polish phrase "first cow." As the youngest girl (at the time) in a household without a mother, she was forced to grow up before her time. Sadly, Mom also confessed to me that she was forced to hide behind the wood stove, as it warmed the farmhouse in the early morning hours, so that she could try to avoid her father's torment. In fact, one of my first cousins has shared deeper knowledge of George with me. She revealed to me that my mom and all of her sisters (except for the youngest) were sexually abused by their father. So, my mother, also managed to survive a home life that had no sense of kindness, caring, compassion, or love from the head of the household.

A Knock at the Door

In addition to their rough and sordid youth, Mom and Dad each had a twisted tale or two about their respective families. For Dad, his Dickensian-type twist involved the death of two infant sisters who were buried in the basement of the family home. Why this situation came about is beyond me; I cannot fathom why a family would bury its own young in the household basement.

As for my Mom's side, she found out at the tender age of eighty-four that one of her cousins was not actually a cousin; he was her *brother*. The family elders had conspired to keep this fact a family secret. Needless to say, the news rattled my Mom very deeply for some time.

As a result of these very dire circumstances, neither of my parents ever learned how to love their own children. They never learned what it meant to be parents because their role models were such poor examples. Therefore, our own family life was a constant argument-filled, corporal punishment based existence.

I am not sure if any "conversation" ever occurred at anything lower than a fever pitch.

Another strange thing that I remember about my youth was that I would stare into the mirror on my bedroom dresser, and I would ask God why I was born into this family. I genuinely wondered what it would be like to have been a child in a family that was normal. I remember the emotions that consumed me when I would beseech God about my placement in this family group. Those feelings were a combination of exasperation and of utter disappointment. I just could not understand why God put me there with those unhappy and angry adults as my parents.

For my entire childhood years, I only wanted one simple thing: to be loved. Specifically, I wished for my Dad to love me. It was a little different with my mother. I thought that she might love me, but I was just never sure because she never really showed me any affection. I don't remember ever sitting on her lap or hugging or kissing her good night. There were no bedtime stories and no help with homework. Every "Parents' Night" the school held for the sports my brother, Karl, and I played meant another opportunity for our parents to embarrass us with their absence. Throughout my school years, I don't recall either one of my parents ever attending a parent-teacher conference.

Wayne Bisek

At thirty-years-old, sitting in the therapist's office, I cried like a baby as I responded to his questions about what I wanted from my parents. I bawled my eyes out as I choked on the words: "I just wanted them to love me!"

Even now, the emotional pain returns when I recall the days of my early life. For example, I recall my first varsity baseball game during my junior year in high school. It was the first year that I could go out for the team. I had convinced Mom to sign the parental release without Dad's approval. I did not have any money for a fielder's glove, so Coach let me use one that a former player had left behind years ago.

That first game, I was hitting in the number three slot and playing right field, I believe. We went into extra innings with the score tied 7-7. Earlier in the game, I had hit a single to drive in one of the runs and then I scored. I was feeling pretty good about my swing when I came up to bat with two outs and a runner on second base. I picked out a fastball and swung the bat with every muscle that I had. I still remember the sound of the wooden bat striking the ball hard. CRACK! I can picture the flight of the ball as it soared out to the gap in left centerfield on its way to the fence. I took off for first base, and I did not stop running until I was almost ready to slide into third. That is when I saw coach jumping up and down and I realized we had just won the game. I had just driven in the winning run in my first varsity game. The thirty or so people at the game were standing and cheering for me. A tremendous rush of happiness swept over me as my teammates engulfed me.

I was so high on the excitement of the game that I floated home from the ballpark. I remember opening the front door to the house, ready to burst into shouts of joy about my exploits, when my father slammed me back into reality. "Where the f___ have you been?" he demanded. In those few words, I went from the penthouse to the outhouse. Not only did he not even care about my experience, he threatened to beat me if I played any more baseball.

There was also the time during my freshman year on the football team that he confronted me. I had won the job of starting fullback on the junior varsity team and was having a pretty good season. In fact, the varsity coach had talked to me about moving me up to play on the big team. It was a Monday, so the JV team was to play its weekly game. I had come home from school to grab a light snack before going back to suit up for the game. For some reason, Dad was home early that day. He was in his usual angry mood so I tried to avoid him. He eventually ascertained that I had a football game that night. When he did find out, the shouting ensued. "If you go and play football you better not come back home because I'll kill you!" He bellowed, and he was a big enough and mean enough man that I did not doubt him at all.

I did find the courage to sneak down to the game that night, after Dad had gone for his nightly visit to his favorite local bar. Mr. Pahl, the assistant coach, spotted me and immediately informed me that they had all of my equipment in the bus and that I could play as soon as I suited up. I told him that would be impossible because if I tried to play and Dad found out, it would get pretty ugly. Needless to say, I did not stay long at the game.

I am sure that other people have had even more difficult times growing up in even more stressful and dangerous environments. The sting of that leather strap across my bare bottom so many nights is nothing compared to the anguish of a child living in a home where incestuous rape occurs. The psychological and mental cruelty that was inflicted on us by our seemingly unloving parents is trivial compared to the twisted lives of children whose own parents have held them hostage in the attic or the basement of their own homes. Yet, the hurt and anguish that I felt were real, deep, and long-lasting.

Forgiveness has been the only genuine cure. It was not easy to do, but at some point, we must all forgive our transgressors or we will never find our own happiness. The amount of energy that we consume with hatred and grudges detracts from our ability to find peace and comfort in our new lives and circumstances. The day that I decided to finally forgive my parents was the first day that I began to attain my own happiness.

I did not go out and tell them face-to-face about my decision, for I doubt it would have meant a whole lot to either of them. The gift of forgiveness that I offered was one that occurred entirely in my own heart, soul, and mind. It was the best gift that I ever gave to Mom and Dad. It was also the best gift I ever bestowed upon myself.

Ice-Capades

MY FATHER IS VERY proud of the forty acres of farmland that he owns in a small rural township in western Wisconsin. One local city is approximately eight miles southwest of his land. Another small city is just about five miles directly north and still one more city is nearly ten miles to the east of the farm. It is within a couple of miles (as the crow flies) of his father's original farm. He purchased the place about ten years after he met Dottie.

It has an old, slightly dilapidated barn that is just big enough to hold eight to ten horses or cows. There is a tin-roof wooden shed that serves as his workshop for his salvage business and he utilizes approximately a third of the land as a storage area for the abandoned or wrecked cars, trucks, and tractors that he acquires for his business. About one hundred feet away from that barn and about one hundred yards up the hill from the workshop, there is a small dam that is used to store rainwater for the cows and as a means of slowing down the flow of rainwater so as to avoid erosion downhill.

The actual house that came with the property is located, along with the workshop, very near the center of his land. It is surrounded on three sides by hills that, in turn, form a natural ravine down that center area. The house is a firetrap with an electrical wiring system that has not been updated or refurbished in over forty years. There is a very antiquated heating system that provides very little comfort for the two upstairs bedrooms, and the trip up the steps to those two rooms is difficult, at best. Treacherous is the only word to describe the eventual trip that you will have to make back down those six-inch wide and extremely steep steps with the doorway to the right at the bottom of the journey. A small kitchen and dining area and a tiny bathroom greet you immediately as you open the door from the enclosed porch into the living area.

A Knock at the Door

A long, narrow living room with a fireplace takes up one side of the back thirty feet of the house, and the other side is the master bedroom. The home gives the appearance of being a trailer house with a basement.

My father loves this place so very dearly. It is all his. He owes nothing to anyone when it comes to this land and its buildings. These forty acres are the only property that he has ever owned in his entire lifetime. It is his little piece of Heaven on earth.

But, for one cold wintry December day in 1992, it very nearly was a death trap for my three children.

We had been out at the farm visiting with Dad and Dottie with the kids for a couple of hours. As usual, the boys tired of spending time inside the house. There was not much on television for them to watch, and their hand-held video games were not filling the time with enough entertainment value. So, the boys asked if they could go outside to roam the hillsides for a while. Melanie begged to go along with them. Since A.J. was twelve-years-old or so, we were reasonably comfortable with him providing safety for them. The few animals that Dad had at the time were in the upper pasture, so we told them to just avoid that area. That did not take much convincing since none of them was especially comfortable around farm animals. One of the side effects of being city folks is that our children did not spend very much time in the presence of animals that were substantially larger than they were.

As we spent about twenty minutes preparing them for the Wisconsin weather, we tried to remind them all of the restrictions that they would have to follow. We told them to stay away from the junked cars and trucks in the salvage yard. The area was rife with broken glass, and rusty metal pieces were scattered all over the lot. They were told to avoid the dam area because the warm weather that had visited the area had thinned out the ice on the waterways and ponds. The boys were directed not to tease Melanie and not to leave her behind at any time.

Once they were all bundled up in hoods, scarves, and boots, they were ushered out the door into this whole new world of opportunity and excitement. The adults hung back in the house and discussed all of the local news and the family's travails. Dad got us up to date on his inventory of antique tractors and contest tractors. Dottie provided all of the details concerning her side of the complicated family tree. Vickie and I attempted to fill them in on the comings and goings of our children's busy lives. Every minute aspect of their young lives was of great interest to Grandma Dottie and Grandpa Bisek. The time seemed to travel by very quickly. Then, suddenly, the door burst open and the three kids came stumbling and fumbling into the warmth of that tiny house.

As quickly as possible, Melanie, Cole, and A.J. were snuggled in front of the cozy fireplace. They seemed to be a little quieter than normal, but I attributed that to the combination of the cold weather and the hot chocolate that Grandma Dottie had ready for them upon their return. She, of course, made it with actual milk, chocolate syrup, and loads of big marshmallows floating on top and the steam swirled upward toward their rosy cheeks. They seemed none the worse for their time on the hills of Grandpa's place.

It wasn't until much later that evening that the interesting activities of their escapades came to light. During one of their not-so-subtle disagreements, one of them happened to mention something about the ice-cracking sounds that they had heard that day in the pasture. As with most good parents, Vickie and I were at least half eavesdropping on their conversation and we both picked up on the slip right away. Vickie immediately began the interrogation in earnest.

It seems that they were out in the lower pasture because the lure of the "forbidden lake" was just too much to deal with for A.J. He decided that since it was one of the few places that we had told him not to venture, then it was probably the best place to go. We were all informed that Cole attempted to persuade A.J. not to try out the ice, but it was to no avail. A.J. had his heart set on making the brave adventure.

Eventually, though, they all three ended up on the ice. Our eldest son had thought all was fine because his reasoning seemed so complete. He had rationalized that the ice must have been plenty thick enough for them due to the fact that there were lots of cow pie droppings on the snow-covered ice already. He figured that if the ice could hold the cows, then it could surely support their weight.

But their reasoning did not involve the age or exact location of those droppings. Unbeknownst to them, the cows had not been on that side of the barn for several weeks. In addition, the droppings were only on the very perimeter of the pond.

With that scientific reasoning, A.J. determined that he would walk across that thirty-foot long pond in order to make it quite clear to his brother

97

and sister just exactly how brave he was. One, and then the other, proceeded to traverse the distance. Eventually, they all wandered out onto the frozen white slab.

Then, something scared Cole. He thought he heard a crackling noise of some kind. Next, Melanie started to whimper because she heard the same noise and thought she was going to fall through the ice and into the cold water. Apparently A.J. did manage to keep his wits about him and directed them both to take soft, slow steps back off of the pond. He stepped slowly toward the edge of the pond, and then he jumped to the hillside with ease. From there, he went to a spot close to the other two and he reached out to the both of them. He held their hands as tightly as possible while they stepped to safety. No sooner had they made it to the solid ground than the ice separated ever so slightly and water appeared.

As a typical younger sister, Melanie seemed to enjoy sharing this information with the adults. While the boys were not quite as forthcoming with the details, they did manage to confess to the entire escapade. As much as they hated to admit it, each of them had been very, very frightened about the situation, and it was going to be their secret forever. Yet, all three of them seemed quite relieved to get this tale of danger and near death off of their minds.

A Knock at the Door

ONE MORE CHRISTMAS EVE was quickly approaching and, as usual, I could not wait for it to be here and gone. At ten-years-old, Christmas meant so many things to me. Unfortunately, none of them were any good. For example, it always brought the embarrassment of listening to my school friends list their wonderful presents of baseball gloves, leather footballs, model cars, toy trucks, fancy shirts, and new dress pants. Everyone would be filled with excitement as they shared with me the joy of their families' laughter-filled gatherings. I was told about uncles, aunts, and cousins that visited with grandmas and grandpas while the kids all tore open present after present from under some gorgeously decorated tree. I could almost smell the homemade cookies, pumpkin pies, and holiday candies. Every story I heard seemed to be about a different world, not just a different house.

None of my friends ever really understood my deafening silence when they asked me about my own holiday experience. There was not much that I wanted to tell them. All of my holiday cheer was wrapped up in the hope that I would get even a single item that I wanted or that our family would actually enjoy the day together. Since neither of those ever happened, I did not have much to share with my friends. Our Christmas nights were spent alone with no visiting relatives or friends, a starkly decorated tree, and ever-so-few presents. There was no excitement in the air as the evening grew late and we waited for Dad to finally arrive home from a bar stop. There was no laughter throughout the house from a group of siblings playing games. There was no early morning rush of children to see what Santa had left downstairs while we slept. Christmas Eve and Christmas Day were two of the longest, quietest, and most depressing days of every year, and I hated that they even happened because they just seem to draw attention to our family's plight.

Somehow, Mom always managed to place an item or two under the tree for each of us. She scrimped, saved, and paid for them over the course of the entire year. When Christmas came, we would each have a shirt or a pair of pants, if we were lucky. Mom tried as hard as she could. But, she just never had enough money to purchase anything substantial, especially with four of us kids still at home. In hindsight, I am sure that Mom felt even worse than we did because she never had the joy of seeing us happy on Christmas morning.

However, I guess that even wide-eyed children eventually realize their place in life, so they lower their expectations with each and every disappointment. By the time that my tenth Christmas Eve rolled around, I was well aware that this would be just another night of tired television shows leading to a Christmas Day spent in idle entertainment. There would be no great pleasure even with a Christmas meal. In fact, whatever meal we had would be simple and without any fanfare with the usual amount of tension and anxiety as we all waited for the arguments to begin. Since money was always tight in our family and food was seldom plentiful, family meals were spiced with finger-pointing accusations and mournful regrets of poor decisions. Christmas dinner always seemed to bring out the worst in both Mom and Dad.

But, that particular Christmas Eve was very different for me. Something happened late that afternoon as I roamed the house trying to fill my time as the television played in the background. Eventually, I ended up in my favorite position lying on the linoleum floor, three feet away from the TV with my stockinged feet placed in the open side door of the oil heating stove in our living room. Mom was in the kitchen trying to figure out what we could possibly have for Christmas dinner the next day, and Dad was nowhere to be found. My brothers and sister were occupying themselves with various activities. The house was relatively quiet. Then, suddenly, I heard some knocking at the front door.

I jumped up wondering who would be coming to our home on Christmas Eve. When I opened the door, I immediately recognized the balding, middle-aged man holding two overflowing bags of groceries. He was "Booby" Kostner, the owner of the Farmer Store grocery on Main Street. What few groceries Mom could buy were purchased mostly at his shop. Mr. Kostner was always a friendly guy who made sure that he said something to make me laugh whenever I was in the store for an errand.

As I stood there staring at him in a state of confusion and bewilderment, he simply reached out his arms and gave me the bags of bread, meat, ice cream, and fruit. "Merry Christmas, Wayne, and Merry Christmas Mrs. Bisek," was all he said as he turned and left. I would be lying to you if I told you that his act of kindness turned our Christmas into a fairytale holiday. But, it did reach my very soul so deeply that I have never lost touch with that wonderful sensation that somebody out there actually cared about me and my family. Someone actually went out of his way to do something nice and generous for me and my siblings. That man and his random act of kindness gave me a small sense of hope and a brief feeling of happiness in my troubled youth.

It took me nearly thirty years to find a way to repay that simple act of benevolence, and when I did, it sparked a chain of events and an introduction of characters that are very nearly beyond my comprehension.

It all started in the fall of 1995 when I was working with American Express Financial Advisors as an investment counselor/financial advisor. Life was relatively comfortable, and I was looking for something worthwhile to add to my plate. American Express gave me just the opportunity that I was looking for at that time. The corporation was running an extremely successful program called "Charge for Hunger." For every dollar that a cardholder charged through American Express, the company would donate three cents to fight hunger. In addition, the company was challenging anyone affiliated with American Express to raise money for a local food pantry, and they would then match it. As an advisor with American Express Financial Advisors, I fit the criteria.

Since I first discovered the program when there was only four weeks left to do something, I hastily gathered six members of a 35-and-older slow-pitch men's softball team that I was sponsoring at the time. I filled them in on the details of the offer and asked them if they were willing to help me raise some money for our local food pantry through a raffle and celebrity basketball game. In spite of the rather insurmountable odds, nearly every one of them immediately supported my idea.

For that initial year, I decided to gather all of the sports memorabilia items that I could and use them as prizes. Eventually, I wound up with twenty items, including a football signed by the legendary Johnny Unitas. In addition to the raffle, we ran a celebrity basketball game. For that event, I was lucky enough to have contacted a gentleman named Tracy Webster for help. Tracy was a former University of Wisconsin Badger men's basketball star. He helped us out by gathering together four other former UW men's players and coming out to little Oregon,

Wisconsin for an exhibition game against the Oregon High All-Star Alumni Team. Everyone truly enjoyed the event and we raised a total of $3,000 for the food pantries of the area.

I am absolutely certain that none of those original volunteers ever dreamed that sixteen years later, Buckets for Hunger, Incorporated would still be functioning so successfully. Even in their wildest dreams, I doubt that they saw themselves willingly and voluntarily working so hard to fight hunger. In spite of my frequent and wildly divergent ideas for bringing in money to fight hunger, they have stayed by my side for the entire decade. They have all, in fact, taken Buckets under their own skin as if the organization was their own baby.

That core group of volunteers has grown to approximately twenty individuals who run the organization. Together, we have orchestrated a wide variety of events and programs that always have one common theme: we do everything possible to combine our love for sports with our passion to feed hungry people. We have organized parties with celebrity athletes, basketball tournaments, and seminars. There have been a number of times that we have had silent and live auctions at University of Wisconsin basketball games in Madison. In addition, Buckets also has run basketball-shooting contests at over twenty different sites in the state for three years. In 2002, Buckets started its now annual tradition of holding a high-end dinner/auction with celebrity athletes in attendance. It has developed into an excellent fund-raising tool for us. In fact, in March of 2005, Buckets brought in over $61,000 to feed hungry folks on the celebrity athlete dinner alone. Our total annual proceeds have increased every year since then. In 2010, Buckets brought in and paid out over $212,000 in proceeds that helped to purchase over 1,400,000 pounds of food for hungry people.

During the summer of 2000, I had the good fortune to meet with a professional representative of one of our honorary board members. The board member was a former University of Wisconsin basketball star, Michael Finley. I asked them if Michael would be interested in establishing an annual fund-raising event in Dallas where he was an All-Star NBA player. My suggestion was to have Michael challenge the local fans, corporations, and his teammates to help him fight hunger in the North Texas area. He would match all of the money that was raised up to a specific amount. Within a week of my proposal, I received confirmation that Michael was thrilled to take on the project. With his dedicated efforts and the help of several key figures with the Dallas

Wayne Bisek

Mavericks, this program brought in nearly a quarter of a million dollars in just four years.

One of the great joys that I have derived from my commitment to feed hungry people through Buckets is the opportunity to meet my boyhood sports heroes at our dinner/auctions. As a die-hard Green Bay Packers fan, I wanted nothing more than to be the next Jim Taylor. He was the hard-running fullback of the Lombardi Packers. One of his key blockers was Jerry Kramer, the right guard, who is the author of *Instant Replay*. They and their teammates were like gods to me in my youth of the 1960's in a small rural community in western Wisconsin.

In both cases, I met these gentlemen for the first time through a telephone call. They never hesitated when I asked if I could take five minutes of their time to tell them about my efforts to "wipe away the tears of hunger..." through combining my passion to feed the hungry with my love for sports. Amazingly, I seemed to hit it off immediately with each one of them. They were both down-to-earth people. There was not a single ounce of egotism in either one. All they wanted to do was ensure that the organization was legitimate and from there, they jumped on board, full-throttle.

Both of these men have been very dedicated to our program from the very first telephone call introduction. They have donated items, signed memorabilia that I sent to them, did radio call-in interviews, made appearances, and have opened many doors for Buckets. It is very humbling for me to tell you that Jim Taylor, my boyhood idol, is now on a first-name basis with me. He calls me on the phone and leaves the message, "Hi, Wayne, it's Jim, call me." I listen to it. I listen to it again, and then I listen to it one more time. At last, I realize that I am not dreaming. It is Jim Taylor, and he is talking to me.

I cannot possibly tell you about all of the kindness and generosity of Jerry Kramer. He is truly a "Renaissance man." I have found him to be one of the most well read people that I have ever met, and yet, he is one of the most humble people that you could ever hope to know. He is a great person who never stops giving, and he never asks for anything. He just wants to know how he can make the event even better so that we can make more money to fight hunger. It would be impossible to overstate his impact on our program.

Not only has Jerry done everything from autograph sessions to radio shows to dinner/auctions, he has used his impressive influence to persuade other athletes to join our cause. He single-handedly persuaded his good friend, Fuzzy Thurston (another Lombardi Legend) to serve on our Honorary Board. Mark Tauscher, currently with the Packers, is another player that Jerry helped bring onto the Board. Mark and Fuzzy have both done a long list of favors for Buckets. Mark, in fact, introduced us to another fund-raising program in a local community and persuaded them to donate all of their proceeds to Buckets.

These two men, Jerry and Jim, are living legends of the NFL and are idolized by most Wisconsin men who are at least forty-years-old. Yet, they are always willing to help in nearly every way possible.

Another example of a boyhood sports hero who has become a linchpin of Buckets is John Brockington. When I was in high school, I wore the jersey number 42 because John Brockington wore it for the Green Bay Packers. He was a rugged, tough running back who was the Rookie of the Year in the NFL in 1971, when I was a senior in high school. Again, with one simple telephone call in 1999, I convinced John to come to Madison for one of our fundraisers. Since that time, John has been a great addition to Buckets events on several occasions. I grew to know him as a good man who has lived through some tough and physically challenging times. Yet, he doesn't ever complain about them. They are just discussed in a matter-of-fact manner. No matter what I have ever asked of John, he has done it.

These are just a few of the sports figures that have stepped up to the plate for Buckets. There are so many that I am absolutely amazed whenever I see a collection of our autographed items. From Muhammad Ali to the University of Wisconsin's last Heisman Trophy winner, Ron Dayne to Stan Musual to the entire Gold Medal-winning United States Women's Soccer team, over one hundred-fifty different athletes have donated signatures and auction items for our events. With their help and generosity, Buckets has reached an unbelievable level of success in our battle against hunger.

In my own wildest dreams, I never thought that there would be a tenth anniversary celebration of our organization. I never imagined that Buckets would pay out over $2,200,000 to food pantries and agencies in nine different states. I never considered that Buckets would be responsible for helping to purchase over 14,000,000 pounds of food for needy people.

Our goal from day one was to "wipe away the tears of hunger and replace them with a glimmer of hope in the eyes of the needy." Buckets has done that to a level that is astounding to me.

Going into our sixteenth year together, I am honored to state that we have never had any paid staff. The program has functioned completely with many, many hours of volunteer time by my wife, my friends, my children, my associates, my teammates, and me.

At every stop along the way, the athletes, their agents, and staff members, the athletic departments' administrators, the corporate decision-makers, and the volunteers have all heard my story of a Christmas gift that touched my very soul. They have listened and responded in the same manner as Mr. Kostner over forty years ago.

One man's act of kindness has spawned an entire organization and all of its benefactors to reach out to hungry men, women, and children for an entire decade and counting. His generosity will live on for as long as I am alive and, hopefully, forever.

Christmas Eve Tears

ON DECEMBER 24, 1996, I had a bit of a "George Bailey" moment right there in the back pew of the Holy Mother of Consolation Church in Oregon, Wisconsin. Only a few short hours before that 4:00 p.m. Christmas Eve mass, I had been released from the hospital after a double-bypass heart surgery.

Over the course of about a four-month time period, I had been undergoing a battery of physical examinations and medical treatments for some breathing problems that had begun to occur when I exercised. My wife actually convinced the medical world that my problem was not exercise-induced asthma. That is when the stress test was finally given. I failed it miserably after only a couple of minutes on the treadmill. He immediately set up a catheterization examination for the next week.

During that procedure, I remember lying there on the examination table wondering what they would find as they inserted the tubes and devices into my arteries through the groin area. At one point, I recall the doctor telling me that he was going to manipulate the device so as to touch my heart. He explained that it would be an extremely uncomfortable sensation, but that I would be fine. The sensation that occurred was breathtakingly alarming, at best. It felt as if someone had just slammed my heart with a steel hammer. Immediately, the doctor administered several shots of nitroglycerin to help me recover. When I did return to a normal breathing pattern, they continued with the procedure. Soon thereafter I saw with my own eyes the source of my breathing problems. The arteries leading to my heart (the left and right anterior descending arteries) were both nearly shut down completely. In the doctor's words, they were "95% blocked." I remember thinking that the picture on the screen of my arteries reminded me of purchasing hot dogs from the butcher back home. You see the hot dogs always came attached to each other by this thin cord of packing "skin." My arteries looked like the last hot dog in the box because they were so wide and then, suddenly, there was only the narrow, string-like connection to my heart.

106

Wayne Bisek

"No wonder you can't breathe very well," the doctor informed me, "Your heart is getting very little blood flow."

By the time that I had returned to my hospital room my wife, Vickie, and my good friend, Paul Lynde, had already arranged for the surgery to be completed the next week. An anesthesiologist, a perfusionist and the cardiac surgeon had been selected and the surgery had been scheduled.

Everything went well with the actual surgery. Several members of my family even showed up to see me that morning. It was very interesting because two of the visitors were my older brother, Karl, and my father. Karl hated my Dad and would rather not have ever been in the same building with him, but they both stayed there the entire time that I was in surgery and more. Never did either one even mention the other one's presence.

In the hours and days following the invasive procedure of December 19, 1996, I spent a lot of time pondering my life and how it had been saved. While I spent a considerable amount of energy recovering, I also had the opportunity to take a second look at my world. When your body has large tubes running in and out of it and a staff of medical professionals monitors your every heartbeat, you begin to appreciate the preciousness of life itself. I began to realize that a great many people did really care about me and about my wellbeing.

During this time, I came to strongly reaffirm my faith in God. Many, many hours had been consumed by prayers of request from me to God seeking His strength and His Divine Guidance for the surgery. My own personal mantra had been the Twenty-Third Psalm. I remember wanting nothing more than to be able to attend Christmas Eve mass. That was my goal—to be at home with my wife and children for Christmas.

Then on the morning of Christmas Eve, Doctor Bachhuber came in and informed me that I could leave as soon as I could arrange for someone to come and get me. Needless to say, I was on the phone immediately after he left the room. Since my wife was working I had to ask Father Tony to do me the favor and he never hesitated in his response.

Within several hours of my return home for the holiday, I was with my family sitting in the last row of pews at Holy Mother of Consolation for Christmas Eve mass. As I sat there trying as hard as possible to thank God for his gift of a longer life, I was constantly interrupted by well-wishers from the parish. I don't remember if it was five or fifty people who shook my hand or hugged me. But I remember that I spent most of the night with tears of joy streaming down my cheeks.

At one point, my then nine-year-old daughter asked my wife why I was crying so much. In spite of all of those tears, I can still remember that, in those long "George Bailey" scenes of that Mass, I wanted to just bask in the warm sensation of genuine love that I was feeling.

A Son's Pride

Cole created a moment for me, also. It was in 1999 and it was after a long night of running an on-air live-auction to raise money for Buckets for Hunger. The event was held on ESPN radio 1070 am in Madison, Wisconsin. It included call-in interviews from several former Green Bay Packers legends including Jerry Kramer, Jim Taylor and Bart Starr. Now, I should remind you that as a young boy growing up in Wisconsin in the 1960s and 1970s, the Green Bay Packers were gods to me. They were perennial champions of the NFL. They were a true dynasty as acknowledged by everyone in sports. Those three players were among the biggest names on that team.

I had convinced them each to call in to discuss their careers and the issue of fighting hunger. Each of them was extremely eloquent and articulate. They spoke of their time with the legendary Vince Lombardi and of what it meant to be so revered by the people of Wisconsin for so many years. Then they each talked about why they wanted to work with Buckets for Hunger to help eliminate hunger in Wisconsin. Unbelievably, each one of them spoke to me on a first-name basis and demanded that I reciprocate. While they talked about their lives, my associates at Buckets and my family took call-in bids on several sports memorabilia items. The bids were coming in relatively fast and furious and the show raised a decent amount of money in our fight against hunger. The night was filled with excitement and a sensation of fulfillment.

Here I was on a regional radio station talking to my boyhood heroes like they were my high school teammates and they were helping me feed hungry people. I did not think it could get any better than that. But it did.

As the evening's events concluded, my volunteer associates tallied up the bids and boxed up the auction items for delivery the next day. I had not realized how "wound up" I had been during the radio show, until it ended. I remember that only minutes after I went off of the air my friends all told me to just go and lie down for a while. Somewhat reluctantly, I left my office and went across the hall to my home and down to my bedroom.

I had just propped up a pillow and planted my head on it when Cole entered the room. "Nice job, Dad. You were great in the interviews," he told me. "I thought you might want to hear how you sounded, so I taped it all for you."

In spite of the fact that I was nearly emotionally exhausted, I was genuinely touched by his thoughtfulness. But that is not the moment that I cherish. No. My sixteen- year-old son then got onto the bed, stretched out beside me, placed his arm across my ribs and deposited his head on my chest. As the sounds of Bart's voice and mine mingled together on the tape, I sat there quietly enjoying the sensation of success. And then the moment occurred.
"Dad," he said, "I am really proud of you!"

There is something very special about having your sixteen-year-old boy lie down next to you and tell you that he is proud of you. I remember that it hit me immediately that this was a moment in time that I should bask in for as long as it lasted. My normal need to rush through life was not allowed to take over this experience. I simply soaked up every drop of emotion that was spewing out of that scene. Even now, years later, I find it impossible to repeat this story without literally breaking into tears of emotion because of the love I felt from him that night.

Ice Bowl Cometh Event
(left to right, Front row: Ron Dayne [1999 Heisman Winner], Mel Renfro [Cowboys], Jethro Pugh [Cowboys], Jerry Kramer [Packers], Paul Hornung [Packers]; Back row: Boyd Dowler [Packers], Dave Robinson [Packers], Danny Anderson [Packers], Ken Bowman [Packers], Cornell Greene [Cowboys])

Wisconsin's Best 2006
(Left to Right, Front Row: Mike Evans, Clyde Gaines, Pat Richter, Kareem Abdul-Jabbar, Al Toon, Adam Burish, Nikki Burish; Back row: Vickie Carroll, Brett Bielema, Terrell Fletcher, Wayne Bisek)

111

(2003; Left to Right, Front row: Don Schultz, Mike Williams, Bonnie Lynde; Back Row: Wayne Bisek, Tim Scott, Michael Finley [Mavs], Antoine Walker [Mavs], Antawn Jamison [Mavs], Paul Lynde)

Buckets Event, 2007
(Left to Right: Gale Sayers [Bears], Willie Davis [Packers], LeRoy Butler [Packers])

A Brother's Love Saves the Day

THIS IS A TOUGH one to tell. I try as hard as possible to avoid becoming somber and to avoid the tears every time that I ponder this tale. I know I should be absolutely thrilled that both of my sons are here with me, yet, in spite of this dangerously close call. I know that what might have been a life-altering double tragedy of epic proportions did not happen. I know that, for some reason, our oldest child (who was then only fourteen) had the courage to make the right decision and the strength and stamina to succeed with his life-saving effort.

It was a celebration of Grandma Bisek's seventy-fifth birthday with all of my siblings and most of their kids attending. It was very rare for all of us to get together for any reason. So this was special for everyone, especially Mom. She was actually doing quite well, from a health standpoint, so it was a good time to enjoy one of her birthdays. She was still very active around the house and yard and she loved to help out at church for funerals and such. Her mind was still pretty sharp and she would share stories, occasionally, with us about her youth. As always, her somewhat rough language spiced up the stories a little. Grandma almost always found a reason to add a "God d—— it!" or a "Jesus Ch——!" to her conversations.

The event was being held at the new home of my sister, Maggie and her husband, Dick. They had just recently moved from their farm after over twenty-five years milking cows and raising chickens. It was the first time that either one of them had lived anywhere besides their mutual home city, except for the time that they spent in Louisiana, when Dick was in the United States Army. But that move was not really by choice. They had gotten married just before Dick was sent to Viet Nam and Maggie went down there for the wedding. She spent over a year down South waiting for him to return from that nightmare across the world.

As I recall, we were not the first to arrive at my sister's new house near the Mississippi River in a small town named Bluff Siding. There were a number of people already enjoying a beautiful June day in Wisconsin.

113

A Knock at the Door

The sun was shining brightly and there was a little bit of a breeze coming off of the backwater that was only about fifty yards from Maggie's front yard. People took turns handing out "how ya doing?" greetings and parents traded stories about how their children were doing in school and sports. There was talk about playing a little baseball or tossing the football around for a while. Our kids joined up with their cousins and before long everyone seemed to be busy with some activity.

Maggie started out by giving all of the adults the grand tour of the new place. The house was typical for Maggie. It was very nearly spotless and very nicely decorated. Everything was immaculate. She explained that it was much smaller than their farmhouse, but that she wanted it that way. She was not sure that she had the energy to maintain a large house while working full-time. I certainly could not spot any sign of problems with her housekeeping, though. As always, her home was beautiful. It was just substantially smaller.

Another attractive feature of the new home and location was the Mississippi River. This allowed them to fish or boat to their hearts' content and, of course, the view was quite nice. The Mississippi has so many beautiful bluffs along its edges that it is a great example of God's handiwork. Maggie was quite pleased with the home that she had found and revitalized.

The day went quite smoothly as we all enjoyed potato salad, coffee cakes, grilled hamburgers and a wide variety of pastas and vegetables and dips in addition to more desserts than were necessary. Before too long, the candles were lit and we all joined in to sing "Happy Birthday" to Mom. The cake was cut and ice cream was added for all those who wanted it.

Eventually, the lure of the river attracted all of the boys. The talk started that they would trek across the narrow backwater to the sandbar/island that was about fifty yards from the shore. I was not really too excited about the prospects, but everyone assured me that the water was not very deep. All of the adults estimated that it was probably no more than four or five feet at its deepest point. So, our two boys and their four cousins hit the water and headed for the sandbar.

But no one factored into the equation the swiftness of the current of the river. Neither did we consider the relative weakness of swimming ability that our twelve-year-old son, Cole, possessed. I stood on the shore (I am not a swimmer at all and, in fact, I am deathly afraid of the water) and watched the boys all proceeding toward their goal. But, as the rest of the group moved with ease across the water, Cole seemed to be lagging behind. Very soon he was substantially distant from the other five boys.

Panic began to set in me as I noticed that he appeared to be struggling to stay above water. His strokes looked more and more awkward and defensive. Then his strokes became fewer and farther between and he began to struggle somewhat to tread water. A fear began to creep into my heart and soul wondering what I could do to aid him, yet attempting not to panic. I quickly started to plan my strategy to rescue him, yet not drown myself.

Luckily, for Cole's sake, his brother had been noticing that Cole was not close to him. He stopped in the water and yelled to Cole. When Cole did not answer, A.J. decided to go after him. I saw him turn around and head toward his brother with some degree of purpose and with a swiftness and hurried attitude that he usually did not demonstrate. He reached Cole and put his arm around him and together they progressed toward the sandbar. I stood there on that shore and prayed that they would find a way to that other side. And they did.

Apparently, Cole gathered his strength while the others caroused in the water near the sand bar. Then, about a half hour later, they made their way back to shore. This time, though, A.J. stayed with Cole and helped him across the entire way.

AJ and Cole

A Knock at the Door

Even now it frightens me to no end to contemplate the nightmarish possibilities that could have taken place that day. We could have lost both of our sons to the river. But, we did not. Instead, one son's love for his brother gave him the courage and strength to make the right decision and to follow through on it. Now, in looking back on those events, I appreciate, even more, the gifts of that day when a brother's love that was so strong it saved a life.

Brandon James Patch

BRANDON JAMES PATCH. THAT is a name that I had never heard before late August of 2004. Brandon James Patch was the name of a young man being discussed and studied on an *ESPN's Behind the Lines* television show. The subject was the safety issue concerning aluminum bats being used in baseball and softball at all levels, except Major League Baseball. Brandon James Patch was at the center of the research. Brandon was killed on the pitcher's mound as the result of being hit in the head by a line drive hit. Except for the occurrence of a small miracle, that name might have been Ashley Jordan Bisek, my son.

A.J. was just eleven-years-old that first year that I coached Little League baseball. He was, like most boys moving into the puberty years, slightly gangly and a little awkward. He was still growing into his body. My oldest son was neither the tallest, nor the shortest boy in his age group. In fact, in most areas of physical stature and athletic ability, A.J. was just about average. He did, though, have some ability to throw a baseball somewhere around the strike zone. His fastball was not as quick as some of the others, but he was relatively consistent with the location of his pitches.

That summer started out rather enjoyably. I was informed that I would be the volunteer head coach of one of the six local Little League baseball teams. Since I have an absolute love for sports, for coaching, and for kids, this seemed like it would be a great summer for me. Actually, A.J. and I got along great as player and coach. I told him right away that once we hit the practice field or the game field that he would have to view me as his coach first and his father second. I promised to treat him in the same manner, good or bad, as I would any other player on the team. He accepted the stipulation without any hesitation and he was always one of the most coachable kids on the team.

My goal was always to be as positive as possible with the kids. I wanted them to learn all of the various skills and strategies necessary to succeed

117

at the game. If I could teach them to constantly play with all of their effort, then I thought they would also learn to love the game. While there were many times that I was frustrated by a player's lack of ability or effort, I tried to maintain my positive approach. In fact, as a coach, I was much more easily bothered by the behavior of other adults, such as coaches, dads or league officers, than by the kids.

Another interesting fact from that first season was that our team had the only girl in the league. She was a twin sister to one of the boys on the team. Katie was actually a very decent player with good defensive skills and adequate batting ability. Her brother was almost constantly riding her for each and every little flaw that she showed. It made it quite interesting in practice because the other guys were very receptive to her presence while her brother was very irritated by it. In his defense, it probably was not a very good set of circumstances for him. I am sure that when I was out of hearing range, the guys gave him a rough time about her skills or her looks. Either way, he just could not be comfortable so he took it out on her constantly. Eventually I had to have a discussion with the parents and it got only slightly better.

In spite of my trials and tribulations with the adults, I absolutely enjoyed working with the kids. Our team had developed a personality of its own and had become known as the best bunting team in the league. We had two kids who could really bring some heat from the mound. One of them was tall and thin with very long arms and a nice pitching motion. The other one was a heavy-set boy with thick arms and legs who had never pitched before I asked him to do so. Neither one of them was able to throw strikes consistently for more than a couple of innings in a row. That is why A.J. became my third pitcher that summer. He would rarely issue a free base, on a walk, to a batter and I don't believe that he ever hit a batter. When necessary, I would bring him in so that our defense could actually get some fielding opportunities rather than watch the other team strike out or walk to each base.

This approach of handling the pitchers worked reasonably well for the first several games of the summer. Then we had to face the toughest team in the league. If I remember correctly, they had at least five players on the "All-Star Traveling Team" for the city. One of their players was the same age as A.J., but he was the "star" player of the league that year. He was that guy we all remember from our youth. He was the one who was a "god" in all sports when he was in fifth and sixth grade, even into seventh and eighth grade. But once he hit high school, he was just another player.

I think most people who were athletes in high school can recall a classmate who just matured in sports at an early age and peaked before he was fifteen. That summer, though, this guy was an absolute terror with the bat and had a "rocket" for an arm. He could do no wrong.

It was the third or fourth game of the season. Our first pitcher was having his usual difficulty about the third inning, so I decided to put A.J. out on the mound. I knew that the "star" was the next batter, but I knew that he had been used to our "blazer" throwing because he had faced him earlier. Therefore, I thought A.J.'s slower speed would mess him up with his timing. A.J. did his warm-up pitches and he looked fine. The batter stepped into the box with complete confidence and measured up A.J. A.J. went into his deliberate wind-up and delivery. The ball left his hand and rotated toward home plate. As it neared its destination, the "star" took one short, meaningful stride toward the pitcher's mound and launched his bat toward that white sphere.

In an absolute instant, the baseball was screaming at my son's head. I know the whole incident lasted no more than a split second, yet in my mind it was an eternity. I knew my son was in danger, immediately. I could only watch, in total fear, and hope that he would survive. The ball was heading directly toward his face. I swear I saw an almost imperceptible movement of his head as he leaned over, ever so slightly, to his right side. I saw him fall to the ground and grab his left ear. The ball went careening out to deep centerfield, yet it was never more than four and a half feet off of the ground.

I rushed out to A.J. in a state of near panic. He was on his knees, bent over at the waist and holding his left ear. When I got there, I asked him if he was okay. He just said, "I think so." I took his hand from his ear and found that it was actually burned. The very top of his ear was singed and appeared bright red. Another half of an inch to his right side and I am not sure if he would have survived. Instead, he looked up at me and asked if he could keep pitching.

I did not want to let him take the mound ever again, much less right then, but he looked at me with so much confidence that I decided to let him continue. I do not recall the details of the rest of that game, but I do know that A.J. proved something that day. He showed me and everyone else at the game that he had a hell of a lot of guts. He never backed down at all, even after that shot at his head. I have seen much older men, professionals even, act differently and play differently after such a close call. A.J. never did. He just continued to enjoy being on that pitcher's mound whenever I sent him back out there.

Later that summer, in the intra-city tournament, A.J. and his teammates found even greater local fame as they upset the "star" and his team. They did it by bunting every chance that they could against this hotshot pitcher. And they did it well. In fact, A.J. even laid down a suicide squeeze bunt to drive in the eventual winning run.

Not only had God provided that miracle of guiding A.J.'s head just out of the way of that dangerous, rocketing baseball, he also had provided that smaller gift of a bunt single that beat the top pitcher in the league that year. Thank God that A.J's name never made it to *ESPN's Behind the Lines* and I am forever grateful for that.

Rapid City Miracle

THE FIELD OF MEDICINE and the discussion of miracles almost never intersect in the conversations that you have with your personal physician. For me, that rare occurrence did happen in December of 1996.

I am an extremely active, sports-oriented, competition-driven individual with relatively modest athletic gifts. I am neither blessed with tremendous speed, nor with astounding strength. What I do possess is a high degree of desire coupled with an almost obsessive attitude about exerting every ounce of energy on every possible play. In fact, I have been known to make all-out diving and stretching attempts to catch softballs even when the score is 16-1 in an over-35 slow-pitch softball league. That is how I ended up having back surgery at the age of 40. One dive and/or slide too many finally resulted in a herniated disc that was causing neurological symptoms in my leg and foot. The orthopedic surgeon explained my injury as "a lifetime accumulation of beating myself up athletically."

I only mention these facts as a backdrop for the miracle that allows me to write this today.

In the summer of 1996, I began to experience some serious health issues. For several months, I had been consulting with physicians and specialists because of a breathing disorder. For some undetermined reason, my exercise habits were now causing me a substantial amount of discomfort.

I would do my usual routine of running about one and a quarter mile three times a week in the hilly area near our home. In the first couple hundred yards of the run, breathing would be very difficult. Then I would fight through it and gather my "second wind." There was never a problem in finishing the run. On Sunday evenings, I would attend an "open gym" wherein guys, from ten years younger than me to a couple years older than I, would play basketball. It was your typical un-officiated game. There would be spits and spurts of speed blasts followed by the pushing and shoving moves associated with athletes more than slightly past their prime. The flow of friendly competition was usually relatively calm, but there would be momentary interjections of anger and frustration. It always made the evenings a tense means of staying in shape.

That summer I was experiencing a troublesome routine on each of these Sunday evenings. I would go to the gym, do my five minutes of stretching routine, shoot around for about another five minutes and then begin full-throttle scrimmages. My breathing rate and depth would be normal for about five minutes of running, jumping, pushing and shoving. Then I would be driven to the sidelines by an extreme inability to take in air. My lungs would cramp up severely and my chest would feel like I had just swallowed some huge gulp of the iciest drink possible. I would rest there on the bleacher for what was never more than five to ten minutes. Upon my return to the floor, there would be absolutely no lingering symptoms of fatigue or distress. I would stay for the next two hours of exercise inducing gallons of perspiration. Never did I retire early and never did I leave under physical duress.

I did, however, spend several months experimenting with inhalers prescribed for asthma sufferers. At one point, I was using the same type of inhalers that the Olympic athletes used to deal with asthma. Several doctors diagnosed me with "exercise-induced asthma." Their treatment was simply to use the inhalers and continue to monitor their effect. The effect of the prescription and treatment was nil. My breathing rate and depth and control were never even slightly affected by the medical effort. Three different doctors never considered any other possibility.

Vickie and I had planned a family vacation to Yellowstone Park, Mount Rushmore and other points of interest out west for that year. When we left for our vacation, I took along my exercise clothes and my inhalers. My plans would be as usual. I would spend approximately one hour with A.J. on three days doing a series of wind sprints, then walking and then several longer distance runs. The other days I would spend, by myself, doing a 1-2 mile jog at a comfortable pace.

No breathing problems were even slightly evident with this routine on the first several days of our trip. Then we reached Rapid City, South Dakota. It was a beautiful community that was similar to so many others in the United States. For our family, though, it was not any one of the pre-determined destination points for our sight-seeing vacation. "Old

Faithful" geyser, for one, beckoned us. Rapid City was just another hotel with a couple of beds slept in by a thousand different people from various walks of life, heading in various directions for a variety of reasons.

We checked into the rectangular room with the slightly worn carpet and immediately ordered the customary ever-so-comfortable rollaway bed. We then proceeded to endure the seemingly endless debate about which child should sleep on the rollaway this night.

Once it was determined that our ten-year-old daughter would have the pleasure of using the extra bed, I got dressed and prepared for my jog.

As I recall, it was a quite pleasant day. There was a gentle breeze that pushed me along somewhat on my way out from the parking lot. It was an almost perfect seventy-four degrees and the sun was playing hide-and-seek behind a grouping of clouds. As I expected, my breathing was a little difficult for the first several hundred yards. The traffic was relatively calm and I tried to be relatively aware of the movement of cars, trucks, vans and bicyclists.

As I subconsciously sought to catch that usual second-wind, I began to realize that that was apparently not going to happen on this day. Instead, my breathing seemed to be taking on an even more shallow feeling. With each and every stride, I was finding it more difficult to take in any air. By the time that I was about a mile away from the hotel, I was very aware of the fact that something quite new and different was happening to me. I was not sure, at all, why I had entered into a whole new area of exertion. I did know one thing for sure. I was beginning to get worried, very worried.

For the first time in my entire life, I was not sure that I could complete my effort. I was beginning to question whether I was about to regurgitate or simply pass out from exhaustion. My heart seemed as if it was fighting to get out of my chest. My head was spinning round and round as if on some nerve-racking roller coaster for the first time ever. My chest first felt as if it was on fire and then as if someone had slammed me, point-blank, with a two-by-four. I honestly had no idea what was going to happen next when I pulled up short on that long expanse of empty concrete a mile away from the wife and children that I loved so much.

I had only one thought as I bent over at the waist, reeling with the fear of a man who suddenly knows that he may be faced with immediate death. I prayed to simply make it to the very next moment, the very next breath. I used every bit of self-control that I could gather to convince myself not to panic. I stood there for several very long minutes crouched over and fully expecting to vomit or to just drop over into unconsciousness. I wondered to myself how my family would ever find me. Would they have to wait for hours back at the hotel wondering why I had not returned? Would they have to contact the local police to see if there was any news of a jogger being hit or being found on the road? How tortured would they all be as they waited and pondered what had happened to their father and husband?

I struggled as mightily as I could to gather my wits and to regain my physical composure. And somehow, I did both. I pulled myself up and persuaded my body to move forward one slow step at a time. And it worked. I moved onward and I returned to that hotel room where my wife and kids were smiling and laughing and planning the next day. I did not have the desire to share with them my frightening tale, not yet.

Several months later (December to be exact), the incidents had become more frequent and more extended in length. Finally, my lovely wife demanded that I undergo a full stress workout to determine the cause of the problem. She became convinced that asthma was not the root of the problem, when I became completely unable to breathe after having done nothing more than walk up the dozen steps in our bi-level ranch home.

The stress test only lasted two minutes before my doctor asked me to get off of the treadmill. My response was to inform him that I would be glad to do another fifteen or twenty minutes to work up a real exertion level. He told me that that would be neither necessary, nor safe. He had spotted an alarming rhythm in the heart tracing already. He advised me to schedule a heart catheterization procedure immediately.

Within two weeks, I had undergone the catheterization and a double by-pass surgery. My left and right anterior descending arteries were each 95% blocked. Asthma had never been the source of my health problems. My heart simply was not able to receive sufficient blood to function properly. I will never forget the words of my cardiologist, Dr. Bachhuber, after reviewing my history and my test findings. He looked me square in the eyes when I recounted my story about jogging in Rapid City. He stated in a very matter-of-fact manner, "Wayne, it is a miracle that you did not have a heart attack that day."

124

Even in hindsight, I cannot be certain that I was the benefactor of a little miracle or I avoided my possible heart attack because of my previous exercise habits. But, I do know that I have read many, many tragic obituaries of athletically inclined, active men in similar circumstances. Loving children, young wives, life-long friends are all left behind after a massive heart attack has struck. I am still here on this earth because of that miracle.

A Father Grows/ A Son Grows Up

A LICENSE TO DRIVE a motor vehicle is one of the most treasured achievements in a young person's life. It represents freedom, independence, social acceptance and the coming-of-age. For every parent, it is a harbinger of fear for your child's safety and the safety of everyone else on the road or near the road. It is the fear of your child growing up and moving away from your influence and into a whole new world of activities and opportunities. It is the moment at which you realize that your life, as a parent, will never be the same again. Your financial circumstances will be dramatically altered. There will by rising gas bills, soaring insurance premiums and costly speeding tickets. That dearly beloved driver's license is viewed from two very different perspectives depending on whether you are the child or the parent.

In the fall of 1997, our oldest child, A.J., reached that milestone age of sixteen and he could not wait to get his driver's license. He had endured all of the classroom sessions to learn the rules of the road. He had spent hours and hours on the road as a passenger and as the driver with his school instructor and with his parents. In his own estimation, there was nothing more that he needed to know or to learn. He was completely ready to tackle that last obstacle, the official state-proctored road-driving test.

The date was set. It was timed exactly and perfectly with the date of his sixteenth birthday, September 1. He actually awakened that morning with plenty of time to spare before heading into Madison for the test. His Mom was going to accompany him for this major endeavor. They piled into the car and A.J. was shockingly attentive to all of the details of the 1988 Chevy Nova that he was going to be driving. Every minute detail concerning how to leave the driveway was covered with care and caution by A.J. As they drove down the road that day, I said a quick prayer for A.J. to do well. Then I said several longer prayers for myself because I knew I would have to deal with all sorts of headaches and sleepless nights from now on.

126

Our family did not yet have a cell phone for A.J. to call me immediately with the results. I had to wait patiently for them to return to our home in order to hear the news. But the news was not good. It seems A.J. made one questionable right turn at a rather busy intersection and the instructor was having a bad day. Thus, like his father, A.J., did not pass that first shot at getting his license. He was forced to set another date for a second effort.

Luckily, he only had to wait a week or so to head back in to the big city for another road test. He had done more driving in Madison during the interim and now he felt completely confident that he would be officially able to drive on his own within the hour. This time A.J was absolutely meticulous with each and every signal and turn. He traveled throughout the city with that State of Wisconsin Department of Transportation employee for about thirty minutes. When he returned to the DMV offices, I was sure he had done well because he had been gone so long. This official decided that A.J. still needed more practice. He said he just did not think A.J. was totally comfortable behind the wheel.

Now A.J. had to go to high school and face his buddies. He would have to give the dire news of his second failure. He would have to endure an endless amount of teasing and good-natured, but tiresome heckling from his friends. Worse yet, it would now be over one month before he could attempt the test again.

Eventually the time did pass and he acquired that now-even-more-valuable driver's license. With each day that he drove back and forth to school without incident or accident, he swore that he was becoming a pretty good driver. His confidence was growing almost by the minute and he was building to that next higher level of self-actualization. He began to ask incessantly for the right to use the car for that other right-of-passage, the double date.

A.J. and one of his buddies had begun to call and to visit a couple of girls from McFarland (a city about ten miles away) and he was looking for approval to take them all to a movie in still another different nearby city, Stoughton. Needless to say, it took an extended time of nearly three months before Vickie and I were even remotely comfortable with that thought. The very thought of our sixteen-year-old, hormone-raging son driving a vehicle at fifty-five miles an hour while an attractive young lady (who might actually be interested in holding his hand) sat only inches away from him scared the hell out of me. It was all I could do to not pick up a drinking habit as a result of those worries.

But as all parents eventually learn, teenage sons can be extremely focused and persistent when it comes to the pursuit of their two most beloved activities, driving and girls. Therefore, we finally allowed A.J. the chance to simultaneously test his driving skills and control his hormones. Adam and A.J. lined up the girls, the movie, the gas money and the date was set.

The evening progressed smoothly as A.J. moved from one location to another picking up Adam, Jenny and then Tiffany. No problems occurred on the trip from McFarland to Stoughton and the movie allowed for the much-awaited handholding session. All was perfect in A.J. land.

Meanwhile, Vickie and I sat at home pondering the insanity of our decision. Each and every minute was absolutely filled with doubt and concern. Unbeknownst to us, as we pondered his safety, all of our fears were actually coming to life.

On the way back to Adam's house from the movie, A.J. was driving along comfortably when he was faced with having to make a left turn off of the main highway onto the side road. Apparently, he put his turn signal on and approached the center lane in order to make the turn. There was a car coming at him at about sixty miles an hour and another one coming up behind him at about that same speed. A third car was waiting to enter the intersection at A.J's left in order to come out onto the highway. As the first vehicle approached A.J., a problem started to develop. Another vehicle behind the other car that was approaching the corner from the north decided to pass (on the shoulder) at the very intersection. That caused the first car to take the curve at the intersection a little tighter than he had planned. The convergence of the three vehicles at the same curving intersection was not something that had been in A.J.'s driving training experiences.

In addition, another complicating factor had occurred. Unbeknownst to A.J., he had the very tip of the driver's side front bumper hanging about six inches over the center as all of this unfolded. As the approaching car cornered into the intersection, his front bumper smashed into A.J's front bumper. The four teenagers were suddenly spinning around to the left into the southbound lane of traffic and then proceeded to careen across the two northbound lanes of traffic until they finally came to rest in the ditch on the north bound side of the road.

All four kids were rattled emotionally and shaken up physically. Miraculously, they were uninjured. They had traveled uncontrollably across three lanes of traffic with cars moving in opposing directions and at fifty-five miles per hour. Yet, they had no contact with any other vehicles or objects, besides the one that hit them.

The telephone call that interrupted our quiet, but nerve-wrenching evening was at once horrible news and great news. A.J. told Vickie what had happened and she quickly informed me that there had been an accident and that A.J. and the kids were all okay. No one had been hurt, but we needed to go to retrieve our son because the car was not drivable and was being towed away.

As a father, I cannot begin to even describe the feelings and thoughts that race through your mind on the way to the scene of an accident involving your child. I do know that the entire way there I kept thanking God for watching over my son, his friends and the other drivers and passengers. I kept telling myself that the car could be replaced easily and that the really important fact was that I still had a son to love. I can't understand quite how I did it, but I shocked everyone that night. My innate reaction to fear and negative surprises had usually been verbose anger. Yet, this time, I did nothing more than give my son a long hug. I must have told him a hundred times that I did not care about the car being destroyed. My only concern was that he was physically fine and so were his friends. And I, absolutely, meant every word that I said.

Every day accidents like this occur and people are killed. Families are torn apart. Friendships are forever ended. I do not understand why others are taken from us in these horrible tragedies. I only know that for some reason, that night, God was watching over my son and his friends.

A Perfect Match and A Perfect Game

AS MY WIFE WOULD be quick to inform you, the area of competitive sports has played an inordinately large and inappropriately important role in my life. It has been the root cause of several of the worst examples of my parenting experience. But it has also been a wonderful cause for bonding with my children.

AJ and Cole wrestling

One of my most pleasant memories of my two sons involved a wrestling match in which they were both on the varsity squad. I will tell you that neither one of the boys was a star athlete during their high school days. In fact, their athletic experiences were almost entirely negative in nature. Some of that was due to their own level of skills and effort and God-given talent, or lack thereof. Some of it though was due to the politics that affects almost all school age children. In fact, there are times when I wish I had never introduced them to sports because they could have avoided so much headache and heartache.

Yet there is one night in my memory that stands out like a beacon in a storm. It was a wrestling match against a local school and both of them were wrestling on the varsity squad that night. A.J. and Cole each had some areas of the sport in which they had strengths, but neither one had the correct combination of attitude, effort, skills and physique to excel in this difficult one-on-one sport. They were good enough to make their varsity squads but not quite good enough to succeed consistently against the other schools.

On this particular evening, Cole hit the mat first and he did it in his normal exciting and aggressive manner. He was nimble enough and quick enough that he could go from embarrassment to golden opportunity in a matter of seconds. This night was different though as he started out with a quick takedown of his opponent and then he turned him onto his back in just a matter of seconds. With relative ease, he maneuvered the poor fellow into a position of no return with a wrestling move called the hammer-and-half. Before the first period was over, he had pinned his opponent and he was smiling widely as his hand was raised in victory.

I remember sitting in the stands with Vickie and Melanie and praying with great intensity for A.J. to win his match. Since the boys were not immensely successful, it was rather rare for them to each win a varsity match on the same night. This night was different. A.J. took the mat and wrestled with a real inspiration. He was absolutely determined to pin his man and he did just that. Being much more muscular than his opponent, he relied more on intimidation and strength to attain his win. His moves were more methodical and deliberate, but just as effective on this night. Early in the second period he broke his man down to the mat and then he simply muscled his way into a half-nelson maneuver. Once he locked it up it was just a matter of time before he turned him and planted him.

I still remember congratulating them after the team match was over and then snapping their picture together. It was so great to see them both enjoying the moment so much. It was obvious that they were each happy, not just with themselves, but for each other. All I did was smile as the very proud father that I was. It was a moment in time that is etched on my mind forever.

Melanie was the dedicated athlete and student in our family. No matter what she tackled she went in with complete dedication and effort. For softball, her dedication and commitment went to a whole new level. She never hesitated in paying the price to improve and to attain her goals. In fact after her freshmen year in high school, she and her mom and I decided that she should transfer to another school district because we all knew that she would never be happy in her home district with her softball coach.

A Knock at the Door

Mel pitching ace

For the most part the move was one of the best things that I ever did as a parent. She spent three years playing for a coach that she genuinely enjoyed and who helped her in every way that he could to succeed in attaining her personal and team goals. She also ended up being an absolute thorn in the side of her former coach for all of those next three years. In six regular season games and six summer games as her new team opposed him, she never lost to them and she dominated them in every way shape and form as a hitter, runner, shortstop and pitcher.

The coupe-de-grace, though, occurred during her senior year in high school when she played them early in the season. Her own squad had lost seven starters from the previous year's team to graduation. Therefore her team was not expected to do well in the conference and her former team was picked as one of the top in the league.

It did not matter to her as she took the mound that day. She used all of her skills, experience and game-savvy to completely baffle that team. She was so dominant as the pitcher that only one hit ball even left the infield that day. Not a single runner reached a base for any reason at all. She threw a perfect game with no walks, no hits and no one reaching base on an error. In addition, she hit a double to drive in the first run and she then scored the only other run on an error.
I will always remember the look on her face when she came off of that field. She knew full well that she had just accomplished a pitching masterpiece. Her face was filled from ear to ear with the smile of a victor.

What I will never forget, though, is that when she walked through the opening in the fence to leave that field, she came directly to me and hugged me hard and long. All she said to me was this, "Dad, don't start crying because if you do, so will I."

Instead, we both just stood there holding each other tightly. I remember feeling so happy for her because she had reached her goal of throwing a perfect game and I knew that it was very special for her because it could not have come against a more fitting opponent.

The Laugh Was On Me

ANOTHER MOMENT THAT MAKES me laugh and smile immensely occurred during a different Buckets for Hunger fund-raising event. It was in February of 2003 and it was at a dinner and auction that we held at the Maple Bluff Country Club in Madison, Wisconsin. The evening included the attendance of several local sports celebrities including Mark Tauscher (a former UW Badger, playing in the NFL with the Packers), Ron Dayne (the former Heisman-trophy winner for the Badgers who was playing for the Giants), Tamara Moore (a former Badgers women's basketball star currently in the WNBA), Brooks Bollinger (another former Badgers football player about to go into the NFL) and Casey FitzRandolph (an Olympic speed-skating Gold Medalist from Wisconsin). There was a gourmet meal, a silent auction and a live auction of sports memorabilia.

Prior to all of the festivities, though, I needed to circle the city in a limousine in order to pick up each of these celebrities. It was one of the fringe benefits of being the President of the organization I guess. So when the limo arrived, I took my seventeen-year-old daughter, Melanie, away from her duties at the event and asked if she wanted to join me for the ride. She had been working on the event for the last month or so at home doing things like typing up descriptions of the auction items, labeling and packing up the items and helping me contact the celebrities to arrange everything. Of course she said she would love to go with me.

The limousine was a beautiful, sleek black SUV-type vehicle. The chauffeur opened the back door for us to get in and the lights were flashing on the ceiling already. Long, black leather seats were on either side of the center aisle with the requisite iceboxes stationed at three or four locations. A television was running above the front seat area and the moon roof was opened at that time.

134

After Melanie stepped into the "pimp ride," I climbed in and sat down on the far rear seat. She simply smiled widely and announced, "It's really TIGHT, Dad."

I returned her comment with the normal response of an out-of-step, non-teen-speaking fifty-year-old father. "Just move up to the front," I said.

Melanie immediately burst out into hysterical laughter at my faux pas. When she finally ceased with her giggles, she informed me that TIGHT meant it is COOL.

"Oh, I guess that makes me an old geezer then," I admitted.

Then we toured the Madison area from Mark's hotel to Ron's home and to the separate apartments of Tamara and then Brooks. Melanie or I repeated the story of my un-hip-like comment as each new attendee joined our group. Everyone found it to be hilarious every time that it was repeated for the latest addition to the limo. Our last stop was to Brooks' apartment and Ron and Mark were both pointing out that he probably would not know what "tight" meant either. They said he was a great guy and an excellent leader on the field. He was just a little bit shy of being "hip."

Sure enough, we had no more than finished laughing after the latest rendition about my "just move up to the front" comment when we pulled up to Brooks' apartment. As soon as he sat down and said his hellos to everyone, I told him that I thought the limo was "really pretty TIGHT."

"Well, I can move up to the front and give you more room back here if you want," he offered.

Immediately, the entire group broke out into an uproar. I had to explain the whole story to him and he just smiled and shrugged. He was really pretty cool about the whole deal.

As I finally ceased laughing, I glanced over to see my daughter with this huge grin on her face. She was absolutely thoroughly enjoying the moment. At that very instant, I remember feeling tremendously happy that I could be in this situation with my daughter and all of these celebrities and yet we were all just a bunch of friends laughing together. I felt great about being able to share that time with her. There was nothing that I wanted to do except smile and let the moment linger. And I did just that.

Dottie's Influence

WITHOUT A DOUBT, THE single greatest moment of my father's life has to be the day he met his second wife, Dottie. That woman provided him with twenty years of happiness and laughter and love. Somehow, she took a bitter, angry, violent excuse of a man and turned him into a genuinely caring, loving and generous human being. Dottie helped him find an inner peace that, I doubt, he ever dreamed existed before he met her.

When I first met Dottie, I was carrying a lot of baggage about her role in my life and my mother's life. She was the "other woman" who beguiled Dad into leaving Mom with "her sexy ways," according to my mother. She was guilty of convincing him to abandon his children and his wife, as we kids were told. Dottie was, allegedly, nothing more than a promiscuous slut of a woman that was the cause of my own mother's years of loneliness and bitterness. All of that information had been fed to me for ten long years. Animosity, hatred and contempt were the only emotions that I had ever felt for her until I met her and came to know her.

At that point in my life, it had been nearly nine years since my parents had divorced during the beginning of my senior year in high school. It had been all of those nine years, and more, since Dad and I had spoken to each other. Of course, it probably didn't matter that we had gone that long without any conversation. Dad had made my whole life miserable in every possible way prior to the divorce anyway. Everything that I ever enjoyed in life, he had conspired to take away from me. Every day that he had been in my life was a day of anger, frustration, violence and fear.

So, it was no small task to consider letting him back into my life. Then, to top it all off, I was going to attempt to allow this other woman, Dottie, to become a part of my children's lives. This was the woman who had disrupted our family dynamics and who had ruined my mother's life. Yet, something inside of me made me realize that I would never be at peace with myself unless I did all of this.

At first, she was very quiet whenever we got together with the two of them. At times, I think she was almost suspicious of my agenda for bringing Dad back into my life. She had spent a lot of time and effort in rebuilding this imposing man into a gentle husband and father. Therefore, she was extremely protective of her personal investment. No one was going to be allowed to use him or to hurt him in any way, if she had anything to say about it.

I am sure that I came across as being very cautious in the early stages of the rebirth of our relationship. It was obvious that I had not forgotten, or even forgiven, Dad for all of the pain he had instilled into my early life. There was no way that I was going to let him disrupt my own newfound happiness either.

Dad and Dottie

Yet, over time, I came to realize that this "Dottie" woman was less evil than I had been led to believe. She was a genuinely sensitive and loving woman who treated my children as if they were her own. From the very beginning, she relished her role of "Grandma Dottie" with them. They always looked forward to visiting Grandpa Bisek and Grandma Dottie because they knew we would laugh a lot and play a lot of games.

"Spoons" was one of their favorite card games when we got together with them. It is a kids' game wherein you all sit around the table and you place spoons in the center of that table. There is one spoon fewer than there are players in the game. Each player rapidly exchanges cards with the others until someone collects four-of-a-kind. Then that person grabs a spoon and the others follow in an attempt to get a spoon before anyone else. The person who misses out on the spoon loses that hand. It was a game that Grandma Dottie, eventually, had played with my kids a thousand times. But, it did not seem to matter which game they were playing. They just liked to hang around with her because she was always smiling and she was always hugging them.

The more time we spent with the two of them, the more I came to admire her strength and generosity. She had had a rough life herself. There had been a difficult first marriage to an alcoholic. Then there were the three battles with cancer that she fought over a twenty year time period. In addition, she had had a deaf daughter who presented many challenges. Yet, she found it in herself to adopt not one, but two other young girls. If all of that was not enough, then she decided to transform my father into a whole new person.

In some ways, it took many years to come to grips with the reality of my Dad's relationship with his second wife and their children. For a while, I was quite jealous of the fact that their home life was filled with joy and excitement and understanding. It was a completely opposite environment compared to the one that I had had with him as my father.

From my perspective, I saw a man who was a tyrant to me and my siblings and mother. I saw a man who disowned me as his own child. I saw a man who never showed me a moment's worth of love or compassion during my youth. The only reason that I let him back into my life was simple. I did not want to teach my children to hate anyone. I wanted to stop the finger pointing and try to salvage a relationship for my children with their grandpa.

Eventually, Dottie and Vickie helped me to discover that Dad always had the potential to be a good father. He had a lot of love in his heart. He just had never been taught what to do with it. With Dottie's influence and nurturing, he learned how to give it away to the people that he cared about so deeply. This large, burly man with the deep voice and the fearless attitude was like putty in her hands. She molded him into a Norman Rockwell-type grandpa figure. Whenever we visited, he was told to take the time to enjoy us. Every time we went to the farm, he would take the kids to see the animals. Or he would put them on some souped-up tractor and drive them around the yard. Or he would just play cards with them. The message was quite clear from Dottie to him. This is your family and you will love them and they will know it.

A Knock at the Door

It took me a while to understand how she had performed this miracle transformation of my father. I believe that she reached into his heart and changed his attitude and his life by demonstrating every day what love was and is. She listened to his rough language and persuaded him that such talk was unnecessary and ineffective. She watched his anger come out in violent rages and she suggested that there were better ways to deal with the people that you loved. For every day of their twenty-plus years together, she sent him the strong message that he was loved and needed and appreciated. She used her soft ways and her subtle strategies to teach him how to quietly earn respect. I never heard Dottie raise her voice. In her own smooth and effective manner, she simply demanded that Dad should become a good person and he did it for her.

In the conversations with this persuasive and insightful woman, I grew to appreciate all that she did for Dad. With her help, I grew to understand that there was another side to the story of my sordid and sad childhood. Dottie and I spent many, many hours getting to know each other's true feelings. Luckily, we both loved to talk and to share our emotions. Through her eyes, I came to know a different viewpoint of my father.

In all honesty, I will never forget the pain and sorrow that my father wreaked upon me and upon my older siblings, especially. It is difficult, after all, to wipe away the heartbreak of parental abuse of any kind. Yet, with Dottie's influence, I grew to understand that nothing was to be gained by a continuation of the hatred. We would all be happier, she proposed, if we could find a way to move away from those bygone days and start over together. Of course, she was absolutely correct.

Late in her life, as the cancer once again devoured her body, she continued to think only of my Dad's happiness. Every time that we talked in those last several visits, she reminded me about how much it meant to Dad to have me and my family in his life. She constantly asked me to watch over him and to stay a part of his life. Her only thoughts were centered around finding him a reason to continue to live on his own.

As difficult, physically, as her last days on this earth were, she found the strength to drive those three and a half hours to visit us one last time. She convinced Dad to bring her to our home so she could see the grandkids one more time before she passed away. I will never forget her sitting in that tufted-back parlor chair in our living room. Her head was slightly tilted to one side and her eyes were very nearly closed. Every breath she took was an exercise in discomfort and pain. But when the kids came in

140

the door from school, she somehow found the energy to smile ever so slightly and to hold them close to her. She even demanded that we take her to Cole's track meet and then Melanie's softball game in the same day. I am sure that she did not really know what was going on during either one. But, she stayed there until the end of both events for our kids.

Only a month later, on Mother's Day, we were called to the hospital as she was dying. We all stood in that somber room, every eye dripping tears, as death encircled Dottie. Each of us approached her, as she struggled through the pain, and said our last goodbyes. We all knew that the morphine had taken away any ability for her to respond. She died two days later.

At her funeral, I attempted to make a short statement about what Dottie meant to me. My emotions, though, took over and I barely uttered the words as I gasped for air through my sorrowful sobs. What I wanted to say was simple. I wanted to thank her for giving my Dad the gift of twenty years of happiness and love. But I also wanted to thank her for giving me the gift of my newfound father.

Ten Seconds

TEN SECONDS IS ABOUT the amount of time that it takes a world-class sprinter to cover one hundred meters. In ten seconds, I could go from the batter's box to third base on a hit to the gap. It takes about that long to recite the complete Hail Mary. In those same ten seconds, you could drink a full eight ounces of water. In ten of the best-spent seconds of your life you could share a very long, sensuous, wet kiss with the love of your life.

But, ten seconds of the dentist drilling into your infected tooth can feel like an eternity. If you spent ten seconds staring into the eyes of a grizzly bear out in the wild, then you could probably see time travel in ultra slow motion. If you had to wait ten seconds for the response to your proposal of marriage, then you would be an extremely apprehensive individual.

On a bright, sunny mid-afternoon on June 7, 2002, I spent ten of the longest and most harrowing seconds of my life absolutely believing that my wife, my daughter and I were about to be killed.

It all started with softball and revolved around my desire to coach the game. My daughter, Melanie, had both the ability to play the game and a genuine love for the game. Ever since she was in fifth grade she stood out as a fast pitch softball player. She had that wonderful combination of God-given talent, intelligence and burning desire to improve. Melanie was a quick study. You only had to demonstrate a skill once or twice and she could then, usually, perform it perfectly herself. My daughter could hit with authority and she had a rocket for an arm. In addition, she could cover the hole at shortstop or go up the middle equally well. On the base paths, she had a natural aggressiveness coupled with a nimble, quick-thinking mind. Her attitude once she stepped onto the field to practice or for a game was simple and straightforward. She loved to be there and she was going to enjoy every second to the nth degree.
Her leadership skills, her positive attitude and her willingness to work hard to improve made her every coach's dream. But, even more

important, she made friends immediately on every team on which she ever played. And she played on about six different teams each summer. As a player who was as talented at pitcher as she was at shortstop, she was constantly being asked to help out other teams in other tournaments.

Now, since we both loved softball, Melanie and I spent a tremendous amount of time at tournament games or in a car traveling to those games. It was a tremendous bonding experience for the two of us. Not only did we grow to a wholly unique level of communication as coach and player, we developed a father-daughter relationship that was the envy of all of her friends. There were no subjects, at all, that we avoided discussing. We spent hours, upon hours, singing along to the oldies in various vehicles with ever-changing music technology. It was a wonderful situation for the two of us because I was able to meet new people, who also loved softball, and she was able to do something that she thoroughly enjoyed. The real bonus was that not only did I get the thrill of watching my child do an activity at which she excelled and that she loved, but I also had the pleasure of serving as her coach for several of those years.

That summer of 2002 was the second year that I had been asked to coach this particular traveling team. We had been practicing for about two weeks prior to this first tournament. The team looked as if it was starting to really come together. This weekend we were going to have a couple of Melanie's good friends, Erica and Jenna, help us out because of some schedule conflicts with a couple of our regular players.

The tournament was in Rockford, Illinois, so Melanie and I would be making a very familiar trek. I never liked the time that we spent on the highway when we went there. There were just too many semis on the road and traffic seemed to be moving at least ten or more miles above the speed limit. Rockford is a city that put on about six big tournaments each summer and we had been heading down there to play and coach for the last three years now. I am not sure that the competition was any better than in Wisconsin tournaments, but they sure had a lot more tournaments.

Erica, Jenna, Jenna's mom (Jody) and her brother met us at our house and we decided to have them follow us. Vickie, Melanie and I were going to stay overnight at a hotel there and the others were going to go back to their homes for Friday night. It was one of those rare occasions when Vickie was actually going with us to a tournament. She usually either worked at the hospital or just stayed home to do other things. Vickie was not heavy into sports, at all. But, she had decided that she would attempt to understand just what Mel and I saw in all of this traveling and softball playing.

Being a relatively newly licensed driver, Melanie was anxious to drive. For that weekend, I had to study for a certification test for my profession. So, off we went with Vickie riding "shotgun" and me hitting the books in the far backseat of the minivan.

Melanie was actually a very good driver for someone who had only been doing it for about four or five months. She was very observant of the road and of the traffic laws. But, I do remember that the day before she and I had been in Madison and I had to continually remind her to slow down for the intersections and to "never run a yellow light." The poor kid got very tired of hearing it over and over, but eventually she did adhere to the request.

Everything went very smoothly as we headed south from our home toward Janesville. Traffic was rather light on the two lane roads for the thirty-five minutes it took to get from Oregon to downtown Janesville. There were two intersections with lights and Melanie was doing a great job of letting me know that she was stopping for the yellow lights. I was stretched out across the seat with my head propped against the inside of the vehicle, while I was reading and taking notes. Vickie and Mel were chatting up front and Jody was having no problem at all following Melanie's lead.

Then Melanie approached another intersection of our three-lane southbound road. On either side of the streets, there were large parking lots with hundreds of people entering and leaving shopping malls, restaurants and discount stores. Jody was about two car lengths behind as we were moving along at about thirty-five miles an hour, but slowing down for the lights. The light changed from green to yellow when Mel was about a hundred yards away from it. She applied the brakes and prepared to stop for a red light. Jody did the very same.

There was a cement truck coming up behind Jody who chose not to do the same maneuver. Instead, he whipped his vehicle around Jody's car, went into the far left lane and then cut back in front of Jody so as to proceed through the intersection in order to beat the red light. He then came to the ugly realization that there was a green van stopped at the

144

now-red light. And it was only about thirty feet away from him when he jammed his foot against the brake pedal with all of his might.

That is the precise moment when my ten seconds started. I either sensed this impending danger or I heard the screeching whine of rubber sliding hard against the sun-parched pavement. Instinctively, I turned my head toward the rear window. All that I saw was a large, red vehicle. I had seen hundreds of them on the road with their turning, churning barrels of cement located behind the raised, boxed-in driver's seat. But, this time it registered immediately in my brain as a horrific solid steel giant that was about to steamroll directly over me, my wife and my daughter. One second at a time, I envisioned the weight slamming into me and crushing me to pieces then proceeding to roll over my wife and daughter. I knew that there was absolutely no hope for any of us against this massive monster of steel and rubber that was only inches, literally, away from my face at that very moment.

And then my body wrenched with the impact as I was slammed from the top in a downward, forward direction and, simultaneously, jolted hard across the base of my back. It was as if the whole effect of the contact was slicing through my head, shoulders and my sacroiliac. The pain completely filled my body and death was my only thought. There was no doubt in my mind that we were all going to die on this Janesville, Wisconsin, street because some jerk cement truck driver was in a hurry for one last load before the weekend.

Our van lurched ahead, driven by the force of this 32,000-pound intruder, across the four intersecting lanes of traffic and slid another one hundred feet before it finally came to rest. The rear roof was caved in exactly where my head had been resting seconds ago. All of the back door was crushed and the glass was broken and shattered. Our whole passenger side exterior was wrinkled and torn beyond repair and the sliding door could not be opened at all. Somehow, we had been forced across that busy crossroads, against the lights, without any broadside collision or contact.

I sat there for several long minutes, in a state of shock that I was still alive and so was my family. I wanted only to extract myself from this near deathtrap and rip the truck driver out of his seat and then beat him to a pulp. As the adrenaline kicked in to high gear, I growled out that I was "going to go and kill that son-of-a-b———."

But I could not get out on any side. I had to have Melanie pull herself out first. When I crawled out through her door she reached out to hug me. It was a hug filled with anguish and fear and the emotion of a teenager who had just had her life flash before her. (Years later, she informed me that the tears were because she was afraid of what I was going to do to the truck driver.) As I started toward the now-still cement truck and its driver, she squeezed me so tightly that I could actually feel her torment.

And in that instant I knew I would have to set aside my lust for vengeance in order to comfort my little girl. I reached out my hand to my wife, still sitting in her front seat. We held hands and I held Melanie. And together we all shared our remaining strength.

There were physical ramifications for me and all of us were emotionally rattled for quite some time. But, miraculously, we all lived to tell about it. For those ten excruciatingly long seconds, I truly believed that my wife, my daughter and I were all about to die. I, sincerely, believe that it is nothing short of a miracle that we survived that horrendous nightmare.

I was sitting in the far backseat on the right hand side when the impact occurred

Cole's Night of Terror

MY WIFE, VICKIE, WAS working an evening shift at the hospital and I was relaxing in bed. *ESPN* was my companion as usual. Our senior-high school daughter, Melanie, was in her room doing a little reading before going to sleep. Everything seemed quiet and normal at the Bisek house that night as the page-flip clock turned a number to show 11:05 p.m.

But then I was startled as I heard the door to the garage open and someone was heading into the house. I called out, "Who's there?" I thought it was too early for Vickie to be home from work and A.J. had had his own apartment for several months now. Then the bedroom door swung open and there stood my second son, Cole. Immediately, I was curious as to why he was here in our home on a school night. I wondered why he was not at college watching *ESPN* himself. Then the door opened even wider and his friend, Brad, slid into the room. That really bewildered me.

"What's up? Miss your Dad?" I asked Cole

Cole just sort of stood there. It was rare for him to be completely still in any situation. But, tonight, he just stood there and barely responded to my question. He hesitated for what seemed like a very long time before he spoke, at all. When he did speak, his voice was extremely shaky and was filled with heavy emotion. I did not know what was coming next, but I knew it was not going to be good. The air was thick with apprehension and concern. Brad was not saying anything at all and the quick glance that I threw his way was met with the look of a man at a friend's funeral. My heart began to quicken as I turned down the volume of the TV.

Then I repeated my original question, but this time my emotions were dancing around my words as the worrier in me came to the fore. I knew something drastic was going on here. I could only hope it was nothing tragic or irreparable. My mind was quick to jump to a thousand conclusions and none of them was positive. Even if I wanted to list off all of the horror stories that raced through my thoughts, I could never make you understand the depth of my fears. Unless you have been there yourself, as a parent, you cannot empathize with my plight. I sat up straighter and taller in that bed as that gut-wrenching sensation consumed me and inundated me, while I wrestled with all of the possibilities for the cause of Cole's anguish.

Somewhere in my subconscious, I tried to send a message to my brain to be prepared for some shocking revelation and to try hard to deal with it as a loving father.

"Cole, what's wrong?" My voice had changed in attitude and intonation. I hesitated briefly and then I pleaded for him to "Just tell me. It'll be okay."

He could barely get the words out of his mouth before he broke down completely in tears. "I had an accident, Dad," he muttered. And he exploded in a torrent of uncontrollable sobs. I quickly reached out to hold him as he nearly lunged at me seeking comfort. I think he just wanted to be held so that he could know he was still alive.

"I thought I was going to die, Dad. He just came at me out of nowhere. He just ran the stop sign and there he was. He was about to crash into me and I just yanked the wheel as hard as I could to turn away from him. I thought I was dead for sure. It just happened so fast."

He took a short, gasping breath and started again. "I just yanked the wheel and turned and then there was this big CRASH and Mel's car just started to spin in one circle after another. And then I could see some trees and bushes pop up and I thought I was going to be slammed into them. And then I think the car rolled over and landed on the wheels."

He poured it all out like water being released downstream in a lock-and-dam system.

"Dad, I was so scared. I really thought I was going to die. He just smashed into me and I just went spinning and I didn't know what I was going to hit or get hit by. Then when my car stopped I didn't know what to do at first. I guess I realized that I wasn't bleeding and that I did not feel anything was broken," he quickly added.

148

I held him tightly to my chest and shoulders as he shook with the release of all of that torment. I know he wanted to speak more and more. It was as if every word let out more tension. I held him and I stroked the back of his head as if to massage away the fear, the anguish and the flashing thoughts of his real-time, real-life nightmare.

"And then I climbed out of my car and went to check on the other guy, "he continued.

Suddenly, it dawned on me that, maybe, the other guy was not okay. Maybe, the other guy was dead. At that point, I could only hope that Cole hadn't had to witness the guy dying in his car.

"I asked him through his car window if he was okay. He didn't answer me until after the third time," Cole informed me. He was not seriously injured, but he desperately wanted Cole to help get him out of his car.

"Then some guy came out of a house. He told me that he had heard the crash and already called the ambulance and police," Cole continued.

At that point, Brad started adding some details to the night's activities. Cole had called Brad on the phone in the ambulance as soon as he had regained his faculties after the collision. Brad is usually a rather unexcitable, stoic person. But that night when he spoke, even his voice rattled substantially. He explained that when he arrived the EMTs had already loaded up the other guy into the ambulance. Then they examined Cole and suggested that he go to the hospital with them. But Cole decided that Brad could just bring him home.

The car was a total wreck, according to Brad, and some tow truck had pulled it out of the ditch and hauled it away. Brad added that the other guy had gotten a ticket for running the stop sign and that both police officers had commented that wearing the seat belt had probably saved Cole's life. Brad then informed me that the old guy told him that it looked like Cole had saved the other guy's life. According to him, Cole's quick maneuver to steer away from the full force of the impact was a key factor in the lack of serious injuries.

It took some time that night for father and son to let go of each other. I wanted to hold him and protect him as long as I could and to cherish the knowledge that he was, in fact, alive and well. For those twenty minutes or so, Cole wanted only to be hugged and to know that he was safe. When you experience this type of near-fatal car crash, it is difficult to reassure yourself that it is over and that you are alright.

Cole's Accident

Eventually, I asked Cole why he had not just called me to come over to get him after the accident. His answer to that question gave me a whole new understanding of the children that Vickie and I have raised in this family. He told me that he did not call me because he did not want to scare me. He called Brad to get him and to bring him home so that I could actually see that he was not injured before he would tell me about the accident. In spite of the fact that he was nearly killed and that he, himself, genuinely needed to be comforted, his concern was for me. Cole did not want me to make that twenty minute trip to the site of the accident while I was under emotional duress.

Now some would say that this was not any miracle or gift. It was just the result of good reactions by Cole, or a wise purchase of a vehicle with two airbags, or a smart habit of wearing a seat belt. All I know is this. I am grateful for whatever divine intervention may have occurred.

Goliath Goes Down

SOME MEN ARE JUST so massive and inherently strong that any sign of physical weakness is almost unimaginable. My father has always been just such a human being. As long as I have known him, he has been an intimidating and foreboding man. His physical characteristics, in my youth, were fear inducing. He stood about six feet tall, rather slender and he was extremely broad at the shoulders. His arms were long and sinewy with thick bands of muscle at the forearms, the kind of muscle you acquire by carrying a twelve pound mall around for ten hours a day. His chest was immense and thick and his back was "wide enough to plant a row of corn," as they used to say back home.

What I remember most, though, about his physical stature is that his hands were like a pair of vice-grips. When he grabbed you there was an absolute sense of entrapment without any possibility of escape. Even for all of those years that I hated the fact that he was my father, I still took great pride in knowing that he would never back down from anyone under any conditions.

As an addition to the intimidation factor, there was the fact that my father had a wicked temper and absolutely no sense of discretion, tact or diplomacy. He was not just a bull in a china closet. He was more like a bull that had just been spurred hard and deep in the side and then released into a tiny china closet. I actually saw him take on two sheriff's deputies who had the nerve to visit him, about some legal action, at our home. Needless to say, they left without him in tow. In his twenties and thirties, my Dad spent a lot of nights working as a bouncer in our small town bars. He was one tough and mean son-of-a-bitch and everyone in town knew it. It was as if he was Goliath in a town full of Davids.

In his twilight years, though, his personality flaws were changed for the better. He was no longer quick-tempered and ill-humored. This new father figure was able to smile, laugh and to actually show affection. As for his physical being, his body had changed in size and, especially, in thickness. His body-build had transformed into a rather rotund figure of about two-hundred-fifty-pounds on a five-foot-ten-inch frame. There was a slight hunch to his posture and his biceps were no longer taut and bulging. Yet, those "Popeye"-type forearms and those gnarled hands were still impressive. I believe that he could still out arm-wrestle healthy men who were forty years younger than he was.

But all of that changed dramatically and emphatically on a crisp November day in 2002. Dad was at home doing some work in the salvage yard on that Sunday afternoon. As was his custom, he was preparing a load of iron with his brother, Bob. The scrap-iron was to be hauled out the next morning. While the two of them wrestled with the junk cars and the twisted metal, the people who rented his farmland, Sue and Steve, came over to feed the livestock and their horses. The normal pleasantries were exchanged and everyone went about their regular chores. Dad went in the house to have some early dinner and to watch some television shows, when suddenly, his breathing became very strained and a sense of dizziness overcame him. He stumbled toward the dining room table and then collapsed to the floor. A heavy sense of confusion swept over him and an intense headache pounded in his brain as if he had been abruptly submerged into a freezing lake. When he attempted to recover and move toward the phone, he realized that his arms and legs were suddenly "asleep" and his fear-induced effort to scream out was unintelligible. With every effort possible, he tried to speak. But his mouth and tongue would not cooperate. Then the situation worsened as he became aware of the fact that his vision was very blurred. Everything appeared as if he was peering through a heavily fogged-over windshield. At that moment, for maybe the first time in his life, he was totally helpless.

Ever since Dottie had passed away in May of that year, my biggest fear was that just such a medical emergency would occur when Dad was alone. Throughout that early evening and into the night, he made several unsuccessful attempts to telephone for help. It was all that he could manage just to move the receiver off of the hook. Dialing and then speaking was not even a remote possibility. For over fifteen hours, he languished on that kitchen floor as he writhed with the pain of a severely throbbing migraine-like headache. His once-imposing body that had so many times been his savior had now betrayed him completely.

Finally, that Monday morning, shortly before six o'clock, he miraculously dialed up Sue's and Steve's number. When Sue answered

152

the phone, he could only mumble incoherently. His emotions were now in a state of turmoil and he was crying in the manner of a mentally challenged person. Words did not roll off of his tongue, in spite of his mind wishing for the ability. Luckily, Sue ascertained that it was Dad and she rushed over to his farm.

She arrived to find him on the floor unable to move and barely able to speak at all. Her first instinct was to call for an ambulance, but Dad would not stand for it. Somehow, Sue was supposed to hoist him from the floor, then drag him outside to his pickup and push him up the side step and into the passenger seat. It is no small accomplishment that she did manage to pull this off, since she weighs only 125 pounds soaking wet.

Once they arrived at the local hospital, he was incorrectly diagnosed as having a virus. So for two days, the doctors treated him for a virus instead of the massive stroke that had actually occurred. An extremely dangerous situation just continued to worsen until; at long last, someone determined that he should be transferred to a larger hospital.

Shortly after his arrival at the next hospital, the doctors correctly diagnosed his situation and began to treat him for the stroke. But after such an extended time period for the stroke to wreak its damage, his medical opportunities had diminished substantially.

It was not until the second day at the second hospital that I was informed about the situation. The call that I received was from Sue. She simply told me that Dad wanted me to come and see him right away and that he was in the hospital after suffering a major stroke.

I packed up my wife and three kids hurriedly and headed to La Crosse not knowing at all what to expect. My first contact, upon arrival, was his nurse. She was a specialist in dealing with stroke victims and had been doing that for many years. Without taking over the doctor's duties, she did an excellent job of preparing me for my initial visit with Dad.

His stroke had almost completely immobilized his physical abilities, while leaving his mental capacities untouched. The damage to his body was intense and widespread. He could not swallow. His respiratory system was very nearly shut down and his ability to communicate was almost nonexistent. He had lost the ability to control his tongue, so he could not speak understandably. Plus, there was the possibility that it could roll back into his throat and cause him to choke at any time. Paralysis had overtaken his hands and arms so he could not even write things down for us to read. All we could do was guess at what he was trying so desperately to tell us. I could not see how the situation could get any worse, but it did.

Dr. Martin asked to speak to me and to my wife, Vickie, alone. There was no hesitation in her approach, yet she was very compassionate about her message. Dad was dying and it was very likely that he would not last through the weekend. She explained that his body was simply shutting down. All of his systems were failing severely and the odds of them returning to normalcy were diminishing with each hour. Sadly, Dad was fully aware that he was dying and why it was happening. He could no longer manage his own body. Yet, his brain was functioning as if nothing had happened.

Then Dr. Martin informed me that we would have to get Dad's permission to put a "do not resuscitate" order in his file. Even now, in looking back on that dreadful conversation, I cannot fathom how we all got through it. The doctor and I had to explain to this man that it did not appear medically possible to revive his body at all. She told him that it was very likely that his physical system would shut down in less than two or three days. Even if he managed to last the weekend, he was not even a candidate for physical rehabilitation and that meant he would never work again. It meant, she explained, that he would never return to the farm that he so dearly loved. He would spend the rest of his days in a nursing home with no physical abilities at all. Therefore, it was her duty to ask him if he wanted to be resuscitated if his body shut down. Or did he want to let nature take its course.

It is a waste of these words for me to attempt to share with you the depth of pain and grief that is involved in that conversation unless you have, personally, experienced it. But if you have had to actually endure that mind-boggling nightmare of a discussion yourself, then my words can hardly do justice to your experience.

To me, it is almost the worst possible way to die. You are totally aware, mentally, that your body has betrayed you and that there is nothing humanly possible that anyone can do to change it. All I could think about, while the doctor spoke of these tragic circumstances to Dad, was how perversely ironic this all was. Here was a man who had spent an entire lifetime of nearly seventy adult years using his body to try to provide for his family. Here was a man whose mind was not allowed to be developed, neither academically nor intellectually, beyond the seventh grade. Yet, now, his mind was working like a well-oiled machine, while his body had collapsed.

I will never forget that day as I sat on his white-linen hospital bed with him propped upright and the doctor standing on his other side as I held Dad's hand. Doctor Martin asked Dad if he understood her explanations of the medical situation. He just nodded as tears welled-up in his eyes. Then she asked him, pointedly, if he knew the ramifications of establishing a "do not resuscitate" order. She needed him to be very definite in his instructions to let him succumb to his body's wishes to die, rather than having the machines perform his bodily functions. Again, he completely understood that there was nothing else that they could do for him.

Her last question to him concerned whether or not he would want to be transferred into a nursing home for an extended period of time. Since I already knew his strong feelings on that subject, I was not at all surprised when he vehemently and adamantly shook his head "no" in an almost violent manner. He was not about to die in a nursing home.

My family gathered together and cried for some time that day when I tried to inform the kids that Grandpa Bisek was more than likely to die before the weekend was done. None of us wanted to say goodbye forever. Then we just prayed with all of our combined might and we put his life in God's hands.

Miraculously, Dad's health circumstances suddenly began to show signs of improvement and slowly, but most assuredly, Dad began to recover. Almost every hour, there were new signs of rejuvenation with his life-systems. At first, his breathing improved to the point of removing the oxygen. Then he began to regain some control of his tongue. This was so important because it was not only one of the keys to his future ability to speak; it was also vital to his ability to avoid choking to death and to take solid food. In no less than seventy-two hours, he went from his deathbed to physical rehabilitation headquarters.

It was truly a miracle. Even the doctors could not explain the complete turnaround in his condition. Over the next three months, Dad regained his speech, nearly all of his motor functions, most of his mobility, his respiratory capabilities and his ability to eat solid foods. In fact, he had actually moved back to the farm to live with his dog.

The bouts of depression that had been occurring as a result of the stroke were now controlled by medication. Dad was not happy about the fact that he could no longer drive his trucks or work long hours in the salvage yard, but he was enjoying his grandkids and his friends.

Dad

In addition, one of his brothers came back into his life in order to chauffeur him to medical appointments and to drive his loads of iron to the buyers. A sister began to visit him weekly in order to clean his house and to bring him some prepared food. He had developed several newly found pleasant relationships with two of his sisters and with a brother. Not only had Dad recovered substantially from the massive stroke, he had also managed to rekindle relationships with several of his formerly-estranged siblings as a result of the medical crisis. The miracle of his rapid recovery actually led to the gifts of several siblings returning into his life.

High Altitude Hysteria

"LOOK AT THAT, WAYNE," my friend and associate, Jeff, pointed out, "every flight from here to O'Hare is cancelled."

We both stood there, patiently, awaiting any word on our trip to Dallas from Madison. It was a rather brisk November 24th, even for Wisconsin. There was a stiff wind blowing out of the north and the temperature had dropped into the low twenties the night before this long-awaited trip. Jeff and I were looking forward to arriving in Dallas a day early for our third annual "Michael Finley's Buckets for Hunger Thanksgiving Challenge."

This third year we were looking to go back down there and do even better. This time the Mavericks had been promoting the event on television and radio and they were going to do promotional spots on the big screen at the game that night. Michael had gotten two different teammates, Antoine Walker and Antawn Jamison, to commit to matching the fans donations and I had gotten a corporate commitment from American Express Financial Advisors. So, we were off to a record pace even before we left Wisconsin.

Only a short while after his first newsbreak on the airline flights, Jeff added, "Wow! Every flight from here to Midway Airport is cancelled, except ours. I don't know if that is good or bad."

"I just hope we get there on time. That's all I care about right now," was my only comment.

While we waited for our plane, Jeff explained how he had just completed his first solo flight to acquire his pilot's license. It was rather fascinating information. Jeff was an interesting enough individual even without this added bit of knowledge and accomplishment. In his younger days, he served as a backup offensive lineman for the University of Wisconsin Badger football team. In addition, he was an avid hunter, generous supporter of Buckets for Hunger and he was a married father of three young children with a fourth on the way. Jeff was never at a loss for conversation and he spoke his mind clearly and honestly. I considered myself a "straight-shooter" also, so I liked that in Jeff.

Finally, we walked out to board the twin-engine propeller-driven airplane. We both agreed that the weather had turned a little drastic. The wind had picked up substantially and the temperature had dropped quite a bit in the last hour or so. "It sure will be good to get to the 80 degree temperatures of Dallas tonight," I remarked as we climbed the stairs onto the plane. Little did I know that I was about to embark on the most frightening journey of my life.

This particular plane had a capacity of no more than fifty passengers and it appeared to be only half full at that. One by one, we all squeezed down the aisle and found our assigned seats. Ours were very near the back of the plane. I proceeded to take the window seat. Normally, I would not do that. I suffer from claustrophobia so I am not a big fan of the cramped quarters in the smaller planes. But, I did it this time because I figured that Jeff would be more comfortable in the aisle seat. At six foot-three inches tall and about 260 pounds, he had three inches in height and about sixty pounds on me. With only a short twenty-five minute jaunt to Chicago, I thought I could handle the accommodations.

Within just a few minutes of our takeoff, the flight attendant began to pass out drinks to everyone. She started at the back of the plane, so I knew that I would not have to wait very long to quench my thirst. This woman looked liked she had done this particular activity at least a thousand times before this flight; but, she spilled the first two glasses of soda on the passengers as the plane dipped and swerved simultaneously. She simply adjusted her grip on the containers and proceeded onward down the aisle. But before she could continue on with her duties, the plane lurched and bounced at least two more times. Not being a frequent flyer, I have few experiences with turbulence, but these doses of sudden movements were something on a whole different level, though.

When she finally got to us, Jeff stared at me like I was completely insane when I asked her for a glass of soda. Her actions were extremely deliberate in her attempt to serve me my drink. For a moment, I thought she looked as if she was handing off a bottle of nitroglycerin. As she reached across Jeff to deliver the drink, he gave me another quizzical glare. He chose not to order anything.

"I take it you wanted to see her dump that pop all over my lap and then sponge it off of me," Jeff laughed. "Didn't you notice she was praying for you to just say no to the offer?" he added.

Jeff must have been correct because after she spilled three more drinks on the next five passengers, she decided to forego any more airline hospitality. She simply pushed the cart to the front of the plane and tucked it away. She sat down in a free seat, buckled herself in securely and never moved again for the rest of the trip. In those first ten minutes of travel, our plane and all of us passengers had been tossed around and jostled like bags of charcoal briquettes. And the journey was only to get worse.

Jeff turned to me and told me that he did not understand what the pilot was doing with his maneuvers. "We must be on the very edge of some cold front and he can't get permission to fly above it because the plane is too small."

All I could do was nod my head in agreement as Jeff went on to fill me in on the whys and wherefores of piloting such a plane. I was intrigued by his thought process and by his speculation as to the reasons for this very eventful beginning to our journey to Dallas. It was obvious that he was not impressed with the pilot's professional skills.

We sat there and attempted to discuss our hopes for the fundraising event that we would be leading the next night. We could only divert our thoughts from our dire predicament for a few minutes at a time because of the harrowing interruptions of our dialogue as the plane bounced along in a somewhat haphazard fashion.

Whoosh! The plane dropped down like a roller coaster plunging downward after reaching its apex. Then it banked into a hard left turn as if the pilot was Dale Earnhardt, Jr. driving on some NASCAR track. We then bounced hard several times and then, finally, we settled down for a few, short minutes.

Twenty-five minutes into our frightening *"Twilight Zone"* edition of air travel, we did not appear to be anywhere near our destination. There was a young mother sitting behind us with two little girls about two and four-years old. As she attempted to calm them down, she, herself, was beginning to sob. I remember thinking that I should try to comfort her and even turned around to do so. But she appeared to get a grip on her emotions so I let it alone.

Wham!! My knees leaped up toward my chin and my shoulders dropped down, hard and fast, toward the floor.

"Jesus Christ!!" Jeff bellowed out to the pilot. "What the hell are you doing?" he demanded to know immediately. "This is ridiculous. He shouldn't be taking those kinds of banking turns so sharply and so suddenly without letting us know what the f—- he is doing."

In all honesty, at this point in the trip, I was too focused, on praying to God to save us. "How can you be so calm, Wayne," he asked me in a voice filled with anger, fear and doubt.

"Actually, Jeff, I am genuinely scared so I am trying to avoid hyperventilating by doing what I always do when I am this frightened. I am praying as hard and as fast as I possibly can," I confessed to him.

"Well, pray for me, too!"

I absolutely abhor roller-coaster rides or carnival rides of any kind because I have no control over what is happening. In fact, I have only tried to endure them on two or three occasions and I was never able to complete the experience because I screamed for the controller of the ride to let me off. It is just not something that I can do or want to do. And here I was in the most challenging ride of my life with a real possibility of life-threatening danger lurking at every turn. Yet, I sat there, relatively calmly, because all I could do was place my life in God's hands. I hoped and prayed that the pilot's abilities would be good enough to guide us to safety.

Then, suddenly, for the very first time during this entire maelstrom of movement, the pilot came on the intercom and told us that we would be going into our approach to the airport. You could actually feel the tension and fear subside in the airplane cabin as every one of us assumed we were saved.

Our fear-filled journey was not quite over at that point. It took at least another fifteen minutes of hellish drops and turns and swerves. At one point, I actually counted at least seven passengers regurgitating into the vomit bags. The lady behind us was now at a point where she was crying hysterically and she was completely unaware of her two daughters. Luckily, her two girls were concentrating intently on their dolls.

At long last, we arrived in Chicago and our plane came to a stop on the tarmac. I turned around to check on the woman and saw her on her hands and knees in the fetal position in the aisle of the plane. She was crying uncontrollably and her two daughters were in their seatbelts. They were beginning to get looks of wonder and concern for their emotionally rattled mother. While the pilot was standing at the front of the plane explaining the connecting-flights situation, I stood up and asked him to please let this mother and her kids off of the plane. He stated he would do that as soon as possible and then he continued to provide the details of the flight schedules. After another minute of his diatribe, I stood up and requested more firmly that he should let the family leave the plane. Again, he said he would handle it as quickly as possible. I waited only another thirty seconds or so before I interrupted him very aggressively, "God, damn it, sir! Let the lady and her kids off of the plane before she has a full-fledged panic attack right here in the aisle!"

Finally, he walked down the aisle, helped her to her feet and took her and the kids off of the plane and out to the terminal.

Somehow, we did make it to Chicago alive. Eventually, we got to Dallas and we had a very successful fund raiser for the North Texas Food Bank. Most importantly, I learned to always avoid taking the only flight that is not cancelled.

The Walton Family Revisited

AS MUCH AS MY own youth was filled with pain and anguish, my adult life with my own wife and children has been much the opposite. It is amazing what the presence of a good woman will do to a man. My wife, Vickie, has been the focal point of our family since the birth of our first child, A.J. She has never stopped massaging my personality and my parental behavior in order to improve my effectiveness as a father. The one constant in our married life has been her steadying influence on our family dynamic.

Rarely does she ever lose her cool or raise her voice. No matter what the circumstances may be she manages to stay calm and to cajole or coerce me into a somewhat similar demeanor. Vickie, the joy of my life, has figured out a method of handling me whereby she knows exactly when to hold my hand and hug me, or when to give me a verbal kick in the pants. After thirty years of marriage, she is still my confidante, my sounding board, my personal advisor, my in-house medical professional and my best friend. I still find her to be extremely attractive and very sexy. She makes almost every day interesting for me.

Vickie, Mel, Cole, Me, AJ

I believe that every man needs someone to push him along when necessary. Every man wants someone to slap his back and celebrate with him whenever a victory is won. It is imperative that every man should enjoy a good laugh as often as possible. More importantly, every man needs to learn to laugh at himself and especially at his mistakes and flaws. We all need a best friend with whom we can bare our soul and find our place in life. Every man needs a true partner with whom to face all of life's trials, tribulations, and tragedies and every man should have a soul-mate to help point out every one of life's great moments. Vickie has been all of that and more for me and she has also been the guiding force for our family life.

I am here to tell you that our family is no better or worse than the vast majority of families in this world. We yell at times, we get angry at each other, we make poor decisions and we make mistakes. But we do some wonderful things together. It is not unusual for us to trek to a park to play softball together or just head out to the yard to do a little wiffle-ball home-run derby. Many, many times we will attend a movie together. I can't begin to count how many times we have played cards or board games. And we have learned what great therapy it is to laugh together with each other about each other.

Mel, Me, Cole, AJ

Over the years, we have developed a whole list of family traditions. A lot of them have come about by accident, but they work. For example, we go out each year and cut our own Christmas tree; our fourteen-foot tall and eight-foot wide door-scratching ceiling-scraping evergreen. Our family watches certain movies at certain times of the holiday season, too. Thanksgiving is for *Planes, Trains and Automobiles*. On the evening of the same day that we get our tree, we watch *Christmas Vacation* and on Christmas Eve we spend time with *It's a Wonderful Life*. But we also do things together like decorating Christmas cookies and Easter eggs.

The three children that Vickie and I have raised are each unique, challenging, fulfilling and enjoyable in so many different ways. Our eldest, A.J. is an artistic individual with a talent for both music and art. He also thoroughly enjoys weightlifting and works very hard at it.

One of the great memories that I have had as a father is when A.J. and his jazz band performed at a local coffee shop when he was still in high school. The evening's music was quite pleasant and spirited, until A.J. took the microphone to lead them with his trumpet and his voice. I was blown away by the manner with which he took over the stage and carried the entire group to a whole new level of performance. Even his younger brother and sister, a tough audience, were filled with pride that night.

A.J. has a great sense of humor that he utilizes quite often. He has a wonderful sense of timing that allows him to turn a tense situation into sidesplitting laughter with some humorous comment. We will all be embroiled in some tumultuous disagreement about household chores or driving habits and then A.J. will utter some great line from one of our family's favorite comedies. He will blurt out, "That there's what you call an RV," or "Those aren't pillows." Suddenly the whole family will be laughing hysterically, partially because of the memory of that line from the movie, but more so because of A.J.'s deadpan delivery.

Cole is our middle child and can be a real handful at times. He has, probably, provided the most challenges to Vickie and me as far as our parenting experience is concerned. In so many ways, he is the reincarnation of me because of his manic-depressive type of personality and his penchant for trying to avoid work through horseplay. When he is in a good mood he can make the entire room buzz with excitement. But when he is irritated about something, he can exasperate and infuriate a clown. He also possesses a great deal of charm and wit. On an athletic field, he is gifted with excellent speed and quickness in addition to being intelligently aggressive.

164

Similar to A.J., Cole has a strong sense of humor, but Cole's greatest strength and joy is the fact that he tends to be rather passionate about a great many things. Whether he is discussing college professors, friends or sports, you always know what he is thinking. He is relatively articulate and he loves to share his views of life with anyone willing to listen. I especially enjoy spending hours and hours with him reviewing every aspect of the sports world and its' inhabitants. Like his Grandpa Bisek, though, Cole can be overly focused on one subject at times. No matter what topic the rest of the family is discussing, Cole will interject his latest sports commentary– abruptly and fervently– right into the middle of the discourse. All fathers should be so lucky, though, as to have a son like Cole to talk with about sports.

Melanie is our youngest child and our only daughter. She is an outgoing, vivacious young lady who makes every day happier for anyone that she meets. At more parent-teacher conferences than I can count and from nearly every coach that she has ever played for in any sport, Vickie and I have actually had the coaches and teachers thank us for having Melanie and for letting them teach or coach her. She has a joy for life that is almost contagious and she is constantly striving to do her best at whatever she does. Wherever she has gone, she immediately makes friends and she earns respect from her peers because of her commitment to excellence and her humility.

Our daughter has taught me so much about life and has influenced me in so many ways. It is because of her that I have learned to control my own emotions during sports events and that I have ascertained how better to deal with parents, coaches and players. It is through her eyes and heart that I have found an actual pleasure in being a coach, a player and a father. She has inspired me to appreciate and understand the viewpoint and actions of others even when it is not comfortable to do so. On more than one occasion, Melanie has actually been the person who was able to calm me down in the middle of a tense situation during a game that I was coaching. She is able to put things in perspective for me with just a few well-chosen words. Of course, she is far from perfect, but she has always brought a shining light into our family circle

After experiencing the torment and anguish of a dysfunctional family as a child, I can now, honestly, state that the gift of a good family has brought untold joy and happiness to me.

AJ, Cole, Melanie, Me, Vickie

My Own Donna Reed and Friends

FRANK CAPRA IS A legendary Hollywood movie director who is responsible for several of my all-time favorite movies. He has done such classic films as *Mr. Deeds Goes to Town*, *Meet John Doe* and *It's a Wonderful Life*. In all three movies, he makes his feelings and values quite clear. His characters state repeatedly that any man is rich if he has good friends.

I have been very blessed that at every juncture of my life I have had good friends who have supported my dreams, goals and beliefs. Never have I had a friend that attempted to sway me from my ethics or values. On an occasion or two in my earlier life, I have had a friend or two that has turned on me. Admittedly I, myself, have betrayed a friend on an occasion or two in my earlier life. For the most part, though, I have had the good fortune to have met and enjoyed friends that have helped me become a better human being.

During my grade school years, my closest friends were Mark, Jim, and Joe. Each one of us had our own particular personality idiosyncrasies but the common thread that linked us was our love for sports. We spent every recess involved in some kind of game alternating between softball, football or pom-pom pull-away. We also spent a great deal of recess time doing punishment for some stupid thing we had done to irritate one of the nuns. But while we may have spent some time between fourth grade and high school doing "detention" for small indiscretions, we never even dreamt of any serious misdeeds.

When high school started for me, I widened my circle of close friends to include Steve, Paul, Bob, Gary, Randy, and Bernie to name a few. Some of my friends smoked marijuana and drank beer, as did a lot of teenagers in the 1970s. But none of my user friends ever pressured me to try either one. There seemed to be a mutual understanding that I and the other non-users would not hassle them about doing it and they would not razz us about avoiding it. In spite of the fact that I grew up in a town with a population of only 2,104 people yet had fourteen bars (that is a loud

167

A Knock at the Door

statement about the town's attitude toward drinking), I managed to avoid drinking parties and alcohol completely throughout high school. I think it is pretty amazing that none of my friends who partied ever excluded me because of my choice to not drink or smoke.

As it is with most high school cliques, graduation split us all up and we headed into various directions. Yet, whenever people got back to town for a weekend, we seemed to manage to bump into each other and we kept the friendships. Even when I dropped out of college and moved back home to start my own business, the friends that I had who stayed in college always treated me with respect whenever they came back to visit. Whenever they had parties at college, I was invited. There was never a time in my young adult life that I was without my friends.

For a great many years, I looked to my buddies to help me cope with a home life that was rife with pain, suffering, disappointment and relative poverty. No matter what happened in my home, I always knew that I could escape through my friends. They found a way to help me laugh at my circumstances and to enjoy every moment that I was away from my house. It must have been a thousand times that one of them would show up at my home to pick me up only to be yelled at or treated rudely. Yet, they never stopped coming back to get me. And none of them ever made me feel less than totally comfortable when I was with them. The subjects of my home and of my home life never caused any tension or problems with any of my friends.

While each and every one of those friendships means the world to me and each served to help me through various and sundry difficulties in my life, none compares to the friendship of my wife, Vickie.

Our relationship began when I spotted her photograph in the local newspaper. She was a registered nurse who was working at St. Joseph's Hospital as the result of a college scholarship program. I was immediately attracted to her petite good looks and assumed she was intelligent because of her profession. It took me a while to convince her to date me because she was already involved with a boyfriend and had been for over six years.

At first, we just talked on the phone for hours at a time. I would call her and we would discuss her day, her life, my day, my life and everything else possible. Our friendship blossomed so quickly and so completely that it

168

surprised even me. In fact, I believe that Vickie is the only woman that I ever went out with who was a friend before we went on a date.

Our conversations flowed so naturally that you would have thought we were life-long companions. We laughed and joked constantly, yet we had great philosophical discussions about our hopes and our dreams. Whenever I was around her I was unafraid to share anything at all with her. I knew that I could trust her with my life and with all of the ghosts in my closet. She allowed me to show my weaknesses and she helped me find and enhance my strengths.

I cannot even begin to count how many times Vickie told me that we would never be more than friends because she was committed to marrying George. But I persisted because I just knew that she was the woman for me. I knew that she reached into my heart and soul and that she always found a way to make me believe in myself. I knew that she was the key to my happiness and I just had to persuade her that she would find happiness with me.

As I look back now at our relationship, I understand more completely the depth of our friendship. I recall so many times when she stood by me no matter what the circumstances. For example, when I explained to her all of the emotional and psychological baggage that I would bring to a marriage and to a potential family she did not shy away. Instead she made a commitment to help me forge a new relationship with my father and his second wife. She forced me to come to grips with all of the demons of my past and then she walked through that dark valley with me.

October 4, 1980, Wedding Day

Shortly after our wedding, I ran successfully for a spot on the city council in my hometown. For the two years that I served in that position, Vickie helped me to make intelligent and well-researched decisions. She prepared me to endure meeting after meeting in an extremely hostile

169

environment. As the upstart young, aggressive and irritatingly curious new councilmember, my associates did not like having me around for discussions or votes on city business. Literally, every session was filled with animosity and verbal sparring at an extremely high level of intensity. Yet, Vickie would absorb all of my shared information and then she would calm me down so that I could be more effective in seeking out my initiatives.

After I failed in my attempt to unseat the fourteen-year incumbent mayor, she convinced me that it was time to leave that city in order to seek new challenges and find new opportunities. The result was that we ended up with me taking a position in city government in Elm Grove, Wisconsin. After thirty years of being a "big fish in a little pond," we moved across the state to start over completely.

Without exaggerating even slightly, I never would have survived that move without her loving support and her firm determination. She nursed me through the difficult transition and she persuaded me that my decision to change my life would eventually help me blossom into a stronger person. Every time I told her that I had decided to quit she convinced me that the future was very bright if I could make it through the present.

I can remember that on at least a couple of occasions she gave me exactly what I needed to get over my "cry-baby" attitude. She, basically, kicked me in the ass and said to stop whining and grow up. Not exactly what a thirty-year-old man wants to hear from his wife. But it was necessary and it was effective.

In the first six years of our relationship, I made at least five career moves and four geographical transfers and she never hesitated in her psychological and financial support. But, more importantly, she always served as my sounding board and my confidant. I never considered making any major decision without her input and influence.

As our family grew to three children, we finally settled down in Oregon, Wisconsin. Throughout these last twenty-five years of living in the same home, she has withstood all sorts of problems and challenges because of the psychological baggage and my health circumstances that I brought to our marriage.

Vickie has never wavered in her willingness to be by my side even when I very nearly suffered a nervous breakdown. She was my guiding light during and after my double by-pass surgery. She was with me every step of the way during my back surgery and recovery. When my first job as a city administrator turned into a nightmare, she walked with me through every twist and turn of that horrible adventure.

No matter how many times I messed up as a parent she stayed with me and she found a way to help me to become the father that I wanted to be. She persuaded me into attending parenting classes. She nudged me into reading magazine articles about approaches to parenting and she even worked with me through my therapy sessions and my anger management courses. Never did she give me the impression that I was on my own in my battles against my own mental demons.

Oct. 1980

After thirty years of marriage and two years of courting before that, Vickie is still and always has been my confidant, my advisor, my lover and my best friend. She is the reason that I am where I am today– in a state of relative happiness. She has helped me to understand that my weaknesses, faults and flaws don't have to control or dominate me. She has helped me to overcome them substantially and she helps me to work around them when necessary.

In that Frank Capra Christmas Classic *It's a Wonderful Life*, Donna Reed plays the role of Jimmy Stewart's resourceful wife. She is the real unsung heroine as she first saves his business with her quick thinking and then she saves him from financial ruin and scandal through her initiative. My wife, Vickie Carroll, is my Donna Reed because she has used her resourcefulness, her intelligence, her initiative and her sense of humor to inspire and to save me hundreds of times.

For every day that I am with her, I become a better husband, a better father, a better friend and a better human being.

One More Message, One More Chance

IN SPRING OF 2004, I was having some slight chest pains during exercise in the weeks leading up to a Buckets for Hunger event. Since I was completely focused on the details of the program, I ignored the telltale signs of my own body and continued on as though everything was fine.

Just a few days after the event, though, I was working out on the stair-stepper in our family room when a serious incident occurred. Vickie was working an evening shift at the hospital, Melanie was gone for the night and the other two kids were at college. I was only a few minutes into my workout when my entire chest area began to ache and every breath became an intense experience in physical effort. Rather than stop the exercise, I attempted to fight through it. Since I had just played full-court basketball pain-free for nearly two hours a few days prior to this, I denied what I knew was wrong.

Eventually, I ended up doubled over the stair-stepper and holding on to its sidebars as strongly as I could to avoid from dropping completely to the floor. My chest felt as if someone had just pounded me with a baseball bat smack across it. I glanced at my heart monitor to check my rate. It was only 86 beats per minute. I took note of the fact that I had no shortness of breath, just painful breathing. I hung on to that stepper for several minutes before I struggled to the couch to lie down. Something was dreadfully wrong and I was scared to know, so I denied that there really was a problem.

When Vickie got home from the hospital I explained to her what had happened and she began to quiz me. She wondered if I had had similar pain prior to this. I admitted, reluctantly, that I had had several substantially less frightening bouts of a similar nature. She suggested that we keep a close monitor on the symptoms and on the circumstances that were present when the symptoms occurred again.

172

Only a day later, Vickie was watching television while I got on the stair-stepper to work out. It took only a minute or two and I began experiencing chest pain once more. She told me to stop exercising and note whether the pain subsided. It did. We immediately made plans to see a cardiologist about the problem.

Then something truly strange began to occur. It was interesting because it was similar to that situation that occurs when you learn a new word. Suddenly the new word pops up everywhere that you go. You begin to wonder if that word was always a part of your life experiences and you just avoided it. The same thing happened with my chest pains. They became extremely more significant in nature and much more frequent in number. In fact, on the short walk from the parking lot to the doctor's office I was in nearly total discomfort. Yet, my blood pressure was perfectly normal, my heart rate was only 56 and my electrocardiogram printout was fine.

My cardiologist, Dr. Moses, no less, decided that my history of heart disease warranted an immediate scheduling of a heart catheterization to determine whether or not there were any problems.

It was scheduled for Good Friday. There I was, once again, in a hospital operating room with another doctor looking into my heart and arteries. As much as I did not want it to be true, I was relatively certain that he would find another serious problem and he did. This time I had a 90% blockage "downstream" from one of my previous bypasses. I was told that he was going to insert a medicated stint once he cleared out the blockage problem.

While I did not endure the same intrusions into my body as my first surgery (It is interesting to me that the medical world speaks of this as a "procedure" not as surgery) I still felt as frightened and as concerned. In fact, I was now absolutely convinced that my heart disease was an issue that was going to play a major role in my life on a daily basis. I was no longer going to be lulled into thinking that I was "over it."

My first thoughts were that living a long, full life probably was not going to happen. I actually began to wonder if I would be around to see my children get married or to spoil my grandchildren. In the short time that I spent in the hospital, the vast majority of my time was consumed with thoughts of my own mortality. Apparently, the fact that all of my "numbers" concerning my heart disease were in good order was not enough. On paper, I appeared perfectly heart-healthy and stable. The issue of my anger and my habit of concocting self-induced stress came charging to the forefront of my conscience. Maybe after all of the soul searching and all of the mention of positive aspects of my life, I was still the same person to a large degree.

It frustrated and disappointed me that I had not learned to avoid or even to reduce the stress from my life. I still became extremely indignant when I thought my daughter was being misused and mistreated by her softball coach. I still was short-tempered with my older son when he did not complete his tasks in a timely fashion and I still was overly sensitive about every comment that my wife or kids made to me. Stress and anger were still both present in my life and I was still creating them for myself. I am still my own worst enemy.

I vowed to enjoy my life, my wife, my children and my friends more completely. I vowed to meditate every day. I vowed to return to my anger management practices and I was determined to reduce the stress in my life by learning to say "no" to more requests for my time.

Then, again, God interrupted my world with a blunt message.

It was just a night after I returned home from the hospital. I was lying in bed trying to fall asleep, switching from channel to channel to find something that could relax me and coerce me into complete rest.

There was Dr. Wayne Dyer pushing his compact disc version of his book *The Power of Intention.* I listened closely as he spoke, seemingly directly to me. He kept telling me that as soon as I could "change the way [I] look at things, the things that [I] look at will change." It was another way of reminding me that my glass has always been nearly full, if I would just open my eyes and see it.

His story of childhood trauma and of parental baggage was different than mine in so many ways, yet it was similar in a number of areas. On one hand, he spent time in foster homes and his father abandoned him and his family early in his life. Like me, though, Dr. Dyer had carried his anger and pain from that situation for many years into his adult life.

He states that his life had been filled with abundance in many areas in spite of all of his psychological and emotional torments, while I remember only emptiness and disappointment from my youth. Similarly to my own situation, forgiveness toward his father played a major role in his journey.

Dr. Dyer's story reminded me of my own and it made me stop and ponder whether I could imagine all of the things that I wanted in life and act and think as if I already had them. Could I find a way to accept all of the love, comfort and success that already existed in my world?

I have stated before in this book that I believe that everything happens for a reason and that God has always been with me for every step of my life. I believe that I stopped flipping the channel that night for a reason. God was sending me another message that it was time for me to take some definite steps to change my life and my attitude. I believe that God does want me on this earth for a while, but I believe that I have to start helping myself get better or I may not be spared the next time.

None of the changes will be easy. I will have to constantly work at learning to relax. My tendency to become indignant for all things great and small will have to be eliminated. The unreasonable and unnecessary habit of worrying about every aspect of my children's lives must cease. I must take the time each and every day to meditate, to talk with my God, to practice anger management and to focus on avoiding stress rather than creating it.

I still need to learn to show more love and understanding to my own family members. I know the pain that I can inflict with my acerbic, quick tongue and I need to bite that tongue. I still need to accept and believe that the only truly important things in life are my family, my health, my friends and my God.

I pray that I can accept these things, believe them and practice them before I drive myself to the grave.

A Death in the Family

IN ALL HONESTY, I cannot give you the minute details surrounding that dreaded telephone call in the summer of 2007. I am not sure if it was one of my brothers that delivered the news or if it actually was my sister, Maggie. In fact, I am not entirely sure if it was June or July. Of this much, I am absolutely sure. My sister's fate could not have been more definite. There was no hope. There was no miracle for which to pray. It was simply a matter of time and the prognosis was that it would be a very short time till her death.

Maggie had been visiting doctor after doctor for many months to ascertain the source of her frightening symptoms. In spite of a battery of tests at numerous clinics and with various well-educated and highly-trained physicians and specialists, the mystery remained. She could drive thirty minutes to work without any problems. But, she could not hold a pencil at arm's length without her body falling over to the floor. She could traverse a mile-long course on an evening walk. But, she did not have the strength to set the table for dinner. For days at a time, she would require the use of a wheelchair. Then she would return to her eight hour a day bookkeeping job.

It was during her second tour of the famed Mayo Clinic in Rochester, Minnesota, that a collection of specialists told her and her husband, Dick, their now-final analysis. She had Amyotrophic Lateral Sclerosis—Lou Gehrig's Disease. As vividly as I can recall my reaction to hearing those words, I cannot begin to comprehend what Maggie and Dick felt at that moment. I will only tell you that my first reaction was, that it is a terminal disease that left no room at all for the possibility of a cure.

Immediately after I received that communication, I went to the internet to learn as much as I could about ALS. Unfortunately, none of it was even remotely hopeful. It seems this wicked ailment has been around for many decades and many millions of dollars have been spent researching it. Yet, almost nothing of value is known about it. We do not know how to cure it. We do not know what causes it. We do not know why one person contracts it but another does not. We do not know what to do to lessen the severity of its symptoms. We only know that it is an absolutely ruthless killer. And for my sister, Maggie, it showed no mercy whatsoever.

The first time that I spoke with her about her situation she wanted me to tell her everything that I had read about it. She was never overly comfortable with her home computer so she could not gather the information on her own. Yet, when she asked me for this simple favor I could not bring myself to share with her my findings. This was, after all, my older sister whom I loved dearly. Instead, I informed her that most people that are diagnosed with it live between three and ten years. About ten percent of those afflicted with the disease live over ten years. While this was not wildly hopeful news, it was the best that I could honestly give to her.

In the next few short and quick months of her life, I tried to talk to her at least once a week by phone. She was dealing with her circumstances remarkably well. It did not take her long to realize that her life was to be much shorter than she had anticipated. Yet, she almost always shared a laugh with me during those calls. She never actually complained to me either. In fact, she told me that she was convinced that there was a reason for her to be a victim of this dreaded affliction. Each time that we spoke she grew weaker and weaker.

It so happened that in early August, I had my high school class reunion. In addition, that same weekend, my nephew/godson was getting married. I decided that I would go home a couple days ahead of my family so that I could visit Maggie and Dick. When I arrived, Dick told me that he had to take Maggie to physical therapy the next day and he was going to be a little rushed because of some work commitments. I offered to take Maggie instead.

Little did I know the shock that I was in for. I watched as she tried hard to feed herself at the kitchen table as she sat in the wheel chair. She struggled tremendously to simply move a single grape from her plate to her mouth. Her inability to grasp with any strength at all made it a challenge to lift the single small green oval. A completely thoughtless action for me was a tremendous accomplishment of effort for her. On two separate occasions that weekend, she went into a state

177

of near panic because she was in a position wherein she could not breathe at all. She would suddenly begin gasping and her green eyes would reveal her absolute fear that her last breaths were now happening. Only after being repositioned in the wheel chair, did she relax and breathe normally.

The evening before I was to take her to therapy, I thought I should practice transferring her from a heavier more equipped wheel chair to the lighter wheel chair. Dick and Maggie both tried to warn me of her lack of ability to assist in the move. If I did not get myself aligned correctly with her prior to my lift, then her shoulders would pop out of joint and she would be in absolute agony. My practice transfer went relatively smoothly except for one comment that Maggie made before I started. She simply said, "Wayne, I am just a lump. I can't help you."

Only seconds after that statement, I realized she was not exaggerating at all. She was completely unable to do anything more than a small single shuffle step. First, she moved her right leg and then her left leg. It took all of the strength that I could gather to avoid breaking down into tears as we moved through this poorly choreographed dance of brotherly-sisterly love.

That Friday afternoon, I proceeded to take her to the hospital. Unfortunately, our first transfer from the chair to the car resulted in her shoulder problem occurring, as I was not properly positioned. She immediately screamed in pain and her voiced begged me, "Wayne, Wayne, stop, stop. My shoulders." The sounds that shook me to my very heart were that of a human being in as much pain as she could stand, yet with barely the energy to cry it out to you. I apologized and reset to do it again. Luckily, we made it much better that time.

It was at that therapy session that some very strange things began to happen. Prior to my arrival, I had just completed reading a book, *Ninety Minutes in Heaven*. It is an amazing and wonderful story of a minister who describes his experience in heaven while he goes ninety minutes without a sign of breath or any location of a heartbeat following a horrific car accident. The gist of the story is that all things happen for a reason and that death is not to be feared because heaven is so divine. I was completely moved by the story. But, I knew that Maggie was so close to death but clinging as hard as she could to this life. I did not know if I should share the book with her or not.

At the therapy session I mentioned the book while the therapist worked with my sister. The therapist, who had been working with my sister for several weeks at that point, immediately suggested that I should give her the book. She had read it herself and opined that it would be good for Maggie to read it.

When we left that session and went back to Maggie's house it got even stranger. Dick had hired a lady, Mary, to assist in some of Maggie's care giving needs during these demanding days. Upon our return to Maggie's home, Mary was waiting for us. We put Maggie to bed to rest and then we started to converse. I shared with her my dilemma about the book. In spite of the therapist urging me to give her the book, I still was not sure. To my amazement, as soon as I stated the title of the book Mary blurted out immediately, "I just finished that book myself. You need to give Maggie the book."

My last question mark about the book was Dick, Maggie's husband. When I explained to him my concerns, he simply said that if I thought it would help her then I should give it to her.

So I did just that before I left her home to head back to mine after the reunion and the wedding. Within the next several weeks, I would call Maggie and Dick to see how she was doing. Each time Dick would tell me that things were getting worse. Twice she was taken to the emergency room to deal with major breathing problems that became worsened by the panic attacks. Eventually, she was placed on a c-pap machine (a device that assists her in keeping her lungs functioning) 24-7. During those weekly calls, Maggie would tell me that she was reading this book and that she was glad that I gave it to her. She told me that she was no longer afraid of dying. She said that the book had helped her to realize that God works in mysterious ways and that she was now ready to go to Him. I knew Maggie well enough to hear in her voice that she had, indeed, appreciated the book and that she was now at peace with dying.

A short two months after that visit, I received a call from my older brother, Karl. He told me that Maggie wanted all of her siblings and our Mom to come to her house to see her. It was arranged that we would do this on October 3rd.

That Wednesday, my wife and I joined with Dick, Maggie, my two brothers and their spouses along with my mother to spend the entire night with her. At first it was very difficult. Maggie wanted to speak with just her husband, her siblings and our mother. She lay there in bed completely helpless at this point. She could do nothing more than speak, softly.

I recall vividly that I went immediately to her side and sat next to her on the bed while I held her hand. She told us that she would not be with us for long and that she wanted to have one last good visit with us all. Everyone began to cry, but I had decided on the way up that I had not come to say good-bye to her. I told everyone that we were here to enjoy a night of storytelling and good-natured kidding of each other. I said it should be like all of the other wonderful times we had had with Dick and Maggie. The family all agreed to do just that.

But Maggie wanted to explain some things to all of us prior to joining the spouses. She had laid out her funeral exactly as she wanted it and she had something for us all to do. She asked me to say some words for her at the wake. I was not sure that I could get through it myself, but I promised her that I would do it. Then I asked her if there was anything else that I could do for her. "Yes," she said, "you can find me a photo of my father."

In this situation, I truly believe that the hand of God was active. The reason that Maggie asked for the picture of her father was that she had never actually met him. Our mom only told Maggie his name very late in Maggie's life. Supposedly, he had already passed away some twenty years before that summer of 2007. Obviously, it meant a tremendous amount to her to get that picture as she asked for that favor knowing full well that she had so little time left.

Since I had no clue of where to start the search, I asked her for whatever information that she had in her knowledge. Maggie explained that this man's sister lived in a nearby city. So I immediately stopped in that same afternoon on the return trip home with my wife. Much to my surprise, the lady allowed me to come into her own home to discuss the matter. She told me that on his deathbed her brother had denied being a father to anyone. His marriage had been childless and he had not fathered any children outside of wedlock. After much heartfelt conversation, she agreed to call her younger brother to see if he had any photos that I could get for Maggie. She, herself, had none as he was eighteen years older than her. Nothing ever came of that lead.

Another approach that I used was to seek a graduation photo of this man. His sister had informed me that he had graduated in 1938 or 1939. But for those years there were no photos taken of the class members. In addition, he had not been involved in sports so there were no photos with him there either. Lastly, the city's historic society had nothing either.

Then I learned at Maggie's wake that she had been very desperately seeking this photo because one of my first cousins told me about my sister asking her to do the same favor. It turns out that this cousin actually had found a photo of this man nearly a year before Maggie's death. Unfortunately, she lost it while she was preparing to mail it to Maggie. Only a week before Maggie died, this cousin found the picture behind a dresser in her bedroom. She immediately wrote my sister a long letter explaining what had happened. The next day she placed it in the mail after the post office assured her it would be there in a couple of days.

That letter with the photo did not arrive until almost two weeks after Maggie had died.

Ironically, my brother-in-law told me that Maggie had wanted that photo cremated with her and commingled with her ashes. I will tell you quite frankly that I do not at all believe that that man was her father. I did not believe it before she died and now I am convinced that God kept that photo from her in life and from joining her in cremation for one reason. He was not her father.

Losing someone you love is heart shattering. But I now know that there are times where the quality of their life is so bad that their death is a good thing for them. That is how it was for Maggie in those last days as she lost her will to live along with her ability to function at all or in any way. When I called to speak to her on November 7, Dick informed me that she was sleeping almost all day long because of the morphine that she needed for the pain. He told me she was now on a morphine drip 24-7.

Only a week or so before that she had told me herself that the doctors explained that eventually she would slip into a morphine-induced coma and die. She knew it and she accepted it.

A Knock at the Door

When I told my wife about the constant morphine drip, she said we needed to get up there again right away. She said that was a telltale sign that she did not have a long time left. The very next morning after I had spoken with Dick, my two brothers called me to say she had died during the night. She simply did not awaken.

While I cannot possibly put in words the role that Maggie played in my life, I do want to try to have you understand what she meant to me.

Maggie was ten years older than me. She started life under extremely difficult circumstances and they only got worse for many years. She was the illegitimate daughter of an uneducated woman in a small, rural community in western Wisconsin in the 1940s. She had every right to be bitter about life and to care about no one else. She always looked out for my siblings and for me. For many years, in fact, she was truly our mother and our sister as she prepared our meals, dressed us for school and kept us safe. We called our run-down, clapboard shack, located next to the stockyards, "home" for one reason—she was there.

Even as she grew up and graduated from high school she did not forget her siblings. In fact, she used money that she earned as a typist to purchase clothing for me to wear to school. She bought me winter coats and shoes rather than new dresses for herself. Several times a month, she would take her hard-earned money and use it to treat me to movies. It was her way to get me out of the house and away from the fighting and arguing.

For much of my difficult young life, she was the one and only source of my self-esteem and of the few smiles and laughs that I knew. She was a selfless person who never treated me with anything less than absolute respect and love. Even though we had different fathers, she never spoke of me as anything other than "my brother."

In a home where education was frowned upon and/or ignored, Maggie inspired and persuaded all four of her siblings to pursue academic success. If I showed any interest in a subject, she would bring me home magazines, newspapers and books about it. She would show so much interest in that subject that I would read the information just so I could share it with her. To this day, I still have many of those gifts in with my personal "memorabilia."

182

In spite of that rough early life, she found a great man to be her husband, Dick Andre. Together, they enjoyed almost forty-five years of love, happiness, family and success. They became parents of three wonderful boys (Shane, Jeff and Cory) and then they were blessed with seven beautiful grandchildren.

She was so generous that she even was willing to share her husband with my brothers, Karl and Richard, and my other sister, Marilyn, and me. Every chance that she could, she would have us stay at her home so that we could experience a home with genuine love. She even had me spend two complete summers

Maggie 1962 approximately

on the farm in spite of the fact that I may have been the worst farmhand to ever live.

Even as a young adult, Maggie always stood by me and nudged me along my path. She was there to cheer for me every time I stepped on to a football field or baseball field or basketball court or wrestling mat. I know that without her I would not be the man that I am today. I would not have known what love was without her presence in my life.

Unfortunately, she contracted this horrible disease that took away her physical abilities and talents. It took away her will to live. But it never took away her dignity, or her willingness to laugh and to smile. And it will never take away my memories of a lady who was a good wife, a loving mother, a kind friend and a sister who changed my whole life.

I will tell you, unequivocally, that this sudden, tragic and merciless death in our family only strengthened my belief that God does hear our prayers and influence our daily lives. For example, somehow God found a way to use me to help my sister shed her fear of her imminent departure. Most subtly and, yet, most effectively God also sent a message to Maggie about the identity of her unconfirmed father. I will tell you also that God did answer my prayers for providing Maggie and her husband the strength and the courage to deal with all that they had been handed. In the end, I will always remember that she was brave and strong in facing her death and in dealing with her disease. And that memory will always make me smile when I recall my big sister, Maggie.

May she rest in peace, forever.

Arrival

THE DAY OF JUNE 20, 2011, will forever be imbedded in my mind and heart as a perfect Father's Day.

I am an early riser so I was out of bed by six-thirty that morning. My wife was still sleeping as she usually rises about 9:00am or a little later. Our daughter, Melanie, was fresh off of her first adventure sailing in northern Wisconsin the day before with a friend, so she was not going to be back until about noon this Sunday. AJ and Cole, our two sons, were planning on coming over to grill a meal for the family as soon as they got out of bed. Unfortunately, that usually means that we could expect them about three or four o'clock in the afternoon. Vickie had left a nice heartfelt note for me on the steps. It started my day off nicely. We headed into Sunday mass at about 10:00am or so.

When we arrived back at home, Melanie was already there and a family friend, Jen, was along as I had invited her to spend Father's Day with us. Another family friend, Brad, was also invited to join us for the day. I thought it would be a lot of fun to eat together, play some yard games and go to see the movie, *Bridesmaids*. It was a movie that Melanie and I had already seen together and we both thought it was hilarious. Since our family loves to laugh, I figured the movie would be a great opportunity to do just that.

As per usual, Melanie had also written me a beautiful note thanking me for my role in her life. She even mentioned that I should feel great about how I had changed my personality traits over time. She pointed out, quite accurately, that I had really learned to control my emotions and to avoid my past anger blowups. It meant a lot to me that she had acknowledged that I had come a long ways in finding more peace and happiness in life. I still let the small things bother me more often than I would like, but I am definitely improving.

185

A Knock at the Door

Earlier in the week, I had texted the boys to tell them not to buy me any gifts for Father's Day. I had suggested that Cole could come over and grill chicken and brats for the family. He loves to grill with his own marinade sauce ideas and meat toppings. I had already purchased the meat so he could save his money for other things. For AJ, I had asked him to bring over his trumpet so he could play me a song on it. I love jazz music and, especially, enjoy listening to AJ play it.

Much to my surprise, the boys actually arrived at our home at about noon. Had I been thinking, I should have known immediately something strange was going to happen this day. Cole immediately got to grilling and concocting his off-the-cuff marinade sauce. AJ talked with me for awhile about his work situation and then dug out his trumpet to do his jazz solo for me. He had been working on the trumpet parts for the song *Cantaloop*. He informed me that he did not have it all down yet. But I did enjoy the pieces that he did play.

We all ate together and shared some stories and laughed a lot about our lives, both current and past. Then out of nowhere, Cole asked if I wanted to take some batting practice. It was out of nowhere because we had talked about going to the 4:30pm showing of *Bridesmaids* and it was already 2:30pm. In our family, softball workouts usually last two hours or more and we are all drenched in sweat at the end of them. It did not seem possible to do softball and get to the show on time. Yet, we headed out with Jen, AJ, Cole, Mel and me for some swings if we could find a softball diamond that was not drenched by the previous night's rainstorm.

We had to try three fields before we settled on a very damp baseball field for our workout. Oddly enough, everyone was taking substantially fewer swings for their batting practice than they normally would do. Heck, no one even wanted to do a second round. Something was beginning to seem strange to me. As I finished my swings, I returned to the outfield to shag balls and commented that "the old man still has a few line drives in him, I guess."

My day got better when my son, Cole, commented," We all know you're a good hitter, Dad. That's why I keep trying to get you to move yourself up to the top of the order on our Wednesday slow pitch league team."

It's always nice to hear that remark from your own children.

Once Jen took her swings, the kids all started rushing around picking up the equipment like there was a fire drill going on. I heard the boys and Melanie talking about the fact that we had to get going if we were going to be on time. Since our boys are never on time I knew something was up.

We barely got back to the house when Cole announced that anyone taking a shower had to do it quickly. We needed to get on the road fast. Now, even Vickie started rushing around loading up the car with clothes and coolers with water and bags with snacks. This was getting really odd but I had no real idea what was going on yet.

Jen told us that she had to go home to let out her two dogs and would meet us at the theater. Brad, apparently, had other plans so he would not be joining us.

Hurriedly, we piled into the car and headed to some, unknown to me, destination. We headed south toward Janesville with Cole driving somewhat excitedly. Just before we got to Janesville, Vickie commented that we should be getting some gas. Now, I knew we must be going to Chicago. I just didn't know why. The several conversations continued as the backseat crew of Vickie, Mel and AJ discussed one thing and Cole and I were talking baseball. Then it hit me like a sharp line drive down the right field line. We were going to the Cubs game at Wrigley at night and the opponent was the Yankees. My first thought was to not announce my discovery but to relish in the joy of the great surprise that these people had planned.

You need to know that I have been a life-long Yankees fan and my kids have all become avid Yankees fans, too. We even went out to New York to make sure we visited Yankee Stadium before they tore it down several years ago. For us, it was like a Mecca to the promised land of Ruth, DiMaggio, Mantle, Maris, Jeter and the rest. Yes, going to a Cubs game at Wrigley at night on Father's Day with the whole family as a surprise gift was amazing, but the topper was that they were playing the Yankees. Still no one would acknowledge that I had correctly guessed our destination.

As if all of this was not enough of a gift, I must tell you that some other fantastically cool things also occurred during this trip.

A Knock at the Door

As you know from the earlier chapters of this book, I have had some issues with anger management and with a negative attitude in my past. Yet, this trip provided me with some opportunities to display my newly found optimistic approach to life. Early in the trip, I could hear my daughter commenting to my wife about the fact we would be late for the game. I knew it could upset Cole to hear this because he has so many of my personality traits. Rather than let the comments float about the car interior like a wasp waiting to land and sting, I changed the mood.

"It won't matter if we are late, this is just a great surprise and I want to just enjoy it all even if we are late."

As we got closer and closer to Chicago, the doubts about driving directions start to creep their ugly heads into the discussion. Some of the family wondered if we had missed our turnoff. Again, in the past I might have joined in the negativity and worsened it all. But, this day, I simply stated that the last time I had been to Chicago the same issue had come up as I approached my downtown destination on that trip. Therefore, I was completely sure that we had not missed it and that we would be fine.

Eventually, we arrived at our remote parking lot location for the game. It was then that I was told that the day had been planned by AJ and Cole. That really made it special. This sort of effort is something that Vickie and Melanie do more consistently. For example, Vickie and Melanie will write me a nice note on all special occasions. AJ and Cole have not done that in years. It is just not a part of their personalities. I know that and I am learning to accept it. That is precisely why it was even more special because they had planned it.

As we boarded the shuttle bus, I overheard the comments that we only had general admission tickets and that we may not get seats together or may not get seats at all. Yet, again I did not let it bother me. We simply proceeded to ride the shuttle to the park and when we got there it was already the bottom of the first inning. No need to get upset, though, we simply entered the stadium.

I will tell you that the sight of every seat filled with a roaring raucous fan did not even irritate me.

"We will find something," I affirmed.
Several open seats in the right field bleachers beckoned us so we headed out. After some quick discussion, the kids each got a seat. Mel and Cole

were placed back to back near the top of the bleachers in the right field corner and AJ found a spot across the aisle. I grabbed a location at the very top of the seats and Vickie went for some food. I kept my eyes open for a spot for Vickie to join me and noticed that the guy next to me was using two spots. I asked him for permission to bring Vickie up and he proceeded to read me the riot act. He blurted at me that if I wanted seats I should have gotten there three hours before the game like he did. He told me, tersely and bluntly, that he was not about to move so that my wife could join me. At this point, I was starting to get more than a little upset, but I shrugged it off. Then, the lady next to him said she would be glad to move so that Vickie could join me.

So, by the third inning Vickie and I were sitting together and the kids were now back to back to back near the top of the bleachers about twenty feet to our left. When the obnoxious man left to use the bathroom facilities, I asked his wife if I could buy him and her each a drink as a thank you.

"No, but I am sorry my husband was so rude to you." she apologized.

Then the day got even better. My daughter waved for us to come and join her because two seats had just opened up. It was the sixth inning. We all enjoyed the game and talked with the other Yankee fans in our area. The game was close until the eighth inning when another little miracle happened in my life.

Nick Swisher is the Yankees right fielder and he was having a decent day hitting in spite of his season batting average being a lowly .230. There were two runners on base when he stepped into the batter's box and the Cubs' crowd was roaring for him to strike out. Loud enough for all those around me to hear, I matter-of-factly stated, "Next pitch, Nick Swisher home run right here!"

To paraphrase Scarlett O'Hara in *Gone with the Wind*, 'as God is my witness' those words just left my lips when that sweet sound was heard. Crrrracckk!! I spotted the ball off of his bat immediately as if it was meant for me. It sliced through the cool, damp Chicago night on a perfect arc toward my outstretched bare hand. I absolutely knew as soon as I saw that leather sphere that it was going to land right by me. As it pierced the air, the crowd was oohing and aahhing and I was preparing to jump as high as I could to catch it. As it approached us, my son Cole (the excitable one) turned and thrust his body back against me while leaping to catch the ball himself. Then it landed and the mad scramble ensued. Hands and bodies were flailing around completely blindly, searching and groping for that most treasured possession of all baseball fans, a home run ball.

I knew that I had just missed touching it, so I observed as everyone scrambled around spilled beer and discarded food containers. I wondered who would be the lucky spectator to come out of that fray with the prize. Then I looked at AJ as he sat there quietly still.

"Where is the ball?" I asked him.

And then I knew my day was complete.

AJ simply smiled as wide a smile as a human can do and slightly raised his right hand caressing this prized object and he mouthed the words, "Right here."

Not only had I called the home run shot and its exact location, but our family ended up with the home run ball.

Father's Day, June 20, 2011, will be forever imbedded in my mind as a perfect day. I spent the entire day with my family laughing, joking, playing softball, watching the Yankees live in Wrigley Stadium and I never let any negativity enter the day. At the age of fifty-seven, I had finally arrived.

Goliath Is Gone

ON WEDNESDAY, JULY 18, 2012, I had just returned home from a softball game. It was approximately 8:30pm and I noticed that there was a message on our home phone. I absentmindedly pushed the button to listen to the message while I got ready to shower. My thoughts were trailing away from the voice mail almost as soon as it started to play. In addition to the just completed game, my wife and I had been gradually working all day long on packing for a business trip to Phoenix, Arizona. The plane was leaving mid-morning on Thursday so we had to be ready to go right away in the morning. As the message played in the background of my mind, I realized it was my uncle Butch Bisek and he was saying that he had taken my father to the hospital earlier in the day. I decided that I needed to call him immediately.

My Aunt Bernice answered the phone and simply said "Butch is right here. I will let you talk to him." So he came onto the line and I asked him what was going on with Dad. He informed me that Dad had called him to say he wasn't feeling very good. So Butch had gone to pick him up and proceeded to take him to Gunderson Lutheran Hospital in La Crosse. He gave me Dad's room number and I ended my call with him in order to check on Dad. The hospital switchboard put me in contact with his nurse. She explained to me that Dad was having difficulty breathing but that he seemed to be improving. He was in the intensive care unit because of his past history of stroke and kidney failure. I explained to her that I would cancel my business trip so that I could come to be with him. She insisted that I need not do that because he would probably be fine in a day or two.

Once I got done with the details of his breathing issues, I said good night to the nurse and then talked with my wife, Vickie, about the situation. Together, we decided that we would continue with our trip plans but would call a couple times a day to check on Dad.

191

A Knock at the Door

The combination of the trip excitement and Dad's health made for a rather short night with little sleep.

I could tell there was an aura of concern and apprehension in the air as we began our travels. The flight went well enough from Madison to Minneapolis. When we landed there, I used the break before our next departure to check in with Dad. I was informed by the nurse on duty that he was stabilized and I even spoke with him for a very short while. As always since his stroke, he was quite emotional with me on the phone. I barely spoke a word and he was in tears. I talked him through the emotion as I had learned to do over the last ten years of dealing with that issue. Eventually, I said good bye and got on the plane to head out to Phoenix.

Again, the flight went fine except for my constant thoughts of Dad's health. I was very ambivalent about my decision to continue my trip in spite of his circumstances. Yet, the conversation with Vickie kept me in a positive light so my trepidation dwindled.

I was rather interested in several of the keynote speakers of the convention for various reasons but mostly because I wanted to approach them about my charity. I was hoping that with some face to face time I could convince them to come to Madison for an appearance for Buckets for Hunger, Incorporated. The two that I wanted to hear and meet were Jim Craig (the goalie for the 1980 Miracle on Ice U.S. Olympic men's hockey team) and Frank Abagnale (the inspiration for the movie *Catch Me If You Can*). They were the entire reason for my deciding to go to this meeting in Phoenix.

When I called back to the hospital later in the day on Thursday, I spoke with a different nurse about Dad. She informed me that he was still in intensive care but that things were going better. I asked if I should head back now and she told me that there wasn't any sense of urgency so I need not do that.

I did get to hear several excellent speakers during the day and Vickie had some nice time to relax by herself so the first day of travel and the convention were worthwhile for both of us. With the nurses' comments on Dad's health being more upbeat, I was beginning to relax a little.

On Friday, once again, the day went smoothly as I talked with my Uncle Butch about Dad and I spoke with the nursing staff also. Butch told me that Dad was doing well. He was moved out of the bed and into a chair.

He was now eating food and was able to talk with some difficulty. He did ask about me. When I called to speak to the nurse that day, she shared with me that he would probably be sent to the Arcadia hospital on Monday. She said he was progressing nicely and that they had changed his medication. She then allowed me to speak to Dad on the phone. He seemed to be stronger and more confident. Again, as always, he started to become emotional as soon as I said hello. When he calmed down, we talked about his going back home soon. Eventually, I even got to hear Jim Craig do his speech (very interesting) and to meet him afterwards. He was very receptive to my request that he attend a Buckets event in the near future. I went to bed that Friday feeling much more at peace with my choice to attend the convention and with Dad's eventual recovery.

Saturday morning I awoke and ate breakfast prior to seeking out my first speaker session. The choice I made for presenters turned out to be disappointing. During the tail end of the program, I noticed that my cell phone was ringing so I walked outside to the hallway to answer it. My whole world was immediately jolted. It was a nurse from Dad's hospital and he immediately told me that I needed to head back to La Crosse as Dad was dying. He thought that Dad had only a few hours to live. He added that they had moved Dad to hospice care over night. Then he provided me with more information that actually angered me. It seems that on Wednesday night the doctors had determined that Dad's problems were not just "difficulty in breathing" issues. He had had a massive heart attack and was in congestive heart failure. While this nurse assured me that just twenty-four hours earlier Dad's prognosis was very bright for the near future, it had all changed overnight. He suggested strongly that I should leave immediately if I wanted to see Dad before he died.

I called Vickie and told her the news immediately, through my tears and sobs. I then ran up to our room and started to pack up to leave. Since our original flight was not to leave until Sunday morning, I realized that I would have to rearrange everything. My calls to the airlines were to no avail. The only flight out of Phoenix back to Madison would not leave until at least eleven-thirty pm on Saturday. I scrambled to call my three kids back in Madison. I, again, fought tears as I informed them that Grandpa was dying and that I needed them to drive to La Crosse as soon as possible to be with him since I could not be there myself. They were each wonderful in their response. Without hesitation, they contacted their bosses and asked to be released from work (yes, the two boys were both working on that Saturday).

A Knock at the Door

Melanie arranged to meet the boys at AJ's house in Madison and then they left for La Crosse.

Meanwhile, I decided to check into the cost of a private jet to fly back. I was more than astounded by the figure that I was told. It was going to be over $13,000 for a one way flight, if it could be arranged. The more likely opportunity was for a round trip charge of $26,000. Vickie and I knew that Dad would not want me to spend that kind of money to get back. So we proceeded to set up the commercial flight that would take us from Phoenix to Atlanta to Madison overnight and then we would drive to La Crosse as soon as we landed in Madison.

At approximately 7pm, I received a call from Melanie that she and the boys were in La Crosse with Dad. He was aware of their presence, but could not speak with them. The nurses kept telling them that he wanted to hang on to see me. They shared with my children that he had last been talking about the three of them and about staying alive to see me one last time. From that point on it was a race with continuous updates.

Vickie and I boarded the plane in Phoenix and travelled to Atlanta. We then waited several hours to board the next flight to Madison. Sleeping in an airport or airplane is difficult enough but when you add in the fact that your mind is constantly aware of a loved one who is dying, it becomes nearly impossible to actually sleep. As soon as we landed in Madison at about 10am, we ran to the car and headed out to see Dad. The kids took turns calling us to let us know that Dad was hanging on and that I should not drive at the speed limit. They told me that his breathing was becoming much more labored and very sporadic. He would not breathe for nearly a minute at a time and then he would gasp out several deep breaths. He would suddenly lurch into an arched position with his spine, his eyes would open and he would then collapse back down from his arched position. This was surely a difficult experience for all of our three children to witness Grandpa struggling so mightily to hold on to see me.

We raced along the interstate highway and as the tension built and the phone calls increased, my foot became much heavier on the gas. The speedometer climbed up from 68 to72 to 75 and, finally, to 81 miles per hour. We were then only about forty-five minutes from the hospital and I was beginning to get a feeling of impending doom. I wanted desperately to see Dad and I felt horrible about not having come back sooner from the trip. I also felt resentment for the doctors and nurses who had not told me about the massive heart attack and congestive heart failure. But, I knew there was nothing that

194

I could do now to change any of that so I just focused on driving as fast as possible and as safely as possible.

At long last we reached La Crosse only to be delayed because of a car accident blocking lanes of traffic. I fretted and started to fume about the situation, but Vickie got me refocused on Dad. We weaved our way through the traffic and emerged out into open road and I restarted my speeding to the hospital. Finally, we arrived there and Vickie and I raced through the lobbies and hallways. At first, I thought we must look strange as we traversed the long walk to his death room. Then I realized that the hospital staff has seen people with these looks of sadness, frustration, apprehension and fear many times before today.

I remember walking into that room and seeing our three adult children standing around Dad. I knew then that they had all been holding in their emotions as they waited for me to arrive. You could feel a deep sense of relief as I went over directly to Dad.

"I am here, Dad. It's Wayne." I uttered the words and then I convulsed into tears. I, also, had been withholding my emotions substantially for over twenty-four hours since I had been told the news. I then held his hand and looked into his eyes. As soon as I had spoken he had lurched forward, forced his eyes to open and stared deep into my eyes, my heart and my soul.

I remember for many years telling my wife that I did not know if I could ever actually, really love my father because of all of the pain that he had caused for me and my Mom and siblings those years ago. I just did not know if I could genuinely feel love for him. Yet, here he was dying and looking straight into my heart and I knew without a doubt that I did love him and had loved him in spite of all of those other issues and experiences. He was my father no matter what and I had learned to love this man with the great sense of humor, the deep love for my children and wife and the generous heart. At that moment, I knew he would not be with us long. I knew that death was here definitively and I knew that I did love him because it hurt so much to know he would not be here for long. At fifty-eight years old, I truly knew that my Dad loved me and that I loved him.

The doctor and the nurses all seemed genuinely happy and relieved that I had arrived as was Dad's wish. They explained to me the details of his current situation and the minute aspects of the events that would be occurring. They described how his body would now be shutting down and how I could help him deal with that. They asked me if I wanted a minister to visit and shared with me that Dad had, in fact, talked with a minister several times already. Without hesitation, I stated that I did want a minister there. A woman then came in and asked how she could help. I asked my wife, children, my Uncle Butch and Aunt Bernice to come and join hands to pray for Dad. The minister said some words and then asked if anyone else wanted to say something. My son, Cole, tried so very hard to speak but just could not get the words out. My daughter, Melanie, finished his thoughts for him. AJ stood next to me with his hand on my shoulder quietly comforting me as he himself faltered. I did say something, I believe, but I cannot remember the exact words. I will never forget that scene, though, as we all said good bye to Grandpa for the last time ever. I felt this profound sense of genuine love that Vickie, AJ, Cole, Melanie and I had had for Dad and that he had had for us. It was such a rewarding feeling to know that we had all touched his life in such a positive loving way and that he had done the same for us.

Shortly after that prayer session, I thanked my uncle and aunt and they left for their home in Arcadia. Then I suggested that the kids and Vickie could head back to our homes in Madison and Oregon, Wisconsin, because they all needed a break and had to get back for work anyway. I remember thanking the kids profusely and telling them how much it meant for me that they had spent so much time with Dad as he was waiting for me to arrive. We all hugged and cried and then they left me to be alone with Dad.

At first, I stood next to him at the bedside as the nurse helped me to understand, even more, what was now happening. As a hospice care nurse of many years, she shared with me that it appeared that Dad could be with us for several hours or for several days. She truly made every effort to ensure that I knew Dad was waiting for me to arrive before he died. She told me how he had talked about me whenever he could speak. She told me that he shared with her that I was the only child he had who spoke with him for these last thirty plus years. She wanted desperately for me to understand how much I and my family had meant to this man. She succeeded quite well with her efforts. Then she left and I was there alone with my dying father, my own thoughts and my God. I watched as Dad's chest would rest completely motionless for a seeming eternity and then his body would leap forward, his eyelids would be forced almost completely open and he would look straight at me. Each time this happened, I felt he was trying hard to send me a message that he

196

appreciated me being there and that he was so grateful for these last three decades of life that we had shared. Then he would gradually close those eyelids again and his chest would slump. I sat there and spoke to him and told him so many times that I loved him and that I was so glad that we had become father and son so long ago. I told him not to be afraid because God had forgiven him for all of his transgressions and that God loved him, too.

As I sat with him, I thought that I needed to inform my siblings that he was dying to give them the opportunity to see him one last time. I called each of them up one at a time. My brother, Karl, was the first one that I called and told. I simply said that Dad was dying and that if he wanted to see him to say anything to him that this was his last opportunity. He responded that he was not interested at all. Then I called my brother, Richard, and his response was the same. I had to leave a message for my sister, Marilyn, as she did not answer her phone.

For about six hours, I stayed there with Dad. I remember the nurse telling me that his "agonizing breathing" was normal for someone at this stage of death. She told me that the morphine drip should be used to help him with his pain and that I should push the delivery button so that he could get more relief from that pain. I could not fathom pushing that button because I felt as if I was causing his death. She assured me that I was simply comforting him from the physical pain and not affecting his breathing or his heart rate. I was glad that she was there to comfort me and to teach me about death.

As I sat there and watched him convulse with each rare breath, I could not help but think back to my visit just ten days prior to this scene. Dad had promised my daughter, Melanie, that he would be there when she received her Doctoral degree in Physical Therapy. He had been constantly telling her this for the last three years. Yet, when the day had come, he and I could not arrange for him to make it. So Melanie and I decided that we would visit him in late July so that we could take him out to eat to celebrate the event. It had all gone so well. He thoroughly enjoyed the time with her and me. He had his usual shrimp meal at Detox Bar in Arcadia and he got to say hello to a couple of old friends even while we were there.

When we drove him back to the farm, I waited until he got out of the car to ask him a question. "Dad, would you be willing to do something for me," I hesitatingly queried.

"What is it?" he replied.

A Knock at the Door

"I would like you to give your mini-rod tractor to Richard. I think he would enjoy it and you aren't doing anything with it any more. It would be a nice gesture to build a relationship with him."

"Why should I do that? He has not been nice to me." He blurted.

I simply told him that he should do it because someone has to take a first step to rebuild our family. I told him that it would be a good thing to do before he died so that we could all be at peace. But, he simply refused. It was so sad to know that no matter what I tried neither of the parties involved in this four-decades-long dysfunction would budge. Several years earlier, for example, I could not get Richard to visit Dad in the hospital after Dad had had his kidney failure bout. Now, I could not get any of the others to reconsider their feelings either. Everyone wanted the other person to apologize first and that was not going to happen. Now, it was obvious that none of them was going to get a real sense of closure or forgiveness.

The last thing that we did during that visit was to present him with all four of his military medals that he had earned during the Korean War. It had taken me nearly a year of working with the U.S. Army to finally get them issued to him and then I had them beautifully framed with a photo of him during his Army days. He was genuinely touched when Melanie and I gave them to him and hung them prominently on a wall in his home. Now, under these circumstances, I could not help but feel good about that visit.

Eventually at about 7:00pm, I decided that I should get something to eat, arrange for a hotel and get some necessities for a possible longer stay. The odd thing about my leaving was this. I actually thought that my talking to him was making him hold on longer. I thought that each time I made a comment to him he would respond by breathing so awkwardly. So I finally determined that I needed to let him die. Before I left, I spoke with the nurse and the doctor and they assured me that it made sense for me to do all of that and then to come back to spend more time with him.

I ran my errands and was unpacking in the hotel room when my sister called me. I told her about Dad and made the offer to her as I had to my brothers. She also responded that she was not interested and that she had no feelings at all for Dad. But, she was very compassionate and understanding about my feelings. She did all that she could to help me with my difficulties. In fact, we spoke for over an hour and a half and I felt better when we said good night. As soon as I got off of the phone, I realized that the hospital had called me at about 8:00pm so I returned the call immediately. The nurse answered the phone and simply told me that Dad had died at 8:00pm. I just stopped talking, listening and crying. I just was motionless and dumbfounded for several moments. Then I said to her that I would be there in a few minutes.

I called my wife and each of my children and tearfully told them that Grandpa had died. I could feel and sense in their voices that they were relieved in some way and deeply saddened in another way. I supposed it is the way we all feel when we get that call that a loved one has died. I then drove back to the hospital.

I remember thinking and realizing that I was walking up to see my father's dead body and I felt empty inside. I walked into his room and there he lay with his mouth agape and his eyelids still open. For a split second, I expected that he might still be alive and was just waiting for me to speak to him. I noticed though that his lips were blue and his hands were cold and his stare was profoundly and obviously lifeless in nature. And then I prayed for God to take his soul into heaven and to join him with Dottie once again.

I knew then that I must now call my siblings again and tell them that he was now dead. Again, I spoke to Karl, Richard and Marilyn and I told them that Dad was gone. Richard was wonderful in his response as he immediately told me, "You don't have to be alone, Wayne. I will help you through this and I will be there with you." It struck me deep in my heart. Marilyn also offered to help me in whatever way she could. Karl barely responded other than to say thanks for telling him.

I then called Uncle Butch and told him about Dad. After that I spoke with Dad's best friend, Frank Klimek, to tell him. They were both grateful for the call.

I sat next to Dad's dead body using my cell phone to do all of that. Then I sat there for some time and just prayed for strength for myself and I prayed for Dad's eternal rest.

Since I had a knee surgery scheduled for just two days after Dad had passed away and since Dad's wishes were to be cremated, I decided that

A Knock at the Door

I needed to plan his funeral services for some time in the near future. Then I returned home and began making the plans for the life celebration. I knew that Dad had wanted a very private funeral when he last talked with me about it all. Yet, I knew that he would not begrudge his friends coming to say one last good bye. I also knew that it would have been important to him to have military rites at his services as he was very proud of his time in Korea during the war. But, I was well aware that Dad did not practice any sort of faith so a church funeral was not in the offing. I wanted also for Dad's siblings to be aware of his passing and to have the opportunity to have closure with his death.

The genuine difficulty of putting together the service was substantially reduced by virtue of the help that I received from my wife and daughter and sons. They each assisted in making key decisions concerning the ceremony, the photo and military medal presentations, the music and the words of the whole service. I spent a great many hours putting together the concept. I knew that I had to be true to Dad and true to myself about Dad. So, I wrote a eulogy in the form of a poem like a country western song. I talked about how I spent my whole life trying to get Dad to love me and how it did not go well for a long time. I explained about how he had hurt so many of the people that I loved. But, then I shared the fact that his second wife, Dottie, had changed him completely into a kind, generous and loving man to me and my children and wife. I pointed out that at last I did have my father's love and I did also love him.

My wife and daughter suggested that I intersperse some music into the ceremony so I researched on the web for "funeral songs". I found many great ones but settled on just a few. I used "I Walk the Line" by Johnny Cash because Dottie truly did make him walk the line and he was glad to do it for her. She really did make him become a better man and a better father. I used a song titled, "Don't Blink" that is about a 102 year old man describing how fast life goes by if you don't take the time to notice it. I used the great song, "America, the Beautiful" as a tribute to Dad and other veterans of military service. The song that I used that truly explained my view of Dad's life and the lives of almost all of us was a tear jerker called, "A Lot of Things Different." The song's lyrics are a man looking back on his life and on all of the regrets that he has. He now wishes he would have told the people that he loved that he did love them. He mentions that he should have been less oppressive with his wife and that he should have enjoyed so much more the people that he loved. At one point, he states that he "should have spent more time with my Dad."

200

Wayne Bisek

It took a while but the whole thing came together because my family helped me so much, especially my wife and daughter.

I knew that I would never be able to actually speak at the service because I am a very emotional person. I truly do carry my emotions on my sleeve as the saying goes. Therefore, I found my good friend, Al Stoppleworth, to do one of the gospel readings and Vickie decided that she could do the other one. For the rest of the service, my very good friend, Bernie Hesch, agreed to do it all. He read, word for word, everything that I had written. He told the one hundred or so attendees that this was going to be an honest funeral service and that everything read was a memory of mine and my family. He further explained that the feelings expressed were mine and mine alone. He handled the whole day very well in spite of being put into a very difficult situation.

My wife and children all did a fantastic job of presenting Dad's life in pictures and words and trophies and mementos. They also did something Dad would have loved. They used a mannequin, some pillows, a white tee shirt, a pair of his bib overalls and his favorite Korean Veteran cap to make everyone take a second look as they walked into the hall. It really did look like Grandpa Bisek standing there at the front of the room.

I knew that I would be in tears that day but it was even tougher than I had imagined. Even before the ceremony started, my emotions erupted over little incidents. A middle-aged man unknown to me walked up to me without giving his name and he just stated that he wanted to come to the service because my Dad had befriended him when he was a stranger in the valley. He told me little stories of the way Dad and Dottie had helped him and his family with food supplies and gas for their vehicles when things were financially difficult. When my sister, Marilyn, showed up at the funeral, I could barely say thanks and I went all to pieces and hugged her for about five minutes straight. A couple of guys that I knew who were slightly younger than me shared with me how much fun they had with Dad when he visited them when they were youngsters. They told me he was always concerned for their safety. It was pretty cool to hear people of all ages and levels of relationship talk to me about my father being a good man.

When the ceremony began, it was very interesting that my son, Cole, sat on my left. My brother, Richard, sat on my right and my sister, Marilyn, sat immediately behind me. It was interesting because at various points in the service each of them was comforting me with their touch. My son held my hand, my brother rested his hand on my leg and my sister reached around to put her hand on my chest. I derived a great deal of aid from their touch and a profound sense of concern for my condition. My wife did a wonderful job of reading, especially, since I had never heard her read in front of a group before this day. As soon as the Johnny Cash song began to play I lost it. I don't know why, I just did. When the song, "A Lot of Things Different" played, I was not alone in crying. When the singer talks about all of the regrets he has in life it drove home the point with many people. When he sings, " I should have spent more time with my Dad......But I didn't", even my brother lost it. Everyone in that room was forced to think about all of the times in our lives when we don't say "I love you" or " yeah, let's do that." Everyone realized that we needed to change that from this day forward.

In spite of a cold, hard rain, we went outside for the military rites. The twenty-one gun salute, the playing of *Taps* and the presentation of the flag to me. I cried because I knew that Dad was so proud of the medals that he earned during the Korean War. That moment took me back almost fifty years in my life to that time when, as a little boy I was so proud of my big, strong father and I ached for him to love me. And now, here I was once again, so proud of being my father's son. He surely had so many faults and had made so many mistakes in his life. He surely had deeply hurt, in so many ways, the people that I loved. Yet, I always was so proud of him and wanted so badly for him to love me and, at last, I truly knew that he really had loved me.

Shortly after the service ended, Dad's friend Frank came up to me, looked me straight in the eyes and simply said, "Your Dad would have been proud of the job you did today, Wayne." I could barely hold back the tears when I thanked him. I was then at peace with myself and my tribute to Dad.

May he rest in peace with Dottie in eternity.

Juxtaposition

ON THURSDAY, NOVEMBER 1, I was in for a visit with my cardiologist of seventeen years. The reason for my appointment was that I was nervous about not feeling too good for a couple of weeks. I explained to him that I had been feeling pains in my chest similar to the ones that preceded my double by-pass surgery seventeen years ago. He asked me what had been going on in my life. I responded by mentioning to him that my father had passed away on July 22nd. I added that I had been having some very serious issues with one of my siblings as a result of Dad's death and its aftermath. In addition, I told him that I was moving my daughter to Waco, Texas, for her new career as a Doctor of Physical Therapy. Then I added that I had been taking Celebrex for about two weeks for knee pain after surgery to remove a bone chip. I commented that his nurse had done a blood pressure reading on me that I thought was relatively high at 152 over 92.

My doctor listened to all of this in his normal calm manner. He listened to my heart and lungs, both front and back as he always does. For some reason, he told me to go ahead with my plans to move my daughter to Texas (a seventeen hour car ride) and to schedule a stress test for a couple weeks out from that Thursday. He chose not to do an EKG (electrocardiogram) procedure on my heart. The procedure usually takes less than five minutes to complete. Instead, he reassured me that I should not worry because my heart was fine. I left his office somewhat baffled and still somewhat concerned about my health. Less than forty-eight hours later, my worries were shockingly affirmed.

Something was definitely not good with me when I awakened that morning of November 3, 2012. All I did was walk to the mailbox across the street from our house to pick up the newspaper as I always do. I came back into the house and climbed the stairs to our main floor. Yet, I was not feeling good at all after the dozen or so steps to our living room. My arms felt so completely weak that I could barely lift them. The back of my neck was drenched with sweat from my head. Worst of all, my chest felt as though it had collapsed and all of that pressure was just sitting there. My breathing was calm, but my heart was absolutely pounding. I went back down the steps to awaken my wife, Vickie. It was then that I knew without any doubt whatsoever that I was having a heart attack.

"Vickie, you need to get up and take me to the hospital," I stated to her after tapping her on the shoulder as she lay there asleep.

"What's wrong, Wayne?" she groggily asked.

"My chest really hurts. I feel just awful," I stated as directly as I know how to do. "I think I am having a heart attack."

Since Vickie is an emergency room nurse, she immediately starting asking questions to determine if she truly thought, also, that I was having an attack. When I explained my symptoms, she decided that she would take me in to Stoughton Hospital (her actual place of employment) to play it safe. She got dressed, walked me to the car and off we went. There was no racing along the highway. There was no ranting or raving from me. We just talked about what I was feeling in my body.

As she pulled into the emergency bay at the hospital, several nurses and a doctor met us. They placed me in a wheelchair and moved me quickly to an examination room. I still vividly remember the bright lights over my head, the purposeful movement of medical staff as they inserted an intravenous needle into my arm, the direct questions to me and my wife and the absolute fear that reached into my brain and grabbed me like a lioness latches onto her prey.

It was no more than a moment or two before I heard the doctor state to Vickie, "He's having a heart attack." I had been praying as hard as I possibly could from the moment that I walked back into the house from my walk for the newspaper. Now, for the first time in my life, I was completely consumed by the thought that I might be dying and that I might never speak to my wife and children ever again on this earth. I am not ashamed to share with you that at that point in time I actually begged God to let me live.

Shortly after I was situated with all of the devices and equipment necessary to monitor my well-being, I informed the medical professionals that I had taken a Cialis pill at about seven the previous evening. I remember reading that if you have done so then you should not take any nitrates in case of a heart attack. (Quite ironically, I need to thank my wife for saving my life by NOT being in the mood for a sexual encounter that Friday night. If she had been interested, then I may not be here writing this story now because I very well may have had a heart attack during that activity. Thus, I need to make every husband's most dreaded comment now- "Thanks honey for not having sex with me that night.") The doctor thanked me for the information and stated that I was right on the edge of the twelve hour window for that drug concern. The nurses and the doctor kept asking me how I felt. I told them that it felt as though someone was slamming a baseball bat into my chest constantly. I asked them for something for the pain. Unfortunately, my blood pressure was so low that they could not administer any pain killers for me. Again, I remember one nurse reading my numbers out loud as I anguished there in that room.

"60 over 30," I heard her announce and I thought "Oh, my God!"

I truly wondered if I was going to make it. I know enough about my health history to know that those were not good numbers. So, of course, I started to cry from fear and concern.

"There you go," the doctor stated, "your blood pressure just went up."

Eventually, the nerve-wracking hubbub of the room left my mind and I only focused on my prayers. All else was background. I heard them talk about the Medflight crew being on the way to pick me up to transfer me to Meriter Hospital in Madison for emergency surgery. The next thing I knew the staff was placing me inside of the helicopter and the doors were closing. My eyes were closed and I was praying as this happened, yet I was very aware of the helicopter seeming to be a very tight fit for all of the crew and me. I remember a sense of claustrophobia intruding into my thoughts but I banished it immediately by refocusing on my prayers. The doctor and nurse in the chopper monitored me constantly and there was always a hand resting on my chest. That hand meant so much to me that it brings tears to me as I write this. That simple caring and kind gesture reminded me of my own loved ones and of how much I wanted to live for their sakes. That simple placement of the hand on my chest let me know that they were watching me and that they would not let anything happen to me. It made me genuinely feel as though these two total strangers cared about me. Don't ever underestimate the power of simple human touch.

A Knock at the Door

Apparently, sometime during my stay in the emergency room in Stoughton or during the flight to Madison, I had been given some drug for the pain. I barely remember arriving at the hospital in Madison and being moved to the operating room. There were parts of the conversation in the helicopter that I vaguely was aware of occurring, but only vaguely.

After that, my next recollection has me in my hospital room with my wife and daughter present along with my good friend and my human guardian angel, Paul. My sons got there shortly after I regained consciousness. They brought along a couple of their friends who happen to be friends of mine, too. Eventually, the surgeon who saved my life came in to explain the procedure. Apparently, a blood clot had formed and was completely blocking one of my main arteries. He removed the clot and placed a stent at that point in my artery to help ensure the integrity of the artery walls. He said they also saw some blockage downstream where a stent had been placed back in 2005. He thought we should wait until three or four weeks had passed since this incident to repair that situation. I thanked him and he left the room.

Before long, a number of people showed up to check on me. In fact, there was a roomful of visitors. Paul, Tony and LuAnn, Mike, Brad, Tim and my whole family were all there. I was amazed that we all spent several hours actually laughing out loud and truly enjoying the moments. It was then that I became aware of the mind-boggling juxtaposition of feelings of life-threatening terror immediately next to feelings of absolute joy and wonder at the gifts of life, love and laughter.

With all of those people in my room sharing memories and giggles of delight, I still kept praying to God. This time, though, my prayers were of profound gratitude.

Eventually, the nurse did come in and hint that, perhaps, I should try to get some rest. With great reluctance on the part of the family and friends (and me), they did head out from my room. Before long, I pushed the call button to ask my nurse for a pain pill that I had been taking for two weeks. The pill was Celebrex and I was given two weeks of samples by a doctor. It was supposed to help alleviate some severe pain that I had been experiencing post knee surgery. It took twenty minutes or so before the nurse returned with news for me. She explained to me that the cardiac doctor who had performed my surgery responded to my request with some startling information. I was not to take any Celebrex "because it causes heart attacks" was the answer the doctor had given to her to pass on to me. I was stunned. Those words still ring loudly with me.

I must confess that I am disappointed in myself because I did not do my own homework. I usually read the side effects flyers that you receive with prescription drugs. Inexplicably, I did not read the flyer this time even though my wife left it on the kitchen table for several days. Yet, in spite of two doctors overlooking the warnings that Celebrex can cause an increase in cardiac incidents, I have never felt any anger toward either doctor. I am thrilled to state that I must truly have changed my attitude about life. Not once during this whole terrifying incident did I ever ask the question, "Why me Lord? What did I do to deserve this horrifying scare?" Instead, I have only thanked God every chance I get for the gift of life. I thank God constantly for every day that I am here because I truly believe that God reached down to save my life again. God must want me to continue His work here for awhile. In fact, maybe, the real questions should be, "Why me Lord? Why am I the one You save so often?"

My second day in the hospital was a Sunday and it was a Packers Sunday. I remember vividly because my two sons, AJ and Cole, arranged to bring in a big screen TV, snacks and beverages so that our whole family and various friends could watch the game together in style. Our "Packer Party" was the talk of the whole floor that afternoon. Many hospital staff stopped in just to check out the festivities. It was a wonderful gesture on the part of my boys and everyone else. It made that day move quickly and with many a smile.

Everything went well during my first several days in the hospital. The nurses were truly wonderful in helping me redevelop a sense of safety. It is only natural for a person to live in fear of another heart attack once that first one has occurred. For me, that trepidation is multiplied substantially because I am a worrier already. Every stress and strain in my chest area had me wondering if something was happening again. The constant hovering presence of my heart monitor directly over my right shoulder next to my hospital bed did not help. In fact, on one occasion it caused more worry than I could handle. It seems the monitor is set to ring an alarm if your heart rate drops below 50 beats per minute. My normal resting heart rate prior to this incident was in the low 50s and very high 40s because of all of my exercise and my medications. I had barely fallen asleep for the night when the alarm went off blaring and the nurse came in to see what was wrong. I immediately looked at the screen that shows my heart activity. It definitely looked out of the ordinary according to the chart readings before and after that alarm. I simply could not return to sleep. Luckily, for me, my nurse came in and talked to me for nearly an hour. When she left at the shift break, her replacement came in and spent almost as much time with me. They were each wonderfully caring, professionally reassuring and genuinely concerned about my mental well-being. Together, they helped me make it through the rough night.

I was scheduled to leave the hospital on that Monday morning. But, the doctor saw a t-wave, or something like that. Needless to say, he did not like it. So he decided to keep me one more day. On Tuesday morning, I was actually in the wheelchair in my room ready to leave the hospital and my wife was outside pulling the car up to the door to get me when I had more chest paint (angina). I told the nurse and she called the doctor. Then I called my wife on her cell phone and informed her that I was not going home just yet. They had immediately scheduled the procedure to clear up the downstream blockage in the old stent for the next morning. I was not heading anywhere just yet. Unfortunately, I spent another restless night concerned about this next procedure. Luckily, my children, wife and friends had been very attentive to me during these days. I got to see each of my three children individually on separate occasions. Those visits meant so much to me as they each shared time with me and each handled the difficult circumstances in their own way. It was so blatantly obvious to me that my deep love for them was returned by each of them. My oldest son, AJ, came to see me and to discuss some issue on which he wanted my advice. I think he just wanted me to know that he was very scared but he could not come out and say that. My son, Cole, came to visit at 9pm after a day of work and brought me some baseball cards to open with him. He explained to me that he thought that was what I would have done for him if the roles were reversed. My daughter, Melanie, tried to have a heart to heart with me. She tried to tell me what I meant to her. But, she had a tough time with it. She kept breaking down in tears and so did I. My wife, also, made the situation so much more bearable because of her matter-of-fact approach to the whole medical circumstances. She talked me through many fears and tears. She never made me feel as though she was scared and that helped me tremendously.

Thursday rolled around and my second procedure had been accomplished successfully. The heart tests had all been run and it looked like I was finally going to leave. Unfortunately, I was stopped again. This time a doctor had seen an arrhythmia pattern that he did not like. He referred me to another doctor who was to check out the "electrical" aspect of my heart function as opposed to the" plumbing" aspect. At nine that morning, I had to inform my wife and daughter that I was not quite ready to go home even now. It was at that point, again, that I began to beg God once more. I asked him to please help me to get good news on my heart so that I would not have to have a pacemaker installed or to do any more procedures with my heart. I actually asked him to do a miracle for me and to heal my heart. I prayed and I cried and I knew I could do nothing more about it but wait.

My wife and daughter and a good friend, Paul, spent so much of that day with me as we waited and wondered. Paul has a very thorough understanding of the heart and its functions since he is a perfusionist. (His job is to keep your body functioning during heart and lung procedures.) He also happens to work at the same hospital where I was located. It was not until approximately 5:30 pm that afternoon when the new doctor arrived. It had been one of the longest days of my life. It was a day spent wondering what kind of life I would have from this point onward. A day spent wondering if my heart was simply no longer good enough to function properly. As hard as I attempted to be patient, it did not work well.

Then, finally, the doctor showed up. He answered every one of our questions. (There were a lot of them considering my wife, my daughter and Paul are all medical professionals.) He went through in intricate detail to explain the concern of the other doctors and his own analysis of the situation. In the end, he advised me to go home and try to get back to living life. I was very impressed with his attitude and with his knowledge. At long last, he released me to go home at 7:00pm that Thursday night. My body was healing properly. Unfortunately, I quickly discovered that my state-of-mind was nowhere near recovered.

My daughter was supposed to have started a new position as a Doctor of Physical Therapy in Waco, Texas, about the time of this incident. She delayed starting until I was back on my feet and home. But she did have to get moved down there so Vickie, Melanie, Vickie's sister, Kay, and Melanie's friend, Jen, all packed up two cars to head to Waco. I was at home on my own but AJ came over to spend a couple nights with me just to be sure. Cole offered to do the same, but I figured that sooner or later I had to learn to be comfortable with being alone. Therefore, I spent another three nights on my own and everything seemed adequate.

A Knock at the Door

Then on that Saturday night, I felt something strange in my chest. I thought it might just be muscle issues from the multiple procedures that had been performed on me less than seven days ago. But, I simply could not get those thoughts out of my mind that I might be having another attack. I hemmed and hawed until almost midnight. Then I got dressed and drove to the hospital and checked into the emergency room, again.

The staff was very calming and very professional. They hooked me up again to the monitors and the IV needle. They checked my vital signs and did my blood draws. It took until almost 2 a.m. but they did help me understand that everything was fine. My friend, Paul, finally arrived after I called to ask him to come to the emergency room. He was great in helping me to understand the various blood draw definitions. Between the ER staff and Paul, I did get back home early that morning and I found a way to relax a little more. The emergency room doctor reassured me that my heart was functioning quite well and that the chest issues were more muscular in nature.

I was not out of that horrible month of November quite yet, though. I was returning home from a business meeting in Middleton with my good friends, Tim and Barb. It was approximately 5:30pm on Thursday, November 29, and I knew that traffic would be heavy. Therefore, I decided to really be cautious with my driving. As per my normal route, I headed off to McKee Road to get home the "back way" as opposed to the busy Beltline traffic. People always seem to drive the Beltline road like idiots with no concern for life or limb. I avoid it like the plague at rush hour. I was travelling past the Star Theater on the right and traffic was slowing down. Even though the speed limit was 40mph, I just set my cruise at 35. As I pulled up to my intersection, I noticed all of the vehicles in the left lane were backed up and dead still all the way to the next lights (about 100 yards ahead) and I saw several cars attempting to enter traffic on my right from a strip mall exit. Suddenly, I spotted a car squeezing between two cars in the left lane and about to cross directly into my path so that they could get into the mall entry. Without a doubt, I thought I was about to T-bone these people in their car as they gave me absolutely no room to stop. I slammed on the brakes as hard as I could. My books and laptop went flying off the passenger seat and into the dashboard and then onto the floor. At that point, I seemed to see everything slow down as I saw my car was not going to stop in time. I took my foot off of the brakes and yanked the steering wheel hard to the right and then abruptly back into the far right lane to avoid a car from the mall. I cruised past all vehicles and somehow never made contact with anyone. I was safe, except my heart was now racing and my blood pressure had just jumped.

I took several deep breaths and headed home to relax. All the while I was thanking God for saving me, again. I did manage to smile to myself several times because I was fairly impressed with my reflexes. I guess I must still have some athletic abilities left in me as proven by those reflexes. Yet, the smiles disappeared when I got home and checked my blood pressure. It had jumped to 150 over 92. That worried me to no end. I sat and thought about it and became increasingly aware of the blood pressure. I attempted to meditate in order to reduce the number but it was not working. When Vickie got home, I shared my experience with her and my concerns. We decided that I would call the doctor in the morning for an appointment.

The next day I arranged a quick appointment with my new cardiologist. He listened to me explain my concerns and the events of the past evening. Quickly, he decided to play it safe and do an EKG on me. Within minutes, he came back into the examination room and informed me that he needed me to have a full-blown stress test done immediately. Needless to say, I went into worry mode full-throttle. I called Vickie and asked her to meet me at the clinic to drive me to the hospital for the test. Again, I sat and waited for what seemed like an eternity with no other thoughts than my own mortality. I truly wondered if I was going to survive November.

Vickie arrived. We talked. We held each other and then we took off for the next test. Wonderful news was discovered. The stress test took my heart rate to 140 beats per minute for three full minutes after seven or eight minutes of buildup without any issues whatsoever. The doctor reviewed the results and sent her assistant to inform me that everything looked excellent. I was now truly on my way to a better psychological state of mind.

That event, coupled with my rehab exercise program, helped me to finally find some peace of mind. The rehab staff at Stoughton Hospital was great in working with me to rebuild my stamina for physical output. But, they were also very understanding in their approach to assisting me in returning to a place of normalcy from a mental standpoint. Throughout my twenty-four visit program, they gradually moved me to a place of comfort and confidence. It was reassuring to do my exercise program while they monitored my heart closely. It was also no small bonus that they were a very attractive group of medical professionals with kind and caring attitudes about all of their patients. Every day we laughed and conversed about a myriad of topics. Yet, they always maintained a completely professional and positive attitude toward me. Jen, Melissa and Betsy truly assisted me in my recovery, both from a physical standpoint and from a mental perspective.

Shortly after the rehab program was finished, I had a lunch meeting with my good friend, Father David Greenfield. He had many pointed questions about my experience. He especially asked me about those moments when I was on the emergency room bed. Father Dave specifically asked me why I had begged God to save my life. My answer was immediate and genuine. I asked God to save me because I did not want my children to see me die so suddenly because of this heart attack. You see, only about three months prior to November 3, they watched my father die (at age 82) from a massive heart attack and its aftermath. They had been with him during the last hours of his life and it had shaken them. I begged God to not put them through that again so soon.

It is now approximately four months since my terrifying experience. It put me immediately in touch with my own mortality. For the first time in my life, I truly thought that I was going to die that Saturday in November. Now, here I sit viewing life so differently again. I have lost almost twenty pounds by ceasing some bad habits of soda and oreo cookies. I have reinitiated my meditation practice. My diet now consists of more hummus, carrots, extra virgin oil olive, dark chocolate and red wine than I ever dreamt of eating and drinking. I thank God every day for the gift of life. I truly believe that God reached down again to save my life.

I don't mean that last statement to sound as if God is more concerned about me than about others. I don't mean it to sound as if God looks at me as someone so worthy of being saved so many times. I only want you to understand that I devoutly believe that God did save me again and that I believe that God must still want me to continue His work here on earth. I will be wiser about how much of His work I feel obligated to undertake.

I will try as hard as possible to thank Him every day for this profound and glorious gift of life. I will take great comfort in knowing that I have indeed changed my attitude about life. For the first half of my life, my attitude had never been that my glass was half-empty, but rather that I had never even received a glass. I was filled with anger in so many ways.

I can now say that my attitude about my life is of a more positive nature. In 1986, a therapist explained to me that I was the "classic example of a love deprivation child". I guess I have done a complete reversal in attitude because now I feel loved by so many. That negative attitude about life and love is now replaced entirely. I now believe that "my cup runneth over with love."

Epilogue

TIME IS A MOST precious commodity. It is demanded of so many and it is sought after by nearly everyone. All of us wonder what we could accomplish if we only had more of it. People are always afraid of running out of it. Self-help authors have made a great deal of money by telling us how to manage it. I have even heard people state that they wished they could buy more of it.

But I am now realizing that we all have just the right amount of time, if we appreciate it while we are in it. Think about the joy you could experience, if you took the time to relish every great moment in your life AS IT OCCURS. If you only would appreciate the entire duration of your child's smile or your spouse's laughter or your own sense of accomplishment, then time might seem tremendously more abundant. Your days would become a series of moments around which you would go about your business with a hopeful smile. That frazzled look of the harried mom or dad would disappear. Your children would come to know that you are actually a loving, funny and enjoyable human being that does not spend every second reviewing a soccer practice performance or a dance lesson. They could find out that you love to read books to them. You could remember to revel in the pleasure of a soft fall breeze blowing across your face as you relax in your backyard.

During the process of reviewing my own lifetime of miracles, gifts and of the occurrence of God's presence in my life, I have realized that I have let too many "moments" slip by completely unnoticed. Too many times I was captivated by my own concern for time or the lack, thereof. While I am now attempting to change that habit, I am thrilled that I do have more than a few episodes that I did enjoy for as long as I could at the time they occurred.

It has taken me nearly four years to write this book of the memories and moments of my life. There has been deep pain in some of those recollections and great joy derived from others. I have literally laughed out loud, smiled broadly, and shed many a tear as I transported myself back in time to each of these chapters of my life. Yet, I was unprepared for the reaction and response of my siblings and my brother-in-law. It very nearly brought me to a decision to never publish.

In early March of 2011, I contacted my family to ask for help in acquiring photos for this book. The response was devastatingly negative. They did not want me to "dredge up old history." I was told to let it all be forgotten. While the threat was never definitively spelled out, my choices were quite clear: I could publish the book, or I could keep my relationships with my family members. They were absolutely mutually exclusive. It was one or the other.

The decision tore at me. All but one had never even read the book, but they were extremely opposed to it anyway. Each one had his or her own memories of our family life that they did not, necessarily, want to be aired publicly.

I proceeded to seek advice from several sources. I talked with my family directly. I talked with friends who had read the book. There were many conversations with my wife. Many, many times I prayed to God to help me understand the correct path to take.

Slowly, one by one, I persuaded my siblings to read the book from front to back and then decide what they thought about it. I asked them to promise to continue reading after the few chapters that described our own family life. They needed to understand that the book is about my whole life and all of the miracles and moments that comprise it. I asked them to be honest and to be fair with their attitudes and their comments.

I remember quite vividly the day that I left my home to deliver the copies of my manuscript to my brothers, my brother-in-law, my sister, and my father. In spite of the fact that I was running late, I stopped in to discuss my situation with a good friend, Dan Behrend. He had read the book several years prior to this time. He studied to become a minister long ago. His father actually was a minister. I share that information because it is a background for our discussion that day. Luckily, like so many of my other good friends, Dan is able to be very coldly honest with me. I explained my dilemma to him concerning my family's reaction to the book.

His response was simple. He surmised that I knew deep in my heart if I was writing the book for myself only or because God wanted me to do so. He told me point blank that God would send me a message with the answer. There was no doubt in his mind that, one way or another, God would solve my dilemma by showing me the path that He wanted me to take. I left Dan's office and drove three and one-half hours to Arcadia. Not once did I turn on the radio because my head was too filled with thoughts already.

My brother, Richard, was my first stop. As always, he was completely candid and very concise in his thoughts. "Wayne, I don't really read a lot of books. I won't be reading this one. I trust you, and I know that you will do what is best. Just try not to do it if you think it will hurt anyone badly," he stated. I then asked him to read the several paragraphs that described him specifically. He did so as I held the book, and we talked a little about it. He did not come out and say it, but I knew that what I had written about him touched him.

Later on when I shared some old pictures of him, me, our siblings, and my dad, he seemed to revel in the photos. He told me story upon story about people in the snapshots. There was an obvious level of pride in his voice that I was happy to hear.

Next, I went to talk to my brother-in-law, Maggie's widower, Dick. He has always been someone that I admired. In fact, he and Maggie were the only ones who had read the book prior to this rendition. Maggie told me that she was very impressed that I could write a whole book about my life. She told me that she thought it was a good book and was well-written. Her only comment was that she wished I could use fictitious names. That conversation, of course, took place back in 2007, prior to Maggie losing her battle against Lou Gehrig's disease. Now, Dick and I discussed the book again. We spoke at great length and with great honesty about it. He stated again that he thought it was "a good read," based on his love of reading. After nearly two hours, I made a statement to him about what I thought Maggie would say if she were alive. "I truly believe, Dick, that if Maggie was here today, she would not stop me from publishing this book."

His response was a genuine surprise to me. "You are absolutely right, Wayne, because Maggie thought the sun set and rose in you."

I never really knew that Maggie felt that way about me. I knew we always had this special bond and that I loved her deeply. Yet, she never told me that herself.

In all honesty, I never told her how much I loved her and how much I appreciated all that she had done for me, either. But, I am very glad that she had read this book before she died because the stories about her portray my love and respect for her. I believe it is obvious that she had a major positive influence on me and that I loved her deeply. I sincerely hope that she got that message from the book.

When I talked with my brother, Karl, and his wife, they agreed to read the book in its entirety. We have since discussed it to some degree, and Karl has now seen that it is not something to be feared. In fact, now his children also want to read it. I believe that it will help them to understand their father much better.

Finally, I drove out to see my sister, Marilyn, and her husband, Jim. They were both wonderfully understanding and open to reading the book. Each of them thought it was only fair to actually read it before judging it. I spent over three hours at their beautiful home that night. I cried more than once at the simple discussion of the painful memories of my childhood. Marilyn shared with me some of her own thoughts and nightmares about our youth. We talked about things that had never before been openly mentioned. That night, in their kitchen, we rekindled a brother and sister bond that I truly cherish and that I had missed for so many years.

In the weeks since, Marilyn has read the book entirely. She has given me her blessing on publishing and distributing it. In fact, she has provided me with some corrections concerning facts in the book. She has shared information with me that supports so many of my thoughts on the life of our mother. I am thrilled that she is once again a part of my life.

In addition to the discussions with my siblings, I knew that I should attempt to read some of the chapters to my father. Since my ninety-year-old mother has Alzheimer's Disease, there did not seem to be any good reason to read her parts of the book. She is now a happy woman with the thoughts that she can recall, and I am glad for that. However, Dad was a different story. He is still quite sharp in his mind. I did not know how that session would go. As I was completely emotionally exhausted after this day of revelations, I held off on until my next trip back two weeks later to see Dad.

When I did return to see Dad and read him parts of the book, I was, again, taken aback. As usual, we made some small talk when I arrived. He caught me up on the local news, and we talked some about political circumstances, too. Then, I asked him if I could read to him some chapters from my book. I reminded him, as I had prior to this, that there were some negative stories about him and some others that were positive. I let him know that I did not try to hide the unhappiness and the dysfunction of our life with him and mom. He told me to go ahead.

I remember reading to him my description of him as this man that I idolized and how he hurt me so deeply by not showing me any love back then. I read about his physical abuse of Karl. He did not argue with me about it as he had in the past months. Instead, my father cried when I read about his treatment of Karl. He broke down and cried.

My father is a strong, stubborn man whose father abused him and his siblings. I don't know that I have ever heard him apologize about anything to anyone. Yet, I believe that by shedding the tears that he did at that reading, he was acknowledging that he was wrong about what he did to Karl.

I have told him that I cannot forgive him for that because that is between him, Karl, and God. It is not my place to forgive him for that.

Then, I read to him about how he became a wonderful father to me and a fantastic, loving grandfather to my children. I read about my thoughts as I watched him hold my first child, AJ, in his arms almost thirty years ago, and I cried to the point of being unable to read any more. Again, Dad surprised me by saying I should stop reading because it was too emotional. Here was my father, consoling and comforting me for the first time in my life, and I was 57-years-old. I regained my composure and finished the story.

After all of this turmoil and all of the revelations, there was one more startling occurrence. If you recall from the beginning of this epilogue, I stated that my friend, Dan, had advised me that God would provide me with my answer. He did just that.

Another of my good friends is Father David Greenfield. He sends me e-mail versions of his homilies three times a week. In one of those Tuesday homilies, unbeknownst to him, Father Dave gave me my answer. His sermon was about the fact that Lent should be a time when we all try to live more like good Christians should live. He suggested we could do that by finding ways to forgive people who had harmed us at all. He mentioned a story about a woman who was doing a book signing as the author of a book about forgiveness. A lady came rushing into the bookstore and asked for eight copies. She said all of her family needed to read the book so they could learn how to forgive. My wife read the homily first and told me that I needed to read it because it had my answer. God, through Father Dave's homily, was telling me that I needed to publish this book.

In reality, there are a number of reasons why I wanted this book published. I truly believe that by sharing my story of a dysfunctional life, where anger and pain were ever-present, there is hope. It took me a long time to realize that my life was somehow filled with love, happiness, and God. I want to help other victims of love deprivation to know that they are not alone. I want to help them so that they might see their lives differently.

I have always wanted to be a writer and this may be my best opportunity to become one. In fact, I am already reaping the benefits of a book that was received, initially, with anger and negative feelings toward me. Yet, it is because of the love and respect of my siblings that it is now accepted by them. There is now renewed love and forgiveness within my own family.

With the help of my wife, I learned to nurture that seed of love with our children. I now see life as filled with love, happiness, and God. For a child whose youth centered around the anguished feelings of love deprivation, I am thrilled now to state unequivocally, "My cup runneth over with love."

It is not enough that we should look back at our lives as we age and then find joy in our past miracles, gifts from God or circumstances of Divine interventions. We need to learn to slow down our lives to the point wherein we understand and acknowledge the "moments" that not only make up our lives but that define our lives.

A Knock at the Door

Every time that a spouse smiles and reaches out to hold the hand of his or her "partner in life" we should embrace that "moment." Every time that a child takes the time to sit on your lap or to utter those wonderful words, "Daddy I love you," we should stop everything that we are doing and experience, completely, the "moment."

Maybe what we all need to realize is that every day that we go through life we have opportunities to fill our glasses a little more. Perhaps if we all spent substantially more time and effort in the joyful pastime of "filling our glasses," then we would stop being concerned about them being "half-empty." Maybe we would finally realize that it is possible for us to fill our own glasses.

Poetic License Revoked

Over the years, I have found poetry to be a catharsis for me. It gave me the opportunity to present my thoughts and ideas and feelings in a different format. I hope you enjoy them.

Lay

Lay thoughtlessly. Lay silently. Lay uncaringly
     Exposed.
Body parched and shrunken. Mind empty and
     Unused.
Heart and soul long ago abandoned. Life merely
     An electronic existence.
Age rules rampant here. Slow destruction
     Its method.
Warp the spirit gradually. Devour the body
     Incessantly.
Loneliness and pain are constant visitors. Death
     Stalks the hallways.
Lay hopelessly. Lay helplessly. Lay pitifully
     Forgotten.
Death will visit here shortly ~ Hopefully ~
     Mercifully.

I wrote this poem after meeting Grandma Clara Sonsalla for the first and only time in my life. She was dying in the nursing home of the hospital in Arcadia.

Cool March Wind

Cool March wind in my face
On a bright moonlit night
A thousand stars share the sky
Two lovers share a stolen kiss.
Sounds of life are all around.
A clanging chain, a crackling branch,
A wind-blown leaf crosses the street
People come and go constantly
Hoping to capture that fleeting feeling.
Spring.

Greatest of All Time

It all started with Olympic glory and culminated with the heavyweight crown.
His charisma and audacity brought him instant recognition and worldwide renown.
It was said that no man ever was better at turning the boxing ring into a glorified stage.
With equal ease he could exude happiness and humor or entertain with false rage.

As a boxer in the ring, he flaunted "The Ali Shuffle" and invented "rope-a-dope."
As a celebrity, he talked with Cossell, Ed Sullivan, the Beatles and even the Pope.
"The Rumble in the Jungle" and the "Thrilla in Manila" highlighted his pugilistic legacy,
While red-tassled shoes and knockout predictions are other parts of his professional history

He fought against both champs and chumps and very nearly beat them all.
Foreman and Moore, Patterson and Liston all went down without a close call.
But the battles were ferocious and unforgettable in "Ali versus Frazier I, II and III."
In his prime and in his time, he truly could "float like a butterfly and sting like a bee."
He redefined the boxing game with his flamboyant style and athletic grace.
But more than anything, he loved to flash that electric smile and talk about his "pretty face."
His quick wit and sharp tongue matched his lightning fists and nimble feet just perfectly.
So the newswires lit up with each rare defeat and with every bombastic victory.
So is the life and legend of Muhammad Ali, the king of the ring and the prince of rhyme,
undeniably and unarguably—"The Greatest of All Time."

Romancing the Colon

She used her wiles and wares so fiendishly on that memorable day.
So seductively she slid to me that most vile and potent mixture.
At once, I knew that there was nothing more that I could say.
The price I paid was sweet indeed as I hugged that porcelain fixture.

By morning's first light, I had nothing at all left inside of me.
Yet, my personal humiliation and physical degradation had barely even begun.
I laid there in that operating room with my derriere in full view for all to see.
No crevice would go unstudied and no orifice would go untouched before all was done.

"Open wide," she whispered as she lubricated the most private of my body parts.
Thanks to the anesthesiologist from then on I was completely sound asleep.
I dreamed of butterflies in my colon and I dreamed of near orgasmic farts.
Then suddenly it all ceased when that camera came out from down so deep.

Had I ever been a smoker, I would most surely have lit one up
to savor the profound and provocative memory
Of that unforgettable day
when my colon lost its virginity.

A Strange Ship

Love is a strange ship.
It can appear suddenly over the horizon,
Or sink quickly into the ocean.
For years love can ride a calm sea,
Or it can be tormented by unending storms.
It can destroy the bravest captain,
Or it can transform a lowly sailor into a legend.
Love's ship may travel the seven seas,
Or it could never venture from its own harbor.
But wherever love carries you.
The voyage more than equals the price of passage.

224

Another Rose

Love visited me a while ago,
Though it stayed for only a brief season.
Like the early rose of spring.
It blossomed suddenly and beautifully.
But, like that same rose it died all too soon,
Fading away gradually, day by day,
Until it was there no more.
Had we nurtured and cared for it properly, it may
Have survived to become the most beautiful rose of
That season ~ or any season.
But, unfortunately, we treasured it only for its
Present beauty,
Not realizing just how red and full it could have become.
We assumed, unwisely, that it would continue to grow and
Bloom, even when left unfed and unwatered.
We discovered, too late, the mistake we had made,
For the rose had wilted ~ the aroma no longer lingered.
We were left with nothing ~ save for the memory of its sweet
Presence and remarkable beauty.
And always, always, the thought of another spring.
And another rose.

Recipe

Catch a glance.
Twice.
Add a slight grin and an inviting nod.
A small amount of conversation.
A sprinkling of charm and debonair.
Just a touch of sincerity
And lastly ~ but most important ~
A hint of desire.
Blend together well.

Usually makes just one serving.

Ego Trip

I sometimes wonder what might have been
Had God not made me the ladies' man
That I am.
Had he not gifted me with this aura of
Sincerity ~ I may have been the
Same as any man.
But not for me ~ that normal life. Not
For one who has as gentle and compassionate
A soul as I've.
If only He had deprived me of this ability.
To love a woman so tenderly.
To melt her heart entirely. To earn her
Devotion so completely.
To have her very soul for mine alone.
I sometimes wonder what might have been.
      And yet I thank Him most often
      It seems
      For allowing me these wonderful dreams.

Marriage

Trust, honesty, respect, sincerity,
Joy, sorrow, pain, security,
Pride, success, failure, humility,
Friendship, protection, cohesion, unity.
Each a part of what the future holds
All entwined by that one necessity –
        LOVE.
A love so strong and true,
That it colors not our perceptions
      Of each other.
It allows us, instead,
      To realize what lies ahead.
That all is not what might have been.
But with our love,
      We will see it through.
And what will be,
      Will be better still.
To have shared together,
      Heart and soul.
For only then can we be whole,
      Man and woman,
      Husband and wife.
Together, from now, till the end of life.

226

Wayne Bisek

<u>My Journey</u>

My journey starts today.
Across the bridge of time.
Yesterday is left behind.
Tomorrow's shores reach out for me.
Doubt is with me every step.
Wondering what the darkness holds.
I know the light of day.
Now I must discover night.

THE IGNITOR

Introduction by Paul Molitor

Over the last eighteen years, I have known of Buckets for Hunger, Incorporated, and its efforts to fight hunger by raising money for food pantries. Wayne Bisek's love of sports serves as the basis for his creative ideas for raising funds. My introduction to Wayne was through my marketing agent who Wayne contacted to see if I would sign various items for the organization. I was amazed at the types of unique items that I was asked to autograph for the charity which Buckets then sold at many memorabilia auctions over the years.

Eventually Wayne contacted my wife, Destini, and talked with her about increasing my role with Buckets. She was persuaded by Wayne's persistence and obvious passion. Destini asked me to helps Buckets out by attending a gathering of my Milwaukee Brewers 1982 World Series teammates in Madison. The evening included a dinner, storytelling, silent and live auctions. I can honestly tell you Destini and I, along with Jim Gantner, Jerry Augustine and Gorman Thomas all enjoyed the evening immensely and were very impressed by the Buckets organization. After that evening, Destini and I decided that I would join the honorary board of directors and make an even deeper commitment to helping Buckets in any way possible

Now Wayne asked me to help him with this book. I happily agreed to provide an introduction to his poem, *The Ignitor.* He wrote it especially for the Buckets dinner/auction that I previously mentioned.

I enjoyed reading Wayne's poem, *The Ignitor.* It very perfectly describes the attitude that exists in that member of the team who starts the much-needed rally and who knows the games well enough to use intelligence, skill and effort to help secure a victory for his team. He has done a great job of helping even non-baseball fans understand the excitement of the game. In fact, Wayne informed me the evening of that even that I was the inspiration for *The Ignitor.* I am flattered and humbled that he saw fit to immortalize me and my attitude about the game of baseball. I have even shared this poem with my own children as a way for them to understand who I was as a player and the particular way that I loved to play the game of baseball.

(Left to Right: Back Row–Destini Molitor, Wayne Bisek, Cole Bisek, AJ Bisek and Paul Molitor. Front Row–Melanie Bisek and Vickie Bisek)

Author's Note: Paul Molitor is a member of Major League Baseball's Hall of Fame and was named the World Series Most Valuable Player in 1993 for the Toronto Blue Jays. He ended his career with 3,319 hits, 504 stolen bases, a .304 lifetime batting average and 114 triples. Paul ranks in the top twenty players in the history of baseball in runs scored for a career with 1,782. Those numbers actually do illustrate quite vividly that Paul Molitor really was *The Ignitor*.

Wayne Bisek

The Ignitor

In the late innings of every baseball game ever played, at any time or any place,
A simple call goes out to one and all, "We need someone to get on base."
The excitement starts with a single player, then spreads to the entire team.
For a simple fact has come to light that gives them hope, that lets them dream.
Their leadoff batter in this final round is a "never-say-quit" fighter.
He is the one they have come to call, quite simply,
"the ignitor."

His history is that he does whatever it takes to light the fire that starts the rally.
And once it has begun, it is nearly completely certain to end in one more tally.
Maybe a well-placed bunt gets him to first, or perhaps, just a simple walk.
The next step might be a stolen base or, better yet, a nerve-induced pitcher's balk.
One way or another he finds a way to travel those ninety
feet from first to second,
And then he stands there and acts as if third base has already beckoned.

From that point on, the opponents know exactly how this burst of activity ends.
A single up the middle of the infield sends him scurrying round the bend.
He heads toward home with his muscular legs churning out his stride.
Then as he confronts the catcher, he begins his patented "fade" slide.
And like a veteran magician pulling the proverbial rabbit-out-of-a-hat,
He gracefully glides past the catcher's outstretched arms and that is that!
A run is scored and the game is in hand.
He calmly gets to his feet and brushes off the sand.
His teammates greet him with jumps and shouts and face-wide grins.
Together, they accomplished one of their hard-fought wins.
And he returns to the dugout like a tired, but victorious, fighter.
With a glowing smile, he tells you, quite clearly, he loves being
"the Ignitor."

I wrote this for Paul Molitor, the great Milwaukee Brewer, when he was a guest at one of our Buckets for Hunger, Incorporated events.

230

Wayne Bisek

After reading the poem, *Five Gold Rings,* I reflect on the good fortune my wife, Cherry, and I have received and witnessed over the years. One of those great blessings was the leadership and talents of those who allowed us to achieve so much while I was with the Packers.

My favorite acronym is TEAM — Together Everyone Achieves More. Organizations such as Buckets for Hunger provide help to families in need with a chance at victory. It is astounding what this team has been able to accomplish.

All of those associated with Buckets for Hunger are to be saluted for their compassion and enthusiasm to serve. Their efforts make a difference in the quality of so many lives.

Finally, every good team needs a leader. Wayne Bisek has been able to rise above adversity and help others do the same. I have had the pleasure of knowing him for many years and I am honored to call him a friend.

Bart

Bart Starr

(Bart Starr with Melanie Bisek, 2005)

Author's Note: Bart Starr is a member of the NFL Hall of Fame and the Green Bay Packers Hall of Fame. He is the only quarterback in the history of the NFL to have five championship rings. He was the NFL MVP in 1965.

Five Gold Rings

Mostly ignored and nearly forgotten on NFL draft day
Then selected in the seventeenth round by God-awful Green Bay
Two years carrying a clipboard and riding the pine
Listening and learning 'til it was his time to shine

He was disciplined and dedicated to succeed
With a quiet, but definite, ability to lead
A field general's mind and the guile of a gambler
Comfortable as a pocket passer or as a wily scrambler

Pinpoint spirals that almost never missed their aim
He was always at his best in a title game
Neither arctic cold nor bitter rivalry ever mattered
He kept his focus even when bruised and battered
An entire decade of victory after victory
His three straight championships stand alone in NFL history
Yet, God, family and the team were the most important things
For Bart Starr, the only quarterback ever with five gold rings

Intro by Jim Taylor

"Born to Play Football" by Wayne Bisek brought back many memories.
I feel humbled by his words.

The third verse really hit home:

"They give all they have on every play,
Everything they do is for the team.
Complete dedication is their only way.
Championship victory is their only dream."

Coach Lombardi instilled these thoughts and values in each of us. This has carried us throughout our lives. I feel the same passion about giving back. Each and every day God has blessed me and my family. It is our duty to go out as Wayne has done with 'Buckets For Hunger' and give back to feed the hungry. We live in a great nation with Americans willing to give their energy and time to help those in need.

Wayne Bisek

Wayne Bisek is one of those great Americans willing to go the extra mile to help see no one goes to bed hungry! He is our hero and a true inspiration for all!

God Bless,

Jim Taylor

Jim Taylor
Pro Football Hall of Fame 1976

Author's Note: Jim Taylor is a member of the NFL Hall of Fame and the Green Bay Packers Hall of Fame. He had five consecutive 1,000 yard rushing seasons and was a key player for four NFL Championship teams with the Packers. He was the NFL MVP 1962.

Born to Play Football

Some men are born to play football.
Their faces appear to be chiseled in stone.
Their chests are solid like a brick wall.
Their muscles are perfectly honed.

A fierce tenacity fills their souls.
They combine athletic grace with brute strength.
Nothing stops them from their goal.
Their threshold of pain knows no length.

They give all they have on every play.
Everything they do is for the team.
Complete dedication is their only way.
Championship victory is their only dream.

Some men are born to play football.
It is as if they were born under a star.
They just answer nature's call
Because it is simply who they are.

On September 20, 1935, Jim Taylor was
born to play football.

Sky Hook

Athletically indefensible.
Physically unstoppable.
Aesthetically enjoyable
Undeniably historical.

It starts so seemingly effortlessly and so innocently;
A simple inlet pass to the low post occurs so efficiently,
A single strong dribble and a drop step to the left with a gliding stride,
A sudden smoothly synchronized raising of the entire right side,
The long lean leg going high off of the floor,
The taut and sinewy arm reaching to the rafters and more,
Those long strong fingers cradling the leather in place,
With absolute domination and resolute determination covering the face.
At the absolute apex of the leap a simple flip of the wrist
And one more two-point goal is about to be added to the list.
The final act is sending the ball on its perfectly precise arc.
The spinning sphere heading definitively toward its designated mark.

Sky hook
Athletically graceful
Physically incomparable
Aesthetically beautiful
Forever memorable

I wrote this as a tribute to Kareem Abdul-Jabbar for his visit to one of our fund-raising events for Buckets for Hunger, Incorporated.

Wayne Bisek

Ice Bowl

On that miserable blustery day, Lambeau Stadium was grim and gray.
There was an arctic wind so brutally raw it froze you to the bone.
Yet, fifty thousand shivering, die-hard football fans were there that day.
They huddled together against the frigid air and slowly turned into stone.

Puffs of frozen breath engulfed the players as they plotted like hunters in search of prey.
Man after frosted man knew that *that* game on *that* day would test his very soul.
Yet, the captains marched out to midfield, stared each other down and said, "Let's play."
And with that simple gesture was born the now legendary "Ice Bowl."

Green Bay surprised everyone when they quickly scored twice by aerial finesse.
But, Dallas' "Doomsday Defense" recovered with a resounding rebirth.
They pressured Green Bay's quarterback into hurried throws under complete duress.
A vicious sack and a fumbled punt brought the Packers' faithful fans down to earth.

At the half, spectators clamored for coffee mugs and whisky jugs, as the scoreboard read
Green Bay Packers 14
Dallas Cowboys 10.
A strategic gem put the Cowboys in front again on an option pass by their halfback.
Then those two mighty teams traded the pigskin back and forth again and again.
Until, in that rugged battle of men and nature, Green Bay set out for their final attack.

A mixture of clever passes and rambling runs put them one yard from victory on that God-forsaken day.
And so it was that Dallas' defenders dug deep to find some solid ground to make a final stand.
And Green Bay's players scratched and kicked and hoped and prayed for one last surge on this one last play.
At that very moment, every player, every coach and every fan knew that no other game would ever be this grand.

235

A Knock at the Door

Just sixteen ticks of the clock remained
when the ball was snapped
the blocks were made
and the quarterback scored
to win the game.

I wrote this for another Buckets for Hunger, Incorporated event when members of the Cowboys and Packers came together to help us raise money to fight hunger.

Shades

Shades of me in you. Shades of you in me.
Someday that is how, I expect, it will be,
As love entwines our souls till we become
        Reflections of each other, mirror images of our
        Lives, and yet we shall remain ourselves,
For I shall only use your eyes to see,
        Not what is, but what can be.
I should only use your heart to discover
        What life is meant to be.
           A series of unselfish sacrificing
           Held together by unflinching loyalty.
Your soul should be a barometer for me
        Against which I can measure the degree
        Of love compassion and sincerity…
        That, then, is my personality.
Time alone will tell us, completely, of my
        Effect on you and of your effect on me.
Unless, or course, God would show us now,
        Somehow, what the future holds for you
           And me.
Or, maybe, he has, already, so subtly,
        By allowing us to see…
           Shades of me in you.
           Shades of you in me.

Wayne Bisek

Woman

Woman
Should highlight your every day
And transform simple moments into
Treasured memories.
She should be feminine enough to enhance
Your masculinity,
Yet strong enough to allow you to have
Weaknesses, also.

Woman
Should share with you her beliefs and emotions,
Yet should not require you to look up to her,
Nor should you look down at her,
But rather there should exist a feeling
Of mutual respect and admiration.

Woman
Should not be something which you possess,
But should be considered more a part of you
And you a part of her.
Parts which both complement and fulfill each
Other's needs and desires.

Woman
Should assist you in reaching your ultimate goal ~
Becoming a man.

A Thanksgiving Prayer

Each night, when I retire, I thank you ~ Lord,
For all the things You've given me.
I thank You for my health and intelligence.
For I've seen some of the less fortunate.
I thank You for lending me the strength and courage
To help me reach the goals I've set.
I thank You for the faith You've given me,
That I can see always beyond the dark.
I appreciate, also, the peace You've granted my generation.
And I pray that others may never feel wars' grip.
I try to use all the abilities You've given me

A Knock at the Door

To help others see Your shining light.
For I realize without You I am nothing.
But because of You I can be something.
So, thank You, Lord for everything

Addendum

Thank you all for coming today to remember and to celebrate Adrian Bisek's life.

I am Bernie Hesch and my good friend, Wayne Bisek, has asked me to be his voice today. Everything that I read was written by him. He has asked me to make it very clear to everyone here that the eulogy is quite personal in nature. He wants you all to understand that it is his and only his recollection of the relationship that he had with his father, Adrian. The memories and the comments belong to him, his wife and their three children only.

Funeral services such as this provide us each the opportunity to recall and to review the life of this man we knew.

I hope you all can do exactly that today and then that you each leave here at peace with yourself knowing that Adrian is no longer of this earth.

(At this point, introduce the Al Stoppleworth and Vickie Carroll who will be reading the two gospel verses.)

23rd psalm
a letter from Saint Paul to the Colossians.

A few short anecdotes about Grandpa

Dad and Willie

For quite a number of years, Dad had a mongrel dog named Willie. Willie was Dad's absolute favorite play mate. At one point, Dad had found a great game to play with him. Dad would place Willie on the floor

239

gently. He would then turn on a flashlight and shine it on the floor next to Willie. Willie would pounce on it immediately. Dad would then quickly move it and Willie would jump to get it. As soon as it moved, Willie would yelp and bark and jump after it. Dad would be laughing so hard he could hardly keep moving it, but he did. They would then alternate between the yelping and barking of Willie and the belly laughing of Grandpa. Unfortunately for everyone else in the room, neither Willie nor Grandpa ever seemed to tire of this game. Eventually, Dottie would tell them both to stop it. Our kids were never quite sure who had more fun at this game, Willie or Grandpa or all of us watching them.

Dad and the Cane

It seems that one of the greatest benefits of Grandpa needing a cane to walk was that it was now a prop for him to play jokes on people. Every chance he got he would tap one kid or the next on his back when he wasn't looking. Even when we knew it was going to happen, it was funny because he would wait for just the right moment and then he would tap you on the back. HIs eyes would light up like he was in grade school yet and he would giggle for a minute or two. He especially loved to do this to Dottie when she was wearing her wide brim sun hat. He would push it from the back to slide down and cover her face and again he would giggle like a school boy teasing his favorite girl.

Grandma Dottie, Grandpa and the fire truck

We all remember when the kids were about 6, 8 and 10 years old and we went to visit Dad and Dottie. It happened that Grandpa had recently purchased an old retired fire truck at some local auction. It was not in top shape at all. The siren didn't sound quite right. It sort of sounded a little sickly as it whined out its squeals. The bell clanged a little strangely and the red paint was rather faded. Of course, there were no seat belts or harnesses atop the flatbed area of the truck. Yet, Grandpa could not wait to take the three kids and me for a ride. We all climbed on top because that is where he said we would get the "best ride". Luckily, we all knew Grandpa well so we held on tightly to each other and to the side rails and off we went. Grandpa was blowing the sickly siren, the bell would clang on each corner and we were bouncing around like pinballs on the back end. I started screaming almost immediately for Dad to stop and about a half-mile down the road he finally did while we were all still in one piece. We all scurried to the enclosed cab by Grandpa and headed back to the farm.

When Grandma Dottie heard the kids' excited stories about their "fantastic ride," she scolded Grandpa for at least ten minutes and threatened to take away the keys and hide them forever. From then on, Grandma Dottie would not let him leave the yard with the fire truck and the kids at the same time.

Proud Grandpa

Whenever Grandpa knew ahead of time that we were coming to visit and go out to eat, he would be dressed in a new pair of bib overalls and a fresh white tee shirt with his hair combed. He would make a point of giving us the tour of the salvage yard and show us any new tractors that he had purchased at some recent auction. He made sure to show the kids and everyone else the power and the speed of his mini-rod tractor. Then we would go on a tour of the neighborhood so he could share some history about the Bisek home farm. He even made sure that he bought the old road signs with "Bisek Ridge" on them and gave them to us. One of them sits grandly above our entry door in our home in Oregon, Wisconsin, with a fresh new coat of both the white and green paint. It will be a family heirloom forever.

This is Wayne's eulogy for his father:

When I was just a little boy, I thought my father was a giant of a man with muscular arms and a booming voice. I wanted nothing more than for him to hold me and to love me. I yearned for it till my heart ached.

But, it never happened at that time.

When I was in my teenage years, I did all that I could to earn his love and to make him proud. I longed to have him at my side.

But, it never happened at that time.

I saw him hurt the people that I loved and I wondered why. I saw the anger and felt his unhappiness and I wanted even more for him to love me.

But, it never happened at that time.

And then he met, Dottie, his second wife and she changed his life. He discovered what love could be and what love was like. She turned him into a different man with a gentle smile, a hearty laugh and a generous heart.

(PLAY "I WALK THE LINE" HERE)

When I met my own wife, she and my God convinced me to find peace through forgiveness because I too had been angry and unhappy. I tried for one more time to seek his love.

And then it finally happened at that time.

In the thirty years that followed that great event, my father proved to be a whole new man. He absolutely looked forward to seeing my wife, my family and even me. He did the things that proud grandpas do. He played "spoons" with us. He took us on wild fire truck rides through Korpal Valley. If you dared to leave the dinner table for even a second, you would come back to find Grandpa had hid your ice cream dish in the oven or on the floor. He showed us all the new tricks that he had taught his dogs, especially Willie. He came to see AJ, Cole and Melanie play their games and to open their Christmas presents.

And then it truly happened that I grew to love him, too.

(PLAY "BLINK")

All the anger had been wiped away.

Forgiveness had saved the day.

242

I loved him for what he was- a flawed man who had made many mistakes but who finally proved to be a great father to me and a wonderful grandfather to my children.

The lesson that I have learned is to never give up on the people you love because someday it might just happen that they love you back.

(WAIT ABOUT TEN SECONDS AND THEN PLAY "A LOT OF THINGS DIFFERENT")

Ask everyone to join in singing," America the Beautiful" in honor of Adrian and all U.S. Veterans.

After the song ends, please ask everyone to proceed outside for military honors for dad.

After military honors simply say, "May the soul of Adrian Bisek rest in peace with the love of his life, Dottie."

Everyone is invited back in for lunch.

This is the entire funeral service that I wrote for my Dad to celebrate his life when he passed away in 2012

I have known Wayne Bisek for over twenty years and I can honestly say that I have never met a man more dedicated to his cause. He is a tireless worker and advocate in his endeavor to feed the hungry. I am proud to call Wayne my friend and brother.

John Brockington

(Left: John Brockington, 2004)

Author's note: John Brockington was an All-American fullback at Ohio State in 1970 and went on to be named the NFL Rookie of the Year in 1971 for the Green Bay Packers. He had over 1,000 yards rushing in each of his first three years in the NFL. He has been a member of Buckets for Hunger Incorporated's Honorary Board of Directors since day one of our existence.

**(Left to Right: Paul Lynde, Cole Bisek, Wayne Bisek, Rebekah Finley, Michael
Finley and Bertha Finley, 2009)**

CPSIA information can be obtained
at www.ICGtesting.com
Printed in the USA
LVOW12s1918230817
546120LV00010B/22/P

9 781602 648159